Unseen World

Unseen World

The Science, Theories, and Phenomena behind Paranormal Events

RUPERT MATTHEWS, RICHARD EMERSON, JEREMY HARWOOD,
ESTHER SELSDON, VICTORIA MCCULLOCH, PAUL DEVEREUX

Reader's
Digest

The Reader's Digest Association, Inc.
Pleasantville, NY/Montreal/Singapore

A READER'S DIGEST BOOK

This edition published by The Reader's Digest Association, Inc., by arrangement with Essential Works Limited.

FOR ESSENTIAL WORKS
Editor: Nicky Vimpany
Layout: Kate Ward, Martin Hendry
Proofreader: Nicola Hodgson
Indexer: Jo Wilkinson

FOR READER'S DIGEST
U.S. Project Editor: Kimberly Casey
Editor: Sandra Kear
Copy Editor: Barbara Booth
Canadian Contributing Editors: Jim Hynes, J. D. Gravenor
Cover Photographer: Erin Paul Donovan
Canadian Project Editor: Pamela Johnson
Project Designer: Jennifer Tokarski
Associate Art Director: George McKeon
Executive Editor, Trade Publishing: Dolores York
Associate Publisher: Rosanne McManus
President and Publisher, Trade Publishing: Harold Clarke

Library of Congress Cataloging-in-Publication Data

Unseen world : the science, theories, and phenomena behind paranormal events / Rupert Matthews ... [et al.].
    p. cm.
"A Reader's Digest book."
Includes bibliographical references and index.
ISBN 978-0-7621-0887-9
1. Parapsychology--Case studies. 2. Supernatural--Case studies. I. Matthews, Rupert.
BF1029.U57 2008
130--dc22

2008010266

We are committed to both the quality of our products and the service we provide to our customers. We value your comments, so please feel free to contact us.

The Reader's Digest Association, Inc.
Adult Trade Publishing
Reader's Digest Road
Pleasantville, NY 10570-7000

For more Reader's Digest products and information, visit our website:
    www.rd.com (in the United States)
    www.readersdigest.ca (in Canada)
    www.rdasia.com (in Asia)

Printed in China

1 3 5 7 9 10 8 6 4 2

"The most beautiful thing we can experience is the mysterious. It is the source of all true art and science." —ALBERT EINSTEIN

Contents

Introduction

The unseen world, the realm of the paranormal and psychic, has fascinated man since the dawn of time. The word paranormal is a relatively recent term, but it defines phenomena that have been around for millennia—occurrences outside normal experiences of reality that seem to originate beyond the five accepted senses and cannot be scientifically explained. Ghostly hauntings, mediums contacting the dead, psychics who seem to read people's thoughts, and predictions revealed in dreams all fall under the general umbrella of the paranormal.

CULTURAL CONSTRUCTS

In the Western world, people tend to hold a rigid view of what is normal and what is not. Anything that science cannot examine and explain empirically is classified as paranormal. However, the Australian Aborigines understand as much of the world through dreamtime as they do through waking hours. Time for them is fluid, and Western constructs of calendar and space-time do not correspond with the Aboriginal understanding of time. Messages from their ancestors and visions of the future shape how they think and live in the present.

Similarly, Native Americans and some individuals of South America virtually step between the worlds, using psychotropic plants, rituals, and initiation rites in an attempt to discover their destiny and purpose. Out-of-body experiences, past lives, and ancestral visions, which many regard as paranormal activity, comprise natural parts of indigenous life. In India *rishis* (seers) and yogis are apparently able to exhibit occult powers, or *siddhis*. By focusing on intuition and understanding the mind/body/spirit connection, they test their bodies to the limit with impossible feats of fasting and breath control, and even travel beyond their bodies through out-of-body experiences.

WESTERN RATIONALISM

In the West a more scientific, rational approach dominates, but on some level society has always acknowledged subtle unexplained realms that seem to affect overall behaviors. Witch trials may be a thing of the past, but police departments and hospitals tend to have more staff on duty when there's a full moon. Police forces sometimes hire psychics in missing-persons cases. Army officials have worked with thought experimentation, and secret service agencies have conducted numerous parapsychological and psychic tests. Despite a lack of evidential proof, millions of people look to astrology, tarot, and other forms of divination to guide them.

Interest in UFOs and beings from other planets has been growing steadily since the middle of the last century, but this is nothing new. The ancient Dogon tribe of Mali drew cave pictures that some people claim depict beings from Sirius B coming down to Earth. Their cosmic mythology includes the existence of Sirius B, which is difficult to observe today, even through a telescope. It was photographed for the first time in 1970.

SCIENTIFIC INVESTIGATION

What separates Westerners from the yogis of the East, the Native Americans, and the Dogon tribe is a desire for proof. Westerners want video evidence, scientific reasoning, and a foolproof explanation for everything. Modern scientists have not completely neglected or rejected the unseen world. In 1882 the foundation of the prestigious Society for Psychical Research in London began a long tradition, on both sides of the Atlantic, of systematic investigation of the unexplained. The society's founders— Henry Sidgwick, Frederick Myers, and Edmund Gurney, and their U.S. counterpart, William James—were the first in a long line of individuals to cast light on areas that seem to defy the categorizations of mainstream science.

The following chapters reveal comprehensive and historical accounts that trace paranormal phenomena, studies, and ideas. The goal of this book is to introduce readers to a wide range of psychic occurrences so that they can draw their own conclusions about the vast and unknown realm of the unseen world.

Mediums, Mediumships & Psychics

Ever since the dawn of time, humankind has felt the presence of spirits, and a select few have claimed they possessed the ability to lift the veil that lies between the worlds, bringing forth the wisdom of the *other side*. From the shamans and priests of the ancient world to Victorian mediums and present-day TV psychics, these communicators have attracted both acolytes and detractors. This chapter examines the history and methods of these so-called gifted individuals, weighing the evidence to the question, Are they gifted or guilty?

Spiritualism: Lifting the Veil

The Spiritualist movement promotes belief in the survival of the human soul beyond death. Spiritualists believe that the souls of the dead stay connected to the human plane of existence and that these spirits serve as a bridge between God and humans. According to Spiritualist belief, mediums, as their name suggests, act as middlemen, contacting the spirits of the dead, relaying messages from this higher realm, and ultimately promising guidance.

Bare Bones

- Spiritualism is a religious movement that promotes belief in the survival of the human soul after death.

- It began in the United States in the 1840s and quickly gained popularity, spreading to Britain and Europe. Although interest in Spiritualism began to wane after the 1920s, it still has strong support around the world.

- Spiritualists believe that spirits of the dead can be contacted through the agency of mediums—individuals who can channel dead souls and bring their messages to the living.

THE EARLY DAYS

Prominent theologian and mystic Emanuel Swedenborg laid the foundation for many Spiritualist beliefs in the 1700s. Swedenborg experienced a spiritual awakening in his fifties and believed he was appointed by God to write doctrine that would reform Christianity. He taught that the afterlife is not divided simply into heaven and hell, but into a series of worlds, or states, through which a spirit gradually progresses. Swedenborg also believed that spirits mediate between God and humans.

The origins of Spiritualism in North America date back to the 1840s, when Margaret and Kate Fox, of Hydesville, New York, claimed they could communicate with the spirit of a murdered peddler. A skeleton found in their basement seemed to further validate their story, and the news caused a stir of public opinion.

With the interest in the afterlife generated by the Fox sisters, séances became a popular form of entertainment, with countless other mediums claiming that they, too, could communicate with the dead. The extravagance of the public performances accelerated, moving from simple rappings to levitation, apports (objects that appear out of thin air), and even physical manifestation of spirits. Home circles, conducted in the privacy of followers' own homes, were also popular, and by the late 1850s the Spiritualist movement had a strong following on both sides of the Atlantic.

Spiritualism saw the height of its prominence between this time and the 1920s. It spread all over Europe but was most popular in the United Kingdom. Born from ties with Mormonism and radical

Quakerism, the Spiritualists believed that humans could directly communicate with God and the angels. However, with accusations of fraud, occult practices, and witchcraft growing, the Spiritualist movement began to decline in popularity. The Spiritualist Church was already formed, however, and is the main vestige of the original movement that survives in North America today.

SPIRITUALISM TODAY

The Spiritualist movement today still has ties with Christianity and is often known as Christian Spiritualism. However, Craig Hamilton-Parker, a prominent medium, holds a view expressed by many in the movement today that Spiritualism should cut its links with Christianity in order to evolve into a universal religion. He also feels that, in fact, Spiritualism has little common ground with Christianity. He believes Spiritualists should look to the East, where the belief systems of Hinduism and Buddhism may have something in common with the Spiritualist faith.

"We need an esoteric system, a yoga to help our mediums develop and flower," he says. He notes that today's mediums and psychic healers often use the chakra and auric system as a healing map within their work, which is a yogic system. Chakras are the spinning vortices of energy within the body that determine physical, mental, emotional, and spiritual well-being. Many Spiritualists believe chakras provide an interface for healing work.

The Fox Sisters of Hydesville, New York, are credited with triggering the birth of the Spiritualist movement in the 1840s when they claimed they could communicate with the spirit of a murdered peddler.

Auras refer to the life force and a person's energy.

Hamilton-Parker acknowledges the important differences between the paths of Spiritualism and those of Eastern faiths, but he feels that the Eastern systems could nourish mediums, their work, their self-knowledge, and therefore the growth of Spiritualism as a whole. "Mediumship and clairvoyance are low down on the yogi's list of priorities," he says. "They are considered *siddhis,* or powers that are acquired on the pathway to enlightenment. The Spiritualist's goal is not nirvana, but a great deal is to be gained by studying Eastern practices."

> ## "Be sure that it is not you that is mortal, but only your body." —CICERO, ROMAN PHILOSOPHER

GOING BEYOND

Another key difference between Spiritualist beliefs and Eastern faiths is the belief in reincarnation. In the East, in Hinduism and Buddhism, people believe they are reborn again and again after they die, until they learn the lessons of their karmic path. They also believe that until these lessons and lives have been played out, an individual cannot attain peace or enlightenment. Spiritualists do not believe in reincarnation. Instead, they believe that spirits can develop and become higher beings in the different realms of the afterlife. They believe that there are many different realms between heaven and hell, and they view the afterlife as a place where spirits can constantly evolve and grow, find peace with themselves, and potentially journey toward heaven.

Despite suspicions and accusations, the practice of mediumship within Spiritualism differs from the psychic practices of Wiccan covens, or other groups that practice mediumship to gain magical powers or esoteric wisdom. For example, in the late 1800s Madame Blavatsky contacted spirits to gain esoteric wisdom. She and her movement, the Theosophical Society, felt that the spirits were higher spiritual beings. Spiritualists believe that the spirits they contact are the souls of dead humans, and they practice mediumship only to facilitate communication between the living and the dead, to bring comfort to the bereaved, and to try to discover more about the nature of human experience after death.

Many people still consider the work of mediums and psychics to be nothing more than smoke and mirrors, but there is a growing acceptance of these abilities, and these practices are crossing over into many mainstream movements. With the multitude of psychic phone lines and online readings currently available, it seems the parallel worlds of the genuine psychics, and the showpeople that characterized the early Spiritualist movement, still live on today.

Craig Hamilton-Parker is a renowned medium who works extensively with the media in the United States and the United Kingdom. He wants to see the Spiritualist movement evolve with the times and become a universal religion.

Spiritism: Spiritual Progress and Past Lives

With its roots firmly in the Spiritualist movement, Spiritism has evolved into a more philosophical path concerning science, spirit, and moral consequences. The practice, widespread in Latin America, is followed by millions in Brazil today, as well as in other countries, where Catholicism usurped pagan or animist faiths. This made for an interesting marriage with a combination of Catholic dogma and heathen rituals.

Bare Bones

- Spiritism is the philosophical movement established by Allan Kardec in the 1850s.

- It is closely related to Spiritualism, but distinct from it in certain aspects of its teaching. In particular, Spiritists believe in reincarnation, while most Spiritualists do not.

- Although the popularity of Spiritism waned in the United States and Europe, Kardecism, as it became known, is still popular in Brazil and the Philippines today.

A PATH OF PERSONAL DEVELOPMENT

Allan Kardec started the Spiritist movement in the mid-nineteenth century, fed by an interest in the Spiritualist movement and influenced by the mediumship of the Fox sisters and the ideas of Franz Mesmer, founder of mesmerism. However, there are key differences between Spiritism and Spiritualism.

Allan Kardec was the pseudonym of Hippolyte Léon Denizard Rivail, the founder of Spiritism.

Like the Spiritualist movement, Spiritists believe that the spirit is eternal and that mediums and psychics can communicate with the spirits of deceased individuals. However, Spiritists also believe that the spirit evolves through different incarnations in the material world, being reborn to learn further lessons. This is a belief system more akin to Hinduism and Buddhism than Spiritualism and Christianity. In contrast to these practices and religions, there is no key prophet or person to be followed in the Spiritist sect. Spiritism represents more of a path of personal inquiry. Followers are encouraged to question the principles of Spiritism as well as their own principles, beliefs, and morals. This path encourages people to seek true meaning or purpose for themselves.

The Spiritist moral and spiritual doctrine closely echoes the teachings of Jesus, Gandhi, Buddha, or Guru Nanak (founder of Sikhism). Its tenets teach living by example, respecting others, and respecting one's own path and potential. There is no ritual within Spiritism, and prayer is more about intention and quality of thought than the actual words. Spiritists often gather together for prayer, guidance, inquiry, and healing circles. A Spiritist seeks to exercise self-examination and faith on an everyday basis, not just at church on Sunday.

SPIRITUAL EVOLUTION

Spiritists often ask the question, "Why are we here? What is our purpose?" These truth seekers embark on a journey to fulfill their potential and to achieve perfection, no matter how many lifetimes it takes. The Spiritist movement openly accepts mediumship as a form of healing and communication with the spirits. In the Spiritist world, all people constitute a population of reincarnated spirits seeking their way toward perfection and God. Spriritists believe that mediums and spirit guides can potentially show people their past lives and point them in the direction of their true path. Another focus of Spiritist doctrine is that there is life on other planets. They believe more advanced life forms exist throughout the universe and that these beings can evolve both morally and intellectually faster than humans can here on Earth.

Spiritism on the Screen

While Spiritism itself may not have a high media profile, its beliefs and preoccupations are ones that show up often on TV.

What Dreams May Come (1998) is a movie that reflects many Spiritist concerns about the nature of the afterlife and the possibility of reincarnation. *Ghost* (1990) and *The Sixth Sense* (1999) both deal with communication between the living and the dead. Whoopi Goldberg's character in *Ghost* provides a rather lighthearted depiction of mediumship: Oda Mae Brown is a woman who earns her living faking mediumship, and then is horrified when she later discovers that she can, in fact, really communicate with the dead.

The TV shows *Ghost Whisperer* and *Medium* both deal with mediumship in a more serious fashion, depicting psychics using their contact with the dead to benefit both the living and those who have already passed over.

The lines of personal inquiry that underpin Spiritist belief are also explored in the film/documentary *What the Bleep Do We Know?*, which delves into humankind's true purpose, creating the perfect self, the power of intention, and quantum physics.

Mediums: The Middlemen

The process by which a person can communicate with spirits is generally known as mediumship, while the incarnate person through whom the communication occurs is known as a medium. Mediums channel information normally unavailable through the five scientifically recognized senses and commonly have the power to heal psychically. They may also exhibit other psychic abilities, such as telepathy or psychokinesis.

Bare Bones

- The term medium was coined around 1860 to describe a person who can contact the spirits of the dead and relay messages to the living.

- Physical mediumship, which was popular in the early days of the Spiritualist movement, involves dramatic phenomena such as table tilting, automatic writing, and spirit manifestation.

- Mental mediumship, which is the most common form of mediumship today, involves verbally channeling messages from spirits.

The term mediumship was coined around 1860 after public interest in psychic phenomena heightened following claims by mediums such as the Fox sisters. The number of incidents has risen steadily, and today various sections of society, including the Spiritualist movement, openly acknowledge the work of psychic mediums.

ALL IN THE HEAD?

Some researchers believe that although mediums claim they can receive messages from spirits, these messages are, in fact, an alternative manifestation of the medium's own personality. Researchers believe that many of the phenomena associated with mediumship also occur in psychological illnesses such as schizophrenia and multiple personality disorders. Spiritualists, however, argue that while schizophrenics have little control over the voices they hear and are disabled by their presence, mediums can control these powers and use them to assist others.

OR A STEP AHEAD?

Some researchers in the psychic field have suggested that the human body is surrounded by and dependent on a vibrating field of energy and that the spirit world is conducted at a higher "vibrational" level than the Earth plane. Therefore, the spirit world represents a higher stage of evolution. Mediums must, they believe, have the ability to self-induce a psychic state that is also at a more highly evolved spiritual level in order to communicate with their spirit guides and with the spirits of the deceased.

WAY BACK THROUGH TIME

The role of the medium evolved from that of the shaman. A shaman was a tribal leader appointed to communicate with the spirit world. They would put themselves into a trancelike state, allowing a spirit to temporarily possess their physical being. This trancelike state is still important to some modern mediums, particularly so-called physical mediums, and once they emerge from their trance, they will often claim no recall of events that occurred, despite the fact that the transformation was clearly marked by physical changes—sudden changes in voice pitch, for example, or the adoption of the body language and gestures of another person.

MODERN MEDIUMS EMERGE

The demand for mediums to assist in communication with deceased loved ones grew rapidly in the mid-nineteenth century when the phenomenon first became public. Realizing the potential for earning large sums of money, hundreds of women, with little or no other outlets for their spiritual creativity, began to hold tea sessions. While shamans had generally been men with revered social standing, these mediums were women with little social standing, and mediumship posed an opportunity for them to gain status and financial independence. Many believe that one of the attractions of becoming a female medium during this period was that women then lived in a restricted patriarchal society, but once working as mediums, they could be possessed by a male spirit and suddenly feel liberated to drink alcohol, swear like a sailor, and most importantly, earn a living wage.

PHYSICAL AND MENTAL MEDIUMS

A medium's ability to communicate with the spirits is generally modulated by an entity known as a control. The control determines whether its messages will be transmitted through mental means or more physical ones. There is generally a clear division between the two, and serious mediums work primarily in only one sphere, though occasionally mediums can control both modes. These days most mediums tend to work in the mental sphere.

Helen Duncan

Helen Duncan, a renowned twentieth-century Scottish medium, communicated with a deceased sailor during one séance in 1941. The sailor informed her that he had died when his ship, the HMS *Barham*, had been sunk just a few days earlier by a German submarine.

Duncan relayed this information to the sailor's relatives, but the British government was horrified because it had not yet revealed the news that the ship had sunk. Helen continued to reveal classified information about absent sons and husbands to anxious relatives, until security forces declared her a war security risk later that year.

The government became concerned that Helen would reveal the date of the D-Day Normandy landings to a worried public, and she was arrested on January 19, 1944. She was tried and found guilty of conspiracy to break the Witchcraft Act of 1735 and sentenced to nine months in prison.

Helen was released but was continually harassed by the authorities until her death in 1956. Her imprisonment led directly to the Fraudulent Mediums Act of 1951, which replaced the much earlier Witchcraft Act.

Physical mediums manipulate and transform physical systems and energies, which may include moving furniture around the room, creating tapped messages on the table, and spelling out messages on a Ouija board. All apparently occur without the interference of the living. Some claim that the physical medium's spirit guide can superimpose his or her image onto that of the medium, who immediately begins to look altered. Some mediums even seem to take the form of the deceased person with whom he or she is attempting to communicate.

"I am absolutely convinced of the fact that those who once lived on Earth can and do communicate with us."

—SIR WILLIAM BARRETT, PHYSICIST AND FOUNDER OF THE SOCIETY FOR PSYCHICAL RESEARCH

In genuine physical mediumship the medium enters a trance and has no recollection of events that occur while he or she is in this state. This form of mediumship, popular during the nineteenth century, involved dramatic procedures such as table tilting, flickering lights and levitation. Although it provided huge spectacle for the onlookers, it was also highly susceptible to fraud, and numerous mediums were caught indulging in fanciful tricks. Arthur Ford, a well-known medium, stated publicly that it was physically impossible to perform on every required occasion and that mediums were, therefore, bound to exaggerate their gifts sometimes for dramatic effect rather than face failure.

Mental mediums, on the other hand, receive information through thought transference and must therefore maintain full consciousness throughout. A mental medium may communicate with an intermediary spirit guide or directly with the spirits of the deceased and will relay information to the sitter or sitters.

The spirit generally begins by citing specific and intimate details, only known to the sitter, allowing the sitter to identify the spirit. This kind of mediumship has become popular because it assumes communication between the living and the dead and can assist in the grieving process. The sitter does not see or hear the spirit at any point, but any message is conveyed through the medium.

During a typical Victorian séance, the participants sat around a table in a darkened room while the medium went into a trance, which allowed the spirits to communicate or to manifest their presence by moving normally inanimate objects, like this mandolin, which appears to be suspended in mid air.

Spirit Guides: Friends on the Other Side

Many believe that spirit guides are spirits that come from the other side specifically to help the living. Mediums and psychics claim they can connect directly with these guides, but some people assert that everyone has a spirit guide who stays with them from birth, whether people choose to acknowledge their presence or not. Spirit guides are considered teachers, healers, or a link to the other world. To some, spirit guides are dead souls who operate from beyond the grave, while others conceive them as energies or entities that operate at a different or higher frequency than that of this universe.

Bare Bones

- Spirit guides are spirits who form a special relationship with a medium and help them to channel messages to the living.

- They may take any form, from an angel to a deceased relative, but many spirit guides appear as Native Americans or other indigenous people.

- Some mediums believe that everybody has a spirit guide who watches over them from the other side, regardless of whether or not they are aware of them or able to communicate with them.

According to author, spiritual doctor, and angel specialist Doreen Virtue, Ph.D., "Your spirit guide is the twin aspect of your soul, with whom you forever seek connection and completeness."

Spiritualists, Spiritists, mediums, psychics, New Agers, Indian *rishis* and yogis, and Native American shamans all believe in spirit guides. Spirit guides might come from one's ancestral lineage or be ghosts or guardian angels; they might be gurus; to shamans they might even be jaguars or plants; to some in the New Age movement, they might be people from other planets.

HOW TO RECOGNIZE A SPIRIT GUIDE

Spirit guides can apparently manifest themselves in a variety of different ways, such as a voice, a light being, a Southern gentleman in eighteenth-century dress, a Native American complete with headdress, or quite simply a fragrance. A spirit guide may come in the physical form they had in a past life. If a spirit guide was once a monk, then this may be the guise he assumes in the spirit world. In a past life, a spirit guide might have been the father, sister, or teacher of the person he or she guides. Other people believe that because Native Americans or indigenous people have a heightened awareness of the spirit world, they are more likely to become spirit guides once they have passed over.

Psychics and mediums can have a whole team of spirit guides with whom they work; some for their personal life and some for work with others. Natural mystic Zachari Van Dyne believes that everyone has a spirit guide, even if they, themselves, do not have contact with the guide. Often a medium works by introducing people to their personal spirit guides or by bringing them messages from the spirit world if they are not adept at hearing them themselves. Mental mediums contact spirit guides and deliver messages as if in a normal conversation, while physical mediums serve as a vehicle for the spirit.

A NATURAL MYSTIC

Van Dyne is a psychic and tarot reader. He has worked around the world giving readings and helping people to experience their own spirit guides. He has worked with families on missing-persons cases and murder investigations as an investigative clairvoyant, finding people or bodies, sometimes within 24 hours. A family in Florida hired him to find their missing daughter. With the help of his spirit guide, Abrum, Van Dyne detailed what she was wearing and where she was, even what state of mind she was in when she was abducted, and relayed clues for finding the perpetrator. He had a strong feeling that she wouldn't be found alive, but he didn't tell the family this. Just 24 hours later they found her in the exact location that Van Dyne had suggested, but unfortunately she was already dead.

"I have three spirit energies that come to me, and another mystery woman who has not revealed herself yet," says Van Dyne. "Abrum comes to me for my own spiritual development and my work with others. He is a cosmic master, and I talk to him the most. There is also a Gaelic fellow; I cannot pronounce his name, so he tells me to call him 'Mr. E.' He appears to me when I need to make a change in my own life. I don't ask him questions. There is also an astral energy—a female form that comes to me when I work in the astral realms. I know that Abrum has been my teacher before in

Florence Cook, a medium from London, England, became famous for manifesting her ashen-faced spirit guide, known as Katie King, during séances in the 1870s. Clad in white robes Katie King would appear to be quite solid and even allowed herself to be weighed and measured.

many lives, and I feel our most powerful connection was in the fourteenth century.

"All my life I had seen the spirit guides of others, but not my own, but when I was around 18 years old, Abrum came to me. I think this is because until the 1990s he had had a physical form, so I started to see and hear him in the late 1990s. I have worked out who he was in his most recent incarnation, and he has worked with a lot of people both in the physical world and in the spirit world. I saw him on the cover of a book, and I have heard his discourses on tape.

"When I do tarot readings, my spirit guides talk to me. I actually receive more information from my guide and from the spirit guide of the person that I am working with than I do from the cards."

TAPPING INTO THE COLLECTIVE UNCONSCIOUS

Some believe that spirit guides have access to something called the akashic record (*akash* in Sanskrit means ether), which is essentially the universal collective unconscious—a cosmic record of everything that has taken place, all the lives people have led, and how people are interconnected. Some yogis and practitioners feel that they can return to the source and tap into the akashic records themselves, while others believe that a spirit guide must assist mediums to navigate the *akash*.

Psychics, mystics, and sages believe that spirit guides play a large part when a person passes to the other side. Whether or not a person believes in reincarnation, psychics believe that spirit guides will assist him or her in the afterlife.

Many people believe that the synchronicities that occur in our lives—a phone call from a friend we had just been thinking about; bumping into someone on the street or even in another country that we wanted to see; a book falling into our lap with an answer we were seeking—are the play of our spirit guides. It is a way for them to help us in the physical world. They might not appear to us, but they throw a few synchronicities our way, and it is our choice whether we toss it up to coincidence or just accept the magic.

Many mediums report that they have a Native American as a spirit guide. Some believe this is because indigenous people walk the line between the spiritual and physical worlds in life and naturally become spirit guides when they pass over.

Séances, Sittings, and Circles

During a séance a group of people meet to communicate with spirits from the afterlife. A medium generally leads the effort and acts as the means of communication between attendees and spirits. Sittings and circles constitute less formal affairs—often held in a person's home, where a medium may or may not preside. The aim is usually to contact spirits, but some other psychic phenomena may be achieved, such as psychokinesis or remote viewing.

Bare Bones

- A séance is a formal meeting, usually led by a medium, with the purpose of contacting spirits of dead humans.

- A sitting or circle is an informal group that meets in someone's home for the same purpose, and may be led by anybody. A medium may or may not be present.

- Séances have been conducted since at least the third century A.D. and reached the height of their public popularity in the Victorian era.

- The optimum number of people to conduct a séance is eight.

Literary references to séances date back to the writings of Porphyry in the third century A.D. In Chapter 10 of his book *Life Of Plotinus*, Porphyry recounts a séance that he attended in the Isaeum in Rome, stating, "It was not a demon that appeared but a god."

The séance was viewed in a positive light by the ancients, and in 1659 the French-English classical scholar Meric Casaubon wrote a serious tome called *A True and Faithful Relation of What Passed Between Dr. John Dee and Some Spirits* without encountering widespread criticism or abuse. However, not until the mid-1800s, with the rise of mediums such as the Fox sisters, did the idea of the séance as a means of communication with the other world permeate the popular consciousness.

THE ART OF SÉANCE

In order to enact a séance, a circular table is placed in the center of a room with about eight people invited to sit around it. These individuals place their palms flat against the table surface with their fingers touching. Though many cinematic recreations of séances show images of the participants grasping each other's hands and closing their eyes in unison, none of these theatrics are necessary.

Over the years mediums have declared that while the number of participants is not strictly important, they do believe that age may be an important factor in conductivity. They maintain that youth exudes a magnetic attraction to the spiritual world. A thorough medium attempts to assemble an equal group of males and

females and does not allow participants to attend more than three séances a week, because of the spiritually exhausting nature of each session. No single sitting should last longer than two hours.

During the séance itself, members are forbidden to touch the medium, because it is claimed that this may result in a sudden and potentially fatal return to consciousness. Wooden furniture is thought to be more conducive to communication with the spirit world than modern alloys such as steel, and although some feel that background music and chanting sets a suitable tone, this is not advised, because it can provide cover for fraudulent noises. Darkness, though traditionally popular, can also enable fraudulent mediums to practice their art more effectively.

The art of the séance is delicate, and novices may not receive the specific communications for which they had hoped. However, the experience itself is almost always positive and can be an important release for grieving relatives.

This still from the 1922 German silent film *Dr. Mabuse: The Gambler* shows a stereotypical séance, with a small group of participants sitting in semidarkness with their fingertips touching.

Ouija Boards: Calling the Spirits

A Ouija board is a tool that mediums use to ask the spirit world specific questions. The name itself is derived from the French for "yes" (*oui*) and the German for "yes" (*ja*). Many Spiritualists slight this controversial form of communication because they believe it draws in negative forces and can be potentially dangerous.

Bare Bones

- A Ouija board is a device used by some spirits to answer questions put to them.

- It consists of a flat board with the letters of the alphabet, the numerals 0 to 9, and the words "yes" and "no" displayed on it, along with a pointer called a planchette.

- Some claim that Ouija boards attract negative forces and are therefore dangerous. Others believe that the unconscious movements of the living participants produce the received messages.

ORIGINS OF THE BOARD

In ancient Greece a small trolley on wheels was used to indicate answers to questions put to the spirits. In 1853 a device called the planchette, the early forerunner of the Ouija board, became hugely popular across Europe. The Ouija board, in its modern form, was designed by American lawyer and inventor Elijah J. Bond. He sold it to businessman William Fuld in 1892 who, in turn sold it to the board game company Parker Brothers. Realizing its potential, Parker Brothers began marketing the concept as "Ouija, the Mystifying Oracle."

ALL IN THE MIND

Parapsychologists have posited that the Ouija board may work as a function of the unconscious by drawing out information the participant wishes to repress. Critics say this sudden release of repressed thoughts is unwise; during sessions boards have been known to fly across the table as if possessed. Practitioners who use the Ouija board, however, say that it is this power that helps them communicate with the spirit world.

USING THE BOARD

The Ouija board set consists of a flat board with the letters of the alphabet marked on its surface. In addition, the numbers 0 to 9 are displayed as well as the words "yes" and "no." A group of participants places the board in the center of a table during a séance. Each participant then places one finger lightly on the central pointer, or planchette. One member of the group, preferably a medium, should first utter the words, "Is there anybody there?" The fingertips, if not the entire hands, of each participant may then be overwhelmed by a chilling sensation, and if the spirit world has been contacted, the planchette should move to the "yes" arrow and then back to the center.

As energy rises, the planchette may begin to whiz around the board, creating ever more disjointed messages. Participants are warned to be cautious if a negative message is received, but if the message is positive and correctly interpreted, the Ouija board can provide powerful insights.

> "It is just an object with letters and numbers printed on it...with no power of its own." —KEITH MORGAN, AUTHOR

GHOST WRITER

In July 1913 a St. Louis housewife named Pearl Curran was encouraged by a friend to try out the Ouija board . As soon as the two ladies began experimenting, they found the name Patience Worth clearly spelled out across their board. Subsequent Ouija sessions produced voluminous correspondence from Patience Worth, who turned out to be a seventeenth-century woman from England. Worth allegedly recounted six full-length novels to Curran, all of which became instant bestsellers.

Spirit boards, or Ouija boards, are flat boards normally made of wood. Advocates believe that spirits use the planchette to point to the letters of the alphabet, numbers, and the words "yes" and "no" to communicate with the living.

Cold Reading

The term "cold reading" is used to describe someone's ability to reveal details about a person they've never met before and about whom they apparently have no prior knowledge. The technique is practiced by psychics, Spiritualists, palmists, and healers, all of whom maintain that their knowledge comes via a psychic or paranormal connection formed with the subject of the reading.

Cynics regard cold reading as little more than a show-ground technique, using simple ploys to encourage gullible clients to reveal personal information without realizing it. This information, critics say, is then relayed back to the client as though derived from a paranormal source. Many people who have experienced cold reading report that the facts revealed were known to no one else and could not have been obtained from any conventional source.

Screen Medium

Perhaps the best-known modern-day exponent of cold reading is the controversial psychic medium John Edward, a U.S. writer and broadcaster whose TV show *Crossing Over* draws audiences in the millions. During his TV readings, Edward reveals information to audience members that he says comes from deceased relatives, and asks for their help in interpreting it.

Edward's critics say his apparent gift is pure illusion aided by techniques such as collecting information about audience members in advance (hot reading) and using vague shotgun comments that could apply to lots of people or ambiguous "rainbow" phrases that could be interpreted in several ways. Edward's opponents also claim that careful TV editing improves his success rate by removing comments that fail to get a positive response. Edward has strenuously denied these claims and says his broadcasts include failures as well as successes.

John Edward is a successful but sometimes controversial psychic medium who has his own TV show, *Crossing Over*.

The Forer Effect

The willingness of subjects to believe the accuracy of vague pronouncements about them is called the Forer Effect and is said to lie behind the success, not only of cold reading but also of astrology and other forms of fortune-telling.

Psychologist Bernard Forer believed that people fail to assess their own personality objectively and willingly accept another's view. This, he said, left them open to exploitation. He revealed his Forer Effect in an experiment he dubbed "A Classroom Demonstration in Gullibility" published in 1949 in the *Journal of Abnormal and Social Psychology*.

Forer gave his students a personality test. Ignoring the results, he then presented them all with the same personality analysis. He asked students to score his analysis for accuracy on a scale of 0 (very poor) to 5 (excellent). Scores averaged over 4, showing that Forer's students believed his bogus profile closely matched their own view of themselves. Forer's analysis encompassed a wide range of personality traits with just enough detail for subjects to personalize it. The use of generalized terminology, Forer believed, allowed subjects to mold a profile to fit their own view.

Reading the Signs

The ability to "read" a person by piecing together such visible clues as body language, expression, demeanor, clothing, age, and state of health is not in itself remarkable. A wedding ring indicates marital status, for instance, and clothing can suggest financial status. Sallow skin or labored breathing indicates a poor state of health. Posture can reveal personality: leaning back with arms folded across the chest and knees together shows a withdrawn, defensive type, while leaning forward with hands on knees suggests a confident, outgoing persona. To be authentic, cold reading must provide more information than can be gleaned by visible clues alone.

Eyewitness

EILEEN BALL, OF SAN DIEGO, CALIFORNIA, VISITED A LOCAL SPIRITUALIST CHURCH.

"At the time, I was finding Gerard, my husband, very inconsiderate in his ways. I would put my makeup bag by the sink, and he wouldn't watch where he'd splash when washing. Makeup and brushes would be soaked beyond use, so we were in conflict about that. One day we went to the church, and after the service the minister asked if she could come to him. She started talking about give and take in marriage and that sometimes one had to make adjustments in the way they lived to accommodate the new partner. My husband nodded but didn't appear to be fully getting it. So the minister said, 'You know, like splashing makeup bags by the sink?' I got a big grin on my face, and he blushed ... I'm sure to this day he thinks that was a setup, but it wasn't. No one knew—just us."

Channeling and Trance Speaking: Stepping Aside

Channeling refers to any process by which a medium communicates information from the unseen world. During direct-voice channeling, a spirit apparently uses the medium as a channel, but words seem to emanate from empty space, not from the medium, who is often in a deep trance. In the majority of cases, the medium wakes up from the trance unable to recall what has taken place. In mental channeling, on the other hand, the medium must be awake to convey the messages to the sitter; therefore, the channeler has total recall of the session.

Bare Bones

- Channeling is a term that can be applied to any method by which a medium conveys information from spirits to the living.

- Trance speaking is a form of channeling in which the medium experiences an altered state of consciousness and is usually unaware of what happens while the trance persists.

- Some psychologists claim that the so-called spirits that manifest during channeling are actually elements of the channeler's subconscious.

- Spiritualists believe that anyone can learn to channel and thus communicate with the dead.

Through channeling, the spirit world conveys messages via a variety of different mechanisms, including automatic writing, Ouija boards, trance speaking, and dreams. It can involve the medium's intuition or some higher psychic wisdom. Physical channeling can involve such concrete manifestations as levitation or telekinesis.

AN AGE-OLD PHENOMENON

Channeling often involves entering a trancelike state, and the trance may be combined with, or induced by, practices such as meditation, hypnosis, and prayer. The word trance derives from the Latin *trans re,* meaning "to cross over," which describes the sensation as channelers experience it. Documented evidence from anthropologists and ethnologists shows that many early cultures explored trance as a state of mind. Its global prevalence suggests that trance experiences play an essential role in human society and may even provide medical and spiritual benefits. The ancient Egyptians, Romans, Tibetans, and Celts all recognized the importance of the trance state to their communities, and each of these cultures had designated channelers to communicate with the spirits and receive instruction from the unseen world.

WHO'S IN CHARGE?

Channeling, used historically for divination and spiritual healing, differs from possession. When a person is possessed, a negative spirit can force control over them to bend their actions toward the spirit's negative inclinations. Because of this, possession was considered to be a demonic state. In the Middle Ages, lawmakers conflated channeling and possession, and anyone suspected of either, would be exorcized, executed, or both. Not until the late nineteenth century, when young women such as the Fox sisters brought channeling into the public eye, did the notion of channeling become distinct from possession.

STRAIGHT TO THE TOP

Channeler Nettie Colburn proffered advice from the spirit world to President Lincoln during his presidency. During the early 1860s Mrs. Lincoln summoned Colburn to the White House on a number of highly publicized occasions to shed light on a variety of topics troubling the President. Colburn offered channeled advice about ways to boost the morale of the Yankee troops during the U.S. Civil War, and it was widely reported that President Lincoln appreciated her advice.

THOUGHTS FROM THE OTHER SIDE

Channeling underwent a revival in the late twentieth century when Jane Roberts published a series of books that she claimed had been channeled to her by a spiritual entity. Roberts and her husband, Robert Butts, had first used a Ouija board in 1963. In December of that year, she began to receive coherent messages from a spirit called Seth. The channeling was so clear that Roberts soon began to hear his voice inside her head. For the next 21 years she held regular trance sessions in which she spoke Seth's words while her husband wrote them down. The text consisted of a series of monologues offering advice about the human condition. Roberts and Butts published much of this as Seth's own work in 1969, and eventually 10 volumes were created including *Seth Speaks* and *Dreams, Evolution and Value Fulfillment.*

Jung

Carl Jung was interested in exploring the forces behind channeling and trance speaking. He suggested that they both sprang from a source that he termed the collective unconscious, which was based in a communal ancestral memory and passed on through the generations by means of symbols and dreams.

According to Jung, even the waking experiences of the average person can be traced back to what he termed meaningful coincidence. Jung acknowledged that moments of apparently irrational insight could be extremely helpful both in understanding the present and in predicting the future. He respected the power of these clairvoyant moments but vociferously denied that they were rooted in the supernatural.

Those who subscribe to their power, he said, attribute prescience to specifically gifted mediums, while he maintained that visions are merely part of the mystery of human consciousness. According to Jung, a medium has chosen not to ignore the interaction between his waking mind and the collective unconscious and has thereby learned accurately to interpret symbols present in everyday lives.

Direct Voice: Out of Thin Air

Direct voice is one of the most controversial phenomena associated with Spiritualism. Spoken words, said to originate from the spirit world, are heard by those present as if emanating from empty space. It is this disembodied aspect that distinguishes direct voice from the spoken words that mediums claim to channel via their own mouths.

Bare Bones

- Direct voice is a form of channeling in which voices are heard that appear to come from thin air rather than from the medium.

- Although similarphenomena have been reported throughout history, instances of direct-voice mediumship were particularly prevalent during the heyday of Spiritualist séances in the second half of the nineteenth century.

- Many allegations of fraud have been made, but some mediums, such as Leslie Flint, have defied investigators and continued to produce voices even when bound and gagged.

Direct voice has its roots in prehistory and the earliest forms of worship. It is strongly associated with the rituals of the shamans, or spirit leaders, of Native American and Siberian tribes. Indeed, a belief in two-way communication with the spirit world, with the shaman acting as an intermediary, is at the heart of shamanism.

VOICES IN THE ETHER

Anthropologist Waldemar Bogoras made one of the earliest recordings of direct voice during a native shamanic ritual in 1901 while studying a tribe in a remote region of Siberia. The researcher was alone with the tribal shaman, who had entered a trance while beating a drum, when Bogoras became aware of voices around him, seemingly coming from thin air. Similar phenomena are reported in Native American sweat lodges and may explain why Western mediums traditionally claimed American Indians as spirit guides.

During the heyday of Western Spiritualism, in the mid 1800s, direct voice came to the attention of a wider public. At this time, the voice was often conveyed via a metal or cardboard trumpet—said to amplify the faint voices of the spirit world. The trumpet would hang, seemingly unsupported, in the unlit séance room, directing spirit messages to sitters. By the 1900s direct voice was reported more often as occurring without mechanical aid.

REAL OR HOAX?

Many claim that direct voice involves secret accomplices, hidden speakers, or recording equipment and is used to dupe gullible clients. One of the most famous direct-voice mediums was Canadian-born Mina "Margery" Crandon, who counted Sir Arthur Conan Doyle among her supporters. Crandon's credibility was badly damaged, however, when an investigator for the Society for Psychical Research claimed that her telekinetic ability owed much to a leather-covered knitting needle held between her teeth. Crandon claimed that what the investigator had touched was ectoplasm—the substance from which ghosts are formed—and promptly fainted.

Another direct-voice medium lauded by Conan Doyle was the Scottish-born Spiritualist Daniel Dunglas Home, who moved to the United States with his family at the age of nine. Home's reputation brought him to public attention at an early age, and while still only in his early twenties, he returned to Britain during a European tour funded by U.S. Spiritualists.

His fame drew many British celebrities to his sittings, including husband-and-wife poets Robert and Elizabeth Barrett Browning. Home proved to be a source of marital conflict to the couple, however, since Elizabeth felt sure he was genuine, while her husband regarded him as bogus, even basing a vulgar poem—*Sludge the Medium*—on him.

STUDYING THE VOICES

Many of the scientific studies conducted into direct-voice phenomena have been inconclusive. In the three years before his death, at 39 years old, Dr. W. J. Crawford, a lecturer in mechanical engineering at Queen's University, Belfast, conducted a series of elaborate experiments to investigate psychic phenomena such as direct voice. They were conducted in a small laboratory at his home and documented in his book *Experiments in Psychical Science (see box, "Studying Direct Voice in the Laboratory")*.

In two experiments held in his laboratory, "with only the dullest glow visible," the medium was seated on a weighing platform with her metal trumpet placed on the floor, out of reach. Crawford monitored the needle of the scales to see if she gained weight, which would indicate she was lifting the trumpet to speak into it.

Studying Direct Voice in the Laboratory

Dr. W. J. Crawford carried out several studies involving a direct-voice medium he called Mrs. Z. Her sittings featured the words of a woman (referred to as Control) emanating from a cone-shaped trumpet. Mrs. Z insisted her sittings be held in complete darkness, which Crawford said allowed "considerable scope for fraud."

In one experiment, Crawford seated Mrs. Z with her feet resting on boards wired electrically to a bell. The device was designed to ring if she moved. Two sitters on either side held her hands while another group (friends of Crawford) encircled the trio. Crawford placed an Edison phonograph recording machine outside the circle, and Control was instructed to sing into the horn of the machine.

Crawford wrote, "I plainly felt the movement of air just at the mouth of the phonograph horn as the song was sung... Moreover, Control's voice emanated from a position just at the mouth of the horn... the nearest distance of the other end of the horn from the medium must have been well over four feet."

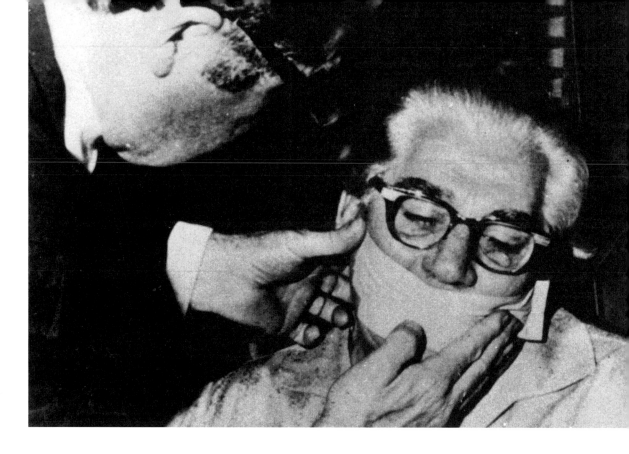

In fact, far from getting heavier, Crawford noted that the medium's weight consistently fell by half a pound (250 g) over the course of a sitting. Crawford wrote, "I did everything I could to prevent fraud; but in an absolutely dark séance-room it is obviously impossible to ensure complete prevention."

FLINT'S VOICES IN THE DARK

Leslie Flint, one of the most famous direct-voice psychics of recent times claimed to be, "the most tested medium…produced (by Britain)." In his autobiography, *Voices in the Dark*, Flint relates how psychic investigators placed a microphone against his throat to check for ventriloquism "so that the slightest sound…would be magnified enormously." All the while, investigators viewed him through an infrared telescope.

Flint's sittings, which did not involve a trumpet, were said to feature the recognizable voices of the departed speaking to relatives in the audience and revealing information unknown outside the family. At one meeting the voice of a young British airman, killed

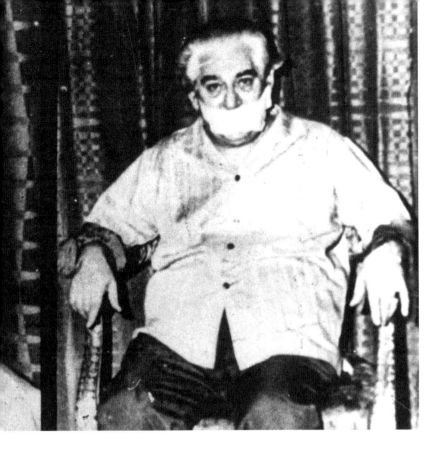

In his writings direct-voice medium Leslie Flint claims to have been, "boxed up, tied up, sealed up, gagged, bound, and held, and still the voices have come...speaking in different dialects, in foreign languages unknown to me, and even in languages no longer spoken on this earth."

in World War II, was heard telling his mother, seated in the audience, that he knew her handbag contained a photograph of his grave in Norway. He also told her he liked the memorial garden she had planted in his memory.

In 1948 *Psychic News* reported a séance in which 12 spectators said they clearly heard direct voices emanating from somewhere near Flint, even though the medium's lips were taped shut with sticking plaster and his hands and feet were tied to his chair. Many researchers continued to regard Flint as a fake, but at least one distinguished investigator was convinced the medium was genuine.

In 1971 electrical engineering professor William R. Bennett, of Columbia University, New York, said that he had used modern investigation techniques to show that the direct voices he recorded were not Flint's. He continued, "...to be thorough, one should consider the possibility of accomplices...The suggestion became untenable to me (during) an impromptu séance in my apartment (in New York), when the same voices...took part in conversations with guests."

Automatic Writing: Authors from the Other Side

Most practitioners believe that a spirit source is responsible for automatic writing when a medium writes down information not emanating from his or her own conscious mind. Often the script will suggest or confirm the identity of the spirit to the sitter. Though the text proceeds from the writer's hand, he or she is normally unaware of what will emerge.

Bare Bones

- Automatic writing occurs when a medium produces written communication that allegedly comes not from his or her conscious mind but from the spirits of the dead.

- The medium may be fully conscious or in a trance when the writing occurs but is unaware of what will appear on the paper before it does so.

- Automatic writing is often produced at great speed and may be jumbled and practically incomprehensible.

UNKNOWN LANGUAGES

People who engage in automatic writing sometimes report a tingling sensation in the arms or writing hand immediately before a message is received. The medium may go into a trance state or may remain conscious, but the writing itself tends to occur at a much faster pace than conscious handwriting. The words often appear jumbled on the page with unusual spellings and peculiar letter formation. Words may appear in mirror script or backward. Some twentieth-century mediums claimed they received messages in unfamiliar languages, even Latin or ancient Greek.

PHILOSOPHERS AND PRIESTS

Nineteenth-century philosopher William James was convinced, having witnessed automatic writing, that it was a way of obtaining information buried deep in the subconscious, and he used it as an early form of psychotherapy. William Stainton Moses, a respected priest, began experimenting with automatic writing in the late nineteenth century despite the fact that it was expressly prohibited by his orthodox Christian views. He believed that he was receiving messages from higher spirits. Another notable automatic writer, Georgie Hyde-Lees, was the wife of the poet, William Butler Yeats. Many people believed it was her experiences of automatic writing that led Yeats to delve further into the mysteries of the universe and, hence, to become a mystical poet.

ART FROM THE OTHER SIDE

The surrealists of the 1920s took a great interest in the creativity and mysticism of automatic writing. André Breton, one of the founders of the surrealist movement, pioneered automatic writing as a creative endeavor, and in the early 1920s he collaborated with Philippe Soupault to write an entire book, *The Magnetic Fields*, by means of automatic writing. The technique became extremely important to the whole movement, and its participants used it to develop a repertoire of creative outlets, including games, tools, and sketches. Later John Frusciante—guitarist for the Red Hot Chili Peppers—dedicated an entire album to the process of automatic writing, claiming, "Music is simply there and we, as musicians, are sucked into its swirling energy."

Skeptics believe that automatic writing constitutes no more than genuine sparks of creativity and maintain that all great works of art produced through automatic writing simply reflect the unconscious mind of the artist. No outside agency or spirit of the dead is involved, they argue. No one can deny, however, that the products of automatic writing have helped many practitioners over the years to divine the answers to some extremely specific spiritual questions.

This is a sample of automatic writing via the medium John Bartlett. The sketches and writings were said to be from long-dead monks of Glastonbury Abbey, England. The architect Frederick Bligh Bond used Bartlett's mediumship to seek help from the purported dead monks in his role as director of excavations at the ruined abbey.

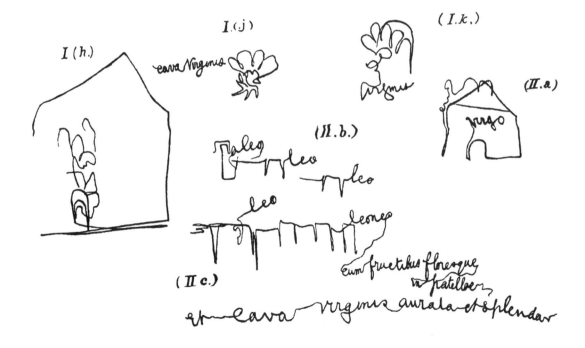

Psychic Healing: The Therapeutic Power of Unknown Forces

A psychic healer seeks to alleviate pain and suffering without using recognized curative agents or techniques. Many practitioners—also called spiritual healers—believe they harness the healing power of prayer. Others say the source comes from cosmic or universal energy or naturally occurs within electromagnetic fields.

Bare Bones

- A psychic healer is someone who claims to heal the sick without recourse to any scientifically acknowledged means.

- Psychic healers often use the power of prayer to effect their cures or may refer to cosmic or universal energy. They may use physical contact—therapeutic touch—or heal without touching the patient at all.

- Although impressive results have been obtained in trials of psychic healing, critics claim that its success can be explained by the placebo effect.

POSITIVE ENERGY

Healing often involves physical contact—called therapeutic touch or the laying on of hands. Many healers focus on the positive energy passing through the patient's body, which may show a disordered pattern that indicates areas of the body affected by disease. Patients may be asked to direct their thoughts inward while the healer intends healing. Healing may even be performed over long distances—called absent or distant healing.

Psychic healing played a part in ancient Ayurvedic medicine, first practiced in India 5,000 years ago, which focuses on the body's chakra energy centers. Reiki, a more recent healing system, is growing in popularity. Reiki, meaning unseen life force, was developed in Japan by Mikao Usui, who founded the Usui Reiki Healing Society in 1922.

PSYCHIC POWER OR SIMPLE FAITH?

A systematic review of the research, published in 2000 in the *Annals of Internal Medicine*, reported that overall psychic healing "showed a positive treatment effect." Critics, however, cast doubt on how the review was conducted and on the choice of studies. Psychic healing remains one of the most studied areas of the paranormal—and also the most controversial. Criticism focuses on the fact that research fails to include the possibility that patients' own minds can effect a cure. Doctors accept that any treatment—even

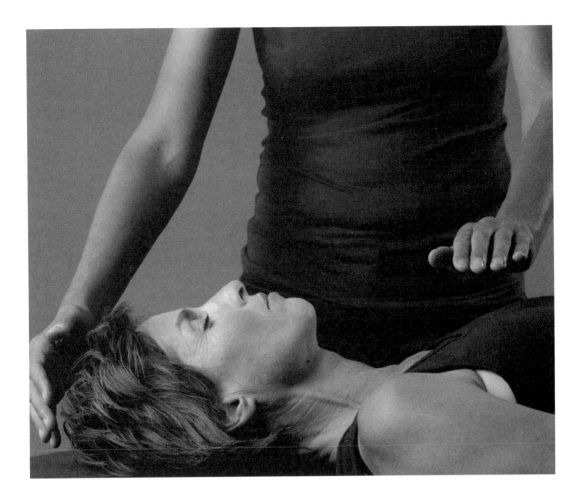

dummy pills or placebos—can alleviate illness if a patient believes strongly enough.

In one experiment involving 20 chronic pain sufferers, reported in the *Journal of Psychosomatic Research* in 2006, a team of psychologists based at Bond University, on the Australian Gold Coast, engaged an unnamed psychic in a healing session for the TV show *A Current Affair*. Patients were placed in two groups: one group received psychic healing, and one did not. Results did not show a significant difference in health between treated and untreated patients but did reveal a big improvement among believers compared with nonbelievers. Researchers summarized the results as such: "Although psychic healing was unable to alleviate pain in the present study, belief in psychic healing apparently was."

During a typical session a reiki practitioner moves her hands over the patient's body—sometimes without making physical contact—to intuitively identify those areas in need of treatment. Practitioners believe reiki stimulates the body's natural healing processes, often felt by the recipient as a warm, tingling, and relaxing sensation.

Absent Healing: Long-Distance Therapy

Absent healing is a form of psychic healing in which the practitioner is separated from the patient by distance—and may even be in another country. Also called distant healing, it plays a major part in many religious and nonreligious disciplines, including Christianity, kabbalah, Buddhism, Ayurveda, reiki, and qigong therapy.

Bare Bones

- Absent, or distant, healing is a form of psychic healing that occurs when the healer and the patient are some distance apart.

- Absent healing comes in different forms and is practiced across numerous traditions, from Christianity to Ayurveda.

- Results of scientific trials of absent healing have been mixed, though some significant studies suggest that it may be effective.

SAY A PRAYER

In the traditional Judeo–Christian intercessory prayer, spiritual healers ask God to heal a patient. But the beliefs behind absent healing are as diverse as the disciplines that practice it. Qigong masters, for example, send harmonizing *qi* energy to heal their patients, while Ayurvedic practitioners use chants and visualization in an attempt to rebalance patients' chakra energy centers. Chakras are spinning vortices of energy within the body. They are described as being aligned in a column from the base of the spine to the top of the head and these practitioners believe they are responsible for our physical, emotional, and spiritual well-being.

Absent healing may be performed in addition to, or instead of, the contact healing of therapeutic touch and may involve one healer or many. Groups of healers often keep a healing book so members can send collective healing to those who request it. Absent healing is sometimes also called faith healing, but many healers reject this term, claiming that patients do not need faith to reap its benefits.

Absent healing has been subjected to frequent scientific scrutiny, but according to the *Skeptical Inquirer*, official journal of the Committee for the Scientific Investigation of Claims of the Paranormal, "results for clinical trials of medical prayer and other distant healing claims have proven inconsistent and are often criticized for methodology."

WORKING WITH AIDS

One celebrated experiment was conducted by psychiatrist Dr. Elisabeth Targ, a clinician and parapsychology researcher (*see box*, "The Scientific Face of Healing Prayer"), who set out to design a gold-standard study involving 20 patients with advanced AIDS, all receiving orthodox medical treatment.

Dr. Targ asked 40 healers from different disciplines to focus on 10 of the AIDS patients. The other 10 were the comparison control group. Healers were given names, photographs, and T-cell counts (indicating the severity of the patients' condition) of members of the first group and asked to send their intention. Dr. Targ used a double-blind protocol so that neither patients nor researchers knew who received healing.

At this time, the mid-1990s, no effective medical treatment for AIDS existed, yet at the end of the study period, all 10 in the healers' group were alive and their medical condition had significantly improved. Four of the control group had died, and the health of the others had deteriorated. One flaw in the methodology was that the control group was older, on average, than the healers' group, which could have accounted for the higher mortality rate. The results of the study were published in the *Western Journal of Medicine* in 1998.

With the advent of triple antiretroviral drug therapy, which helped to prolong the lives of AIDS patients, Dr. Targ and her coresearchers decided to repeat the study with different patients. All survived, but the control group suffered nearly three times as many AIDS-related illnesses and spent six times as long in the hospital as those who received absent healing. Researchers were careful to rule out the patients' own belief in healing as a factor.

Published in 1999 in the *Western Journal of Medicine*, this was held up as a landmark study, although writer Po Bronson, in his Internet article "A Prayer Before Dying," claims the team's biostatistician, Dan Moore, has since cast doubt on the results, claiming that the study was not in fact initially designed to monitor AIDS-related illnesses and had been unblinded, then reblinded, in order to search for significant data.

The Scientific Face of Healing Prayer

Few psychic investigators had a science background equal to that of Dr. Elisabeth Targ (1961–2002). A practicing clinical psychiatrist, Dr. Targ was Professor of Medicine at the University of California at San Francisco and founding director of the Complementary Medicine Research Institute at California Pacific Medical Center when her life was cut short at the age of 40.

Dr. Targ's interest in the paranormal was inspired by her father, Russell Targ, a world-renowned researcher studying extrasensory perception. At the age of 10, she was taking part in his ESP experiments. A child prodigy, Elisabeth graduated from high school at 15 with top science grades and fluent in three foreign languages, including Russian.

Following medical training, Dr. Targ combined clinical practice with investigations into the healing power of the mind (psychoneuro-immunology), including research into the role of spirituality in the well-being of women with breast cancer. While planning a study on the effect of distant healing on brain cancer, Dr. Targ was diagnosed with a highly malignant form of the disease and died two years later.

Clairvoyance: Seeing Beyond

Derived from the French adjective *clair*, which means "clear," and the verb *voir,* which means "to see," clairvoyance means the ability to look beyond the physical or seen world and into the realm of the unseen or spiritual. This could imply an ability to see events that have already happened (for example in a past life or on a different continent) or to visualize events that will happen in the future or in another dimension. This "seeing" occurs by means of senses other than the five normally available to human beings. Three main forms of extrasensory perception exist: clairvoyance, telepathy, and precognition. The boundaries between these three are hazy, but anyone with the ability to "see clearly" is referred to as a clairvoyant.

Bare Bones

- Clairvoyance is a form of extrasensory perception.

- Clairvoyants possess the ability to "see" things that they would not normally perceive using the five commonly recognized senses. This may involve seeing events from the past, from the future, or from a distant place.

- The Oracle at Delphi is an example of a famous clairvoyant from ancient times.

- Clairvoyance has been the subject of scientific investigation for over 150 years, but no firm evidence for its existence has been produced.

ANCIENT HISTORY

In 550 B.C. Croesus, King of Lydia, wanted to ascertain who of his favorite seven oracles had the greatest clairvoyant powers. He sent messengers to ask each of these prophets what he, Croesus, was doing at a certain fixed moment in time. He made the test more complex by choosing to perform a particularly irrational activity—chopping up a tortoise and boiling it with lamb in a brass cauldron. His messengers later told him that the Oracle at Delphi not only accurately reported the correct sequence of events but also accurately described the smell of the tortoise-and-lamb stew in the pot.

Ancient Hindu religious texts, meanwhile, consistently list clairvoyance as one of a list of skills, or *siddhis*, that humans who are more advanced can develop through persistent devotion to meditation and strict personal discipline. These *siddhis* should be employed not only for the benefit of the practitioners but also for the good of their communities.

One of the earliest written references to clairvoyance in Europe is credited to the Marquis de Puysegur, a Frenchman, who treated a, "dull-witted local peasant" in 1784. Apparently, the Marquis used hypnosis to put the peasant into a "somnambulistic clairvoyant state," during which the peasant would suddenly become articulate and accurately predict the future. This ability faded completely once the peasant woke up. The Marquis, however, did not consider this to be clairvoyance but rather some predictable outcome of natural science.

INVESTIGATING CLAIRVOYANCE

Adele Maginot, a well-known psychic in the early 1830s, participated in the first modern scientific experiments on clairvoyance. Although she accurately visualized many of her subjects' thoughts and memories, scientists uncovered no fraud. Since clairvoyance was deemed potentially useful to government agencies, research continued well into the twentieth century with both Soviet and North American scientists conducting experiments throughout the cold war. Secret Services were keen to harness the spying potential of clairvoyance, but the results of all these experiments were mixed, and interest in the topic has apparently waned.

Today scientific opinion remains divided. A 1994 research paper entitled "Does psi exist?" in the *Psychological Bulletin* discussed the evidence for "replicable evidence for an anomalous process of information transfer." This was inconclusive, but after a survey in 1979, two social scientists named Wagner and Monnet established that more than 50 percent of scientists believe that ESP is an empirical possibility, though less than a third of psychologists consider this to be the case.

Some parapsychologists suggest that clairvoyance, telepathy, and precognition all evolved from one basic mechanism, which no one has yet identified. In March 1999 researchers at Harvard University began investigating the ability of the human eye to detect moving objects too fast to be seen. Cricketers, for example, accurately bat balls that their eyes are not technically capable of registering. Researcher and professor Markus Meister discovered that the human eye contains cells called ganglions, which can accurately "predict" the future position of moving objects and transfer this message to the brain before the eye has actually seen the object. Although this does not explain clairvoyance, it highlights the mysteries of human vision, which remain, at present, simply inexplicable.

Edgar Cayce

Edgar Cayce, a U.S. clairvoyant, hugely influenced New Age thought. Born in Kentucky in 1877, he left school at 13 years old and began to study at home, reading mainly the Bible. In 1900 he contracted laryngitis and lost all ability to speak. The following year, a hypnotist heard about Cayce's condition and offered to cure him.

Cayce agreed to treatment, and after some time, his voice returned. While under hypnosis, however, Cayce uttered such clairvoyant truths that the hypnotist suggested that Cayce was clairvoyant and that he should use his skills for a higher purpose.

Initially reluctant, Cayce began to offer free treatment for spiritually afflicted individuals, and his fame spread, with all of his work still occuring under hypnosis while a secretary took notes. After fortune-hunting customers asked him for help, he concluded that he should use his gift only to help the sick. This created a hugely positive image for clairvoyance throughout North America and made him nationally famous.

Clairaudience: Hearing Voices

People who hear voices that are inaudible to others experience the phenomenon of clairaudience. These voices are usually thought to be spirit voices but occasionally have been identified as disembodied voices of the living. Whether these voices come from the percipient's own mind or from some unknown supernatural source continues to be a matter of debate.

Bare Bones

- Clairaudience is the ability to hear voices not audible to others.

- Some claim these voices come from spirit guides, spirits of the dead, angels, or other spirits. There are even reports of disembodied voices of the living being heard.

- Skeptics suggest that these voices actually originate in the subconscious mind of those who hear them.

Many clairaudients believe that the voices they hear are those of angels. Messages attributed to these beings are reported as overwhelmingly positive, offering advice and guidance and even, in some cases, protection from imminent danger.

VOICES IN MY HEAD

Some people claim they hear the voices of angels, whereas others consider this to be speech from their spirit guides; still others hear messages from their ancestors on the other side. The voice may come from within or from outside. It may sound like the percipient's own voice or the voice of another. Some psychics actively seek communication of this sort, while others are plagued with voices that they neither solicit nor control. The scientific establishment is often at odds with believers, especially where clairaudience is concerned. "As a psychotherapist, I was trained to believe that hearing voices was a sign of insanity," says Doreen Virtue, who has written extensively about her communications with angels and hears frequent messages. She even claims that the guidance of these voices saved her life: "When I found myself in the middle of a carjacking, an angel guided my lifesaving actions by speaking to me through an inner voice."

GUIDING VOICES

Individuals gifted with clairaudience have put their skills to many uses. Some hear voices that guide them on their own path in life. Others hear the voices of spirits who want to contact loved ones with a message. Some have been employed by the police to find missing persons because they hear the voices of the missing. It seems clear that these voices are real to the people who hear them, but still the outstanding question remains: Where do they come from? While skeptics argue that they are a product of the percipient's own mind, others believe supernatural forces are at work.

Ectoplasm: The Very Stuff of Ghosts

The term ectoplasm derives from the Greek words *ektos,* meaning "outside," and *plasma,* meaning "something formed or molded," and describes a physical substance from which ghosts and other creatures of the unseen world are said to be formed. This normally invisible substance may become visible or exteriorized once a medium becomes involved with a particular spirit.

Bare Bones

- Ectoplasm is the substance from which ghosts are formed.

- It is normally invisible, but many nineteenth-century mediums claimed to be able to materialize ectoplasm during séances.

- Although many mediums were caught cheating, using substances such as muslin and egg white to fake the appearance of ectoplasm, some famous practitioners, including Mina "Margery" Crandon, were never proved to be cheats, despite careful investigation.

PHYSICAL EVIDENCE

The existence of ectoplasm is much disputed in mainstream scientific circles, particularly because, on the rare occasions when ectoplasm has been gathered and analyzed, the substances have frequently been found to be of wholly human origin, including materials such as chiffon, egg white, and human skin. Observers, however, have concluded that ectoplasm is a whitish substance that comes from any orifice belonging to a medium through whom communication with the spirit world is being conducted. The chosen orifice tends to be the mouth or nose but can be any part of the body.

EARLY ECTOPLASM

The term ectoplasm was coined in the late nineteenth century by the French psychologist Charles Richet who had been observing Madame d'Esperance, a well-known, ectoplasm-producing medium. The couple claimed that at the end of every séance in which Madame d'Esperance participated, she finished covered in a sticky white substance with a gelatinous texture. Observers reported a substance that was sweet-smelling, like freshly picked clover, and sticky, with a membrane-like structure. It was generally recognized that whenever ectoplasm was exposed to daylight, it would immediately be absorbed back into the medium's body, causing him or her maximum discomfort and pain. Skeptics claimed that the detail about the danger of light was invented to mask fraudulent activities. These skeptics, however, could never manage to uncover any such schemes.

In the early 1900s well-known medium Marthe Beraud apparently produced enormous amounts of white and gray material during sittings. A thorough investigation was conducted by the German doctor Baron Albert von Schrenck-Notzing. He examined her before a séance, finding no evidence that she had concealed any chemicals or substances on her body. The baron took careful notes but could see no evidence of sleight of hand. After the séance was over, the doctor declared that Madame Beraud was indisputably covered in an ectoplasmic substance that was white and sticky and which ran "like sticky icicles" down her face and along the length of her body. Having previously eliminated fraud, the baron could think of no adequate rational explanation.

The best-known ectoplasm-producing medium was Mina Crandon. Famous photographs showed her with long spaghetti-like chains of ectoplasm extruding from her ears, mouth, and—most strikingly—from between her legs. Just as with Madame Beraud, no one could adequately explain these photographs using rational arguments, and no cheating was ever exposed.

TWENTIETH-CENTURY SLIME

During the twentieth century, interest in physical manifestations of psychic phenomena has, to a large extent, dwindled, and research has focused more upon mental phenomena. Noel Coward, however, brought the subject of ectoplasm back into the public eye by having his characters mention it in his 1941 play *Blithe Spirit*. Most notably of all, the 1984 hit film *Ghostbusters* features an extraordinary denouement in which most of the central characters end up covered in a viscous white ectoplasmic substance, while Bill Murray's character utters the memorable line, "He slimed me!" This bought heavily into the public consciousness, and interest in ectoplasm was once again ignited.

Charles Richet

French physiologist Charles Richet was made professor of physiology in Paris in 1887 and won the Nobel Prize for Physiology in 1913 for ground-breaking work on allergic reactions. This research made him world famous and, most important, highly respected among his peers.

One of Richet's interests was in extrasensory perception, which meant that other scientists were also encouraged to seriously explore this field of research. In 1884 a colleague, Alexander Aksanov, introduced Richet to a medium called Eusapia Palladino, who so impressed Richet that he founded a scientific journal called the *Annales des Sciences Psychiques* to further research into the paranormal.

After regular contact with many European clairvoyants, Richet was nominated as president of the Society for Psychical Research in 1905 and began conducting experiments on many of the leading ectoplasm-producing mediums of that age, including Marthe Beraud and Madame d'Esperance. He attempted to analyze the chemical makeup of ectoplasm, with limited success, though his work remained the benchmark for many years and lent the subject scientific kudos.

Frauds, Hoaxes, and Skeptics: Bluffing It

A darkened séance room, flickering lights, hidden tape recorders, speaking in tongues, fake ectoplasm, sleight of hand, smoke machines, objects dangling on wires, a few choice words pulled from the depths of the other side...and a medium is born.

Bare Bones

- Popular psychic and paranormal phenomena are relatively easy to fake, and since people have always been prepared to pay to witness such events, fraud is an ever present possibility.

- When Spiritualism was at the height of its popularity in the latter half of the nineteenth century, many fraudulent mediums were exposed.

- As long as there are fraudsters and hoaxers around there will be people who devote their time and energy to exposing them. Harry Houdini was an early example, while James Randi continues the tradition today.

In the realm of the paranormal, evidence and scientific proof are hard to obtain, and in order to convince paying customers, some mediums and psychics have been known to put on quite a show. From the days of Franz Mesmer, who introduced hypnotism, to today's psychic hotlines, clients have accepted without question words from their loved ones, the existence of spirits and poltergeists, bending spoons, and other psychic phenomena. People have always been fascinated by the other world, ESP, spirits, and ghosts, often making them easy targets for fraud—some people are simply gullible, while others ignore the telltale signs of a deceiver. However, from Harry Houdini in the 1900s to James Randi, who posts his encyclopedia of skepticism online today, a group of people has always stood ready to highlight these fraudulent ways.

IS THERE ANYBODY THERE?

Even in the early days of mediumship, competition was fierce, and for some mediums parlor tricks became a way of commanding higher prices. Séances, mind-reading, and psychic phenomena became popular forms of entertainment in the late 1800s, and fraud became widespread.

Mediums claim to channel the spirit of another—they might speak in a loud, booming voice, or they might appear to faint or swoon as a spirit takes hold of them. The reported manifestations of a spirit are drafts, strange noises, or an unusual voice, and these elements are easy to fake. Skeptics argue that mediums pull a very basic trick. If you say, "There is a David here," there is a good chance that someone in a group of 12 seated around a table will have known a David.

Arthur Ford became the United States's best-known psychic in the 1900s and founded the First Spiritualist Church of New York. However, it may be that Ford almost succeded in perpetrating one of the best-known hoaxes of all time. In his lifetime Harry Houdini

Magician and escapologist Harry Houdini went on a crusade to expose fraudulent mediums. He devised a code that was known only to himself and his wife, Bess, to prevent mediums from fraudulently claiming to have contacted him after his death.

The Cottingley Fairies

The case of the Cottingley Fairies in England sparked the imagination of millions around the globe and was even made into the 1990s film *Photographing Fairies,* with Peter O'Toole and Harvey Keitel.

Five photographs taken in 1917 by the young Elsie Wright and Frances Griffiths appeared to show the girls surrounded by cavorting fairies. Media types, Theosophists, photographic experts, clairvoyants, and even Sir Arthur Conan Doyle traveled to Cottingley near Bradford in the UK to see the girls and their photographs. Conan Doyle, a Spiritualist, keen to believe that the photographs proved the existence of fairies, then wrote two supportive articles for *Strand* magazine.

Elsie and Frances maintained their enigmatic silence until their seventies, when they revealed that the photographs had been a hoax. However, they both maintain that Frances did see fairies in Cottingley and was fed up with the scorn she received from adults, so with cardboard cutouts and hat pins, they created a fairy community dancing in the undergrowth.

set out to extinguish fraud from the ranks of Spiritualists and mediums. Although Houdini believed in Spiritualism, he recognized the amount of fraud committed under its banner. He devised a test with his wife, Bess, and after his death, which fell on Halloween 1926, she offered a reward of $10,000 to anyone who could break a code they had devised together before he died. Every Halloween for 10 years, Bess hosted a séance hoping for Houdini's spirit to show up. Although she enjoyed debunking fraudulent mediums and hoaxers, she also missed Houdini and genuinely hoped to hear from him. Having gleaned information that appeared in an interview with Bess in a newspaper, Arthur Ford mentioned the secret word "forgive" during one of these séances. During another séance in January, secret words were again thrown out to the waiting table. Ford had done extensive research into Houdini's life. Eventually Ford tried to bribe a rather ill Bess Houdini into saying that he had broken the code. He never received the $10,000.

Similarly, the housekeeper of famous medium Helena Blavatsky divulged secrets to the media in the late 1800s. One of Blavatsky's skills was to make a cedar wood shrine containing letters from the other side magically appear. According to the *Times* of London, "A faithful disciple, wishing to demonstrate that fraud was impossible, had slapped the rear wall of the shrine saying, 'You see, it's perfectly solid,' when, to his dismay, a panel had shot open, revealing another panel in the wall of Blavatsky's boudoir!"

"YOU WILL HAVE A LONG LIFE AND MANY CHILDREN!"

In terms of clairvoyance and divination, people can be somewhat predictable. Most have been heartbroken at some point and want to find a tall, dark, handsome stranger waiting around the corner. People want to hear that they will have success in their work, their loves, and their lives. "Is there a significant D in your life?" A psychic may ask. This could be a Daniel, a drummer, a dollar sign, a dog, or a druid. Usually people will rack their minds and come up with something. If not, the next question is, "Well, maybe it's a 'B'?" As the character Jesse in *Before Sunrise* says, "I'd like just once for some old lady to go to the palmreader all excited and for her to say, 'You will have no new experiences, no new passions, in fact every day will be exactly like this one.'" Nobody wants to hear that, so they will take what they can get. Leading questions deliver enough information for a tarot reader or palmist to give a successful reading. Fortune-tellers also get clues from clothes, jewelry, hairstyles, and so on, in what is called cold reading.

According to debunker Ian Rowland,

To begin with, we are all much less unusual than we think we are. People are often amazed at what I can "see" in the cards about their early life. What they don't realize is that I give the same account to everyone. For instance, most of us have had one serious accident or know someone who has. And many of us have had a relationship where distance was a problem, and so on. Also people tend to do certain things at certain times in their life. So to a man in his forties I would say: "Something that used to be important to you when you were a child has been coming back into your life." That's because men of that age have the money to indulge in their childhood hobbies and they often do. For a woman in her 30s I would certainly suggest that babies had been in her thoughts.

Psychic hotlines have become big business. Richard Dworman, editor of the *Infomercial Marketing Report*, estimates Psychic Friends Network's gross annual income at $100 million.

On a more sinister note, NBCs *Unsolved Mysteries* heard from many unsettled callers after showing an episode

"What the eyes see and the ears hear the mind believes." —HARRY HOUDINI, MAGICIAN

that highlighted the fraud of a fortune-teller who swindled Mrs. Josephine Wallace, a widow, out of $200,000 in cash and jewelry. The fortune-tellers also persuaded her to buy them a $30,000 Cadillac. Like Josephine Wallace, people from around North America have been duped in similar scams where they were told that a family curse was upon them. In a similar case in Hartford, Connecticut, a mother and daughter team are serving concurrent sentences of 230 years in prison for duping 12 people practically out of house and home. Fraudsters have convinced some victims that they need to spend $100 on a special candle or buy specific jewelry for rituals. Other people have been convinced that money they have inherited is evil and must be cleansed.

PUTTING ON A SHOW

Despite receiving accolades from the *New York Times* and Barbara Walters, as well as convincing researchers at the Stanford Research Institute that he could foresee events, those close to Uri Geller say that his work and skills are merely parlor tricks. Close friends report that they used to give him signals from the audience. One stipulation of his performance was that his "brother" always received a front-row seat. One friend reported:

> One time was when Nasser of Egypt died. Uri was in the midst of a performance, and we notified him of this news through the curtains at the back of the stage. The audience, naturally, did not know a thing about it. As soon as we conveyed the news to him, he exploited this information in a most theatrical manner. He appeared to be fainting, and called for a doctor. A doctor volunteered from the audience and came up on the stage. Uri asked him to take his pulse right in front of the crowd of 700 people. Uri said to him, "I feel terrible. Very, very bad. I feel bad because I think Nasser is dying right now. Right this minute." Naturally, immediately after the performance the audience left the theater and found out about Nasser's death. Thousands of people were convinced that Uri Geller was a prophet.

Professional magician James Randi, also known as The Amazing Randi, has publicly exposed a number of psychics and Spiritualists. In *Time* magazine Randi debunked Geller's tricks of spoon bending and levitation as "nothing you couldn't get off the back of a cornflakes box so to speak."

Similarly, across the globe many people believe that the spiritual work of Sai Baba in India is all an illusion. Baba is reputed to be a living guru who produces watches, jewelry, and holy ash, *vibhutti*, for his followers as proof of his *siddhis*, or powers. A BBC program

The Amazing Randi—professional magician James Randi—sets out to debunk myths, frauds, and hoaxes on stage and on his website. His Educational Foundation offers a million-dollar reward for anyone who can prove that they have psychic or supernatural powers.

called *Guru Busters* set out to disprove his tricks. Even his birth date seems to have been falsified to fulfill a prophecy. On a more serious note, whether he has jewelry or sacred ash up his sleeve seems fairly irrelevant; he has also been accused of child abuse.

THINGS THAT GO BUMP IN THE NIGHT

Fueled by TV shows—both fictional, like *Ghost Whisperer* and allegedly factual, like Derek Acorah's *Most Haunted*—the ghost-buster trade is ever popular. Under the guise of liberating earth-bound spirits or exorcizing ghosts, psychics and exorcists brandish electronic devices that pick up electromagnetic fields. Poltergeist or spirit activity is proclaimed if the needle moves or if sound waves are detected, although the anomoly is more likely caused by an appliance or an extractor fan. Some ghostbusters or spirit detectives receive vibes the old-fashioned way: Spirits are detected by drafts (prevalent in old houses—the preferred residence of most ghosts) or through ESP, which is impossible to prove or disprove.

Theosophy: Blavatsky's Brainchild

Theosophy, derived from the Greek *theos,* meaning "god," and *sophia,* meaning "wisdom," is a spiritual practice rooted in the belief that all the major religions of the world come from one original, universal religion, which has, like a great oak tree, spawned varied offshoots, each using different symbols. Modern Theosophy draws on the spiritual traditions of ancient China and India, among others, as well as on medieval mysticism and magic. The ideas of karma and reincarnation are particularly popular with Theosophists.

Bare Bones

- Modern Theosophy is a spiritual practice that was founded by Helena Petrovna Blavatsky and William Q. Judge in 1875.

- Theosophy is based on the belief that all modern religions come from one original, universal religion, and it draws on ancient mystical traditions from all over the globe.

- The three main aims of Theosophists are to investigate the unexplained and man's latent powers; to "form a universal brotherhood of humanity without distinction of race, creed, or color"; and to study comparative religion.

The term Theosophy first appears in Greek Neoplatonist philosophy but later reappears in Enlightenment thought, particularly in the work of the Swedish philosopher Emanuel Swedenborg. In *Heaven and Hell* he expressed the desire to reform Christianity partially through Theosophy.

BLAVATSKY'S EARLY LIFE

Modern Theosophy, however, was founded by Helena Petrovna Blavatsky, who had a deep interest in magic and the occult since her early childhood in Russia. Blavatsky was born in 1831, the daughter of a colonel and the well-known Russian novelist Eelena Andreyevna Fadeyeva. Sergei Witte, the Russian prime minister under the reign of Emperor Nicholas II, was Blavatsky's first cousin. She grew up in the midst of the Russian Enlightenment, where she was introduced to culture, poetry, mythology, and spirituality at an early age. According to Blavatsky, because she had been born in the seventh month of the year, all the locals referred to her as a *sedmitchka* (a word that translates roughly as "seventh monther"), which, she claimed, indicated she had certain supernatural powers.

Blavatsky spent much of the year 1848 and the following decade traveling the world and, eventually, journied to Tibet to learn about ancient wisdoms. She spent two years studying with a venerable lama in whose company she apparently witnessed many inexplicable events, including a reincarnation ceremony during which a four-month-old baby stood up and spoke the words, "I am Buddha. I am the old lama. I am his spirit in a new body."

A MEDIUM IS BORN

This event had a profound influence on Blavatsky's philosophy of life. She returned to Russia, where she found that other people's interest in the paranormal had also grown, and she began to develop and exploit her skills as a medium. Sergei Witte wrote that on one occasion Blavatsky closed a piano lid, walked into an adjacent room, and then caused the piano to start playing. Following much publicity, Blavatsky decided to travel to New York in 1873, where she continued to impress the public with her psychic abilities, making a small fortune as a medium. In 1875 she founded the Theosophical Society with William Q. Judge. The original idea purported the continued study of esoteric subjects such as the Egyptian mysteries and the kabbalah.

They soon gathered a huge following and began to organize their society in the greatest secrecy, acknowledging each other with secret names and symbols. Blavatsky wrote that all religions were both true in their teachings and deeply flawed in their public manifestations. Much of her work connected esoteric spiritual knowledge with scientific doctrine, and many researchers believe that her writings are the first true expressions of what is now referred to as New Age thinking. A scandal developed, however, when a communication that Blavatsky claimed to have received from ancient Mahatmas appeared, upon investigation, to have been written in her own handwriting. She concluded that she had used automatic writing without being conscious of her powers, but the seeds of skepticism had been sown.

In December 1884 Richard Hodgson of the Society for Psychical Research in London went to the Theosophical Society's headquarters in Adyar, India, to investigate and declared that many of her statements and her writings were fraudulent. However, in 1986, long after her death, the Society for Psychical Research published a partial apology.

The Theosophical Society in Adyar

Madame Blavatsky founded the Theosophical Society's original headquarters in Adyar, India, near Chennai, in 1875. Lawyer, mystic, and occultist William Quan Judge subsequently established a rival branch in North America, but the two are now entirely separate.

Presidents of the Adyar Society have included Annie Besant, Nilakanta Sri Ram, and currently, Radha Burnier, who is Nilakanta's daughter. The society's aims remain the same as Blavatsky's, and a president is elected every seven years by members all over the world. There is also a vice president and a secretary, who acts as archivist. An executive committee implements decisions and oversees the society's financial affairs.

In individual countries members are organized into lodges, and when any one country has seven lodges, these may be reorganized into a national section, where committee members are democratically elected by local members. The only prerequisite for joining the society is support of its three main objects.

After the 2004 tsunami hit Adyar, many inhabitants were affected, and the Theosophical Society played a key role in helping to reestablish their daily lives.

BASIC TENETS

In 1877 Blavatsky produced a book entitled *Isis Unveiled*, which contained more than 1,300 pages of her thoughts on life. This was followed by the *Secret Doctrine* of 1888, which she claimed had been dictated to her by the Mahatmas and included material on the creation of the universe, the evolution of humankind, and the traditions underlying various religions and philosophies. Blavatsky later published two more books, *The Key to Theosophy*—a basic introduction to her work, and *The Voice of the Silence*, a mystical and poetic guide to enlightenment. Each of these works highlights the three main tenets of Theosophy. The first is the attempt "to investigate the unexplained laws of nature and the powers latent in Man." The second is an attempt to "form a universal brotherhood of humanity without distinction of race, creed, or color," and the third is to study comparative religion.

The ideas constituted an extremely modern philosophy founded on the ancient belief that nature does not operate by chance. Theosophists believe in an omnipresent, inexplicable principle behind all human life and that the human soul, being a mirror of the divine universe, is immortal and indestructible. The soul reincarnates into successive lives, they believe, from the mineral to the animal. Once the soul has attained self-consciousness, it does not regress back to animal form; instead, it embarks upon a long journey toward physical and mental perfection. Humankind, they believe, possesses a sevenfold constitution, extending from the physical to the purely spiritual, and the three higher planes form the higher self or essential soul, which can reincarnate and refine itself through the different spiritual planes. For Theosophists religion, philosophy, and the arts all assist in a soul's elevation to these higher planes.

Blavatsky also proclaimed that the true teachers of Theosophical wisdom were the Mahatmas, the old souls or

> ## "We are outwardly creatures of a day; within we are eternal."
>
> —H. P. BLAVATSKY, FOUNDER OF THE THEOSOPHICAL SOCIETY

Helena Petrovna Blavatsky emigrated from Russia to New York City in 1873 where her fame as a Spiritualist medium spread rapidly. In 1875 she founded the Theosophical Society, which still thrives today.

masters of wisdom, who had completed their own cycles of earthly incarnations and returned to Earth to spread their message among those who might be open to learning. Blavatsky declared that through the Mahatmas, she had knowledge that the planets and solar systems are also conscious beings, fulfilling their own evolutionary paths.

FALL FROM GRACE

Since Blavatsky had also declared that humanity was descended from "root races" and that the so-called "Aryan race" was descended from the superior "Atlanteans," some of Blavatsky's ideas were later interpreted by Nazi sympathizers who used elements of her work to declare that Aryans were intellectually superior and that certain other races were degenerate offshoots of the original tree. After World War II this misinterpretation led to a decline in Theosophic converts, but in recent decades, with a renewed interest in spirituality, the movement has undergone a resurgence. There are now Theosophical organizations in more than 60 countries and each one with solid membership.

Anthroposophy: Steiner's Way

Anthroposophy is a philosophy based on the teachings of Rudolf Steiner, an Austrian philosopher. He stated that the world is an intellectually comprehensible, spiritual place that can be studied, understood, and therefore lived in a more spiritual way. According to Steiner, the best way to achieve this is through directly experiencing inner spiritual development, which can occur only via a "sense of thinking," independent of the five normal human senses. To this day Anthroposophy aims to achieve the rigor and clarity of the scientific world to demonstrate the possibilities of the spiritual one.

Bare Bones

- Rudolph Steiner founded the Anthroposophical Society in 1912.

- Steiner was originally involved with the Theosophical Society but split from it as he moved toward a more Christian, science-based outlook.

- Anthroposophy sees itself as a way to extend the positive aspects of scientific rigor into the realm of the spiritual, with the development of creative techniques to enable humans to fulfill their spiritual and intellectual potential.

In Rudolf Steiner's early work, *The Philosophy of Freedom*, he developed the idea of free will based on inner spiritual experiences, especially those that arise out of creative activities. By the early twentieth century his research had become more explicitly spiritual, and he had become involved with his local Theosophical Society, of which he soon became the local secretary. By 1907,

Rudolph Steiner designed the striking Goetheanum in Switzerland as the headquarters of the Anthroposophical Society. It was built entirely in cast concrete after an earlier, wooden version burned down.

however, he had veered away from Theosophy's Eastern approach and moved toward a more Christian, science-based outlook.

BREAKING AWAY

Steiner was, by this stage, a well-known spiritual leader with a large following, and as the schism solidified, the entire German chapter of the Theosophical Society seceded from London, becoming an independent entity. Steiner believed that spirituality could be available to everyone but that a person's spiritual development could follow only from his or her moral refinement.

Steiner founded the Anthroposophical Society in 1912 and, after World War I, used its facilities to start projects in schools, centers for the handicapped, and organic farms. By 1923 Steiner had realized that, although the older members were more interested in spiritual concerns, younger followers engaged in projects geared toward social welfare. In a successful attempt to be inclusive, he founded the School for Spiritual Science.

SCIENTIFIC MYSTICISM

Anthroposophy still sees itself as a way to extend the positive aspects of scientific rigor into the realm of the spiritual. Steiner said that traditional mysticism was too vague to be useful and that natural science was too narrow to be inclusive. He believed humans consist of physical, etheric, astral, and spiritual parts and that creative techniques like imagination and inspiration allow people to combine scientific thought with these four areas to achieve self-awareness. Steiner believed the capacity for enlightened rational thought enables humans to think and reason independently and that this would eliminate the need for external authority. This was clearly antithetical to National Socialist ideology, and the Nazis banned the movement for a number of years. Since World War II, however, the movement has undergone a renaissance, and there are now more than 10,000 institutions worldwide. Modern Anthroposophists now successfully apply Steiner's principles to practical applications like the production of medicines, organic farming, and education.

Biodynamic Agriculture

Biodynamic agriculture is a method of farming based on Rudolf Steiner's philosophy. He began lecturing on the subject in 1924 after local farmers complained about soil deterioration. He concluded that soil, plants, and animals are interconnected systems requiring natural balance and nonchemical fertilizers. He advocated the use of astronomical calendars to determine when to plant and harvest crops.

These ideas caught on, and many now regard this as the first modern ecological farming system. Steiner believed that the farm was a self-contained, holistic entity with its own individuality. Crops should be rotated and recycled. He prescribed nine preparations to use as fertilizers, which are numbered from 500 to 508. Fertilizer 500, for example, is a humus mixture made of cow manure left to decompose throughout the winter. Number 501 is composed of powdered quartz sprayed gently during the wet season. Various studies have shown that biodynamic compost contains relatively high amounts of nitrate and greater organic matter than other types. Although there is no significant difference in yield, crops often taste better.

Paranormal Experiences

Those who have undergone a paranormal experience rarely doubt that what has happened to them has not only been odd but inexplicable. Some find their experiences disturbing, even terrifying. Others feel comforted and reassured by what has happened. A few people are changed forever, so awesome has been the impact of the event. A great many more simply move on with their lives, always aware that they have been touched by the paranormal. The reaction to a paranormal experience seems to depend as much on the person as on the experience. But all can agree on one point: Paranormal experiences are extraordinary affairs.

Defining the Paranormal

Anyone who spends time researching the paranormal will sooner or later experience the recurring problem of how to define the term and what it seeks to describe.

Bare Bones

- The word paranormal was coined in the early twentieth century to lend respectability to the study of psychic phenomena.

- Its literal meaning is "beyond normal."

- While some researchers include any phenomenon that has no obvious explanation as paranormal, others prefer to limit its application only to phenomena that can be studied scientifically.

The word paranormal itself is fairly modern. Forty years ago it would have had people scratching their heads and reaching for the dictionary. It is, in fact, a made-up word that began its life in the early twentieth century and was generally ignored until the 1980s.

It is composed of two elements. *Para* is taken from ancient Greek and in modern parlance means beyond or additional. For example, paramilitary forces are units that undertake military duties without being formally part of a military organization. "Normal" is a perfectly ordinary English word with a meaning similar to "ordinary." Therefore, a strict dictionary definition of the word might be rendered as "beyond the ordinary." That, however, fails to cover the wide range of phenomena included by the word. In fact, the history of the word and how it is defined says much about society's attitudes toward the paranormal.

A VENEER OF RESPECTABILITY

The word was invented to lend scientific respectability to the subject. By adopting a word with Greek roots, those seeking to conduct scientific investigations hoped to distinguish themselves from the rather unfortunate connotations already established with earlier words and phrases used to describe the same thing.

Some used the word psychical, coined in the nineteenth century, to describe most of what people today refer to as paranormal. Several serious institutions were founded with the words psychic or psychical in their titles. One of the most prestigious organizations to undertake serious scientific investigations into the paranormal is the Society for Psychical Research in London. Before long, all sorts of individuals and groups more interested in the sensational and bizarre than in rigorous investigations adopted the term psychical into their vocabularies. By the 1920s the word had become inextricably linked to mediums, séances, and similar less-than-scientific activities.

The search was on for a term that had the respectability that psychical had lost. Supernatural was the next word to surface, but that swiftly adopted a more general and sensationalist meaning as well. A variety of other terms surfaced, among them perceptual studies and anomalous processes, before the word paranormal gained a following in the latter half of the twentieth century.

CASTING THE NET WIDE

After establishing that paranormal phenomena include events that lie outside what science teaches is possible, the problem then becomes what types of occurrences to include. There are as many answers to this questions as there are investigators.

Some paranormal investigators want to include almost anything people claim to have witnessed or experienced that has no immediately obvious explanation. They spread the net wide to embrace all sorts of odd occurrences, such as fish falling from the sky or monsters in Loch Ness.

Others prefer to limit the paranormal to include only those phenomena that lend themselves to rigorous scientific study. Prophecies, for example, can be written down so that the outcome can later be observed to see how closely it resembles the prediction. The subject provokes highly charged debates. Some researchers would classify religious visions as paranormal experiences, while others would find this offensive. By its nature the paranormal is a shifting and uncertain subject, and researchers must handle deep-seated beliefs with sensitivity, while also investigating to eliminate fraud and expand the boundaries of current scientific understanding.

The English philosopher Henry Sidgwick was famous for his many liberal and unconventional activities. In 1882 he became the first president of the Society for Psychical Research.

"By far the most usual way of handling phenomena so novel that they would make for a serious rearrangement of our preconceptions is to ignore them..."

—PROFESSOR WILLIAM JAMES, PSYCHOLOGIST AND PHILOSOPHER

Near-Death and Out-of-Body Experiences

The terms out-of-body experience (OBE, or sometimes OOBE) and its variant near-death Experience (NDE) describe an event known for many years, but in the past such events were viewed as tricks played by mischievous spirits or sometimes as some sort of religious vision.

Bare Bones

- Out-of-body experiences have been recorded in different cultures for thousands of years.

- During an OBE the soul, or astral body, apparently separates from the physical body and moves around independently.

- A near-death experience is similar but occurs at the point of death. Typically, people report seeing their body from above before moving on through a tunnel toward a source of light.

- Documented reports of NDEs are consistent throughout different periods in history and across different cultures.

SOUL SEPARATION

The Christian tradition has long held that the body and the soul are distinct entities. In his Second Letter to the Corinthians, Saint Paul wrote about a man who had an experience that researchers today might easily classify as an OBE. "I knew a man whether in the body, I cannot tell; or whether out of the body, I cannot tell; God knoweth. He was caught up into Paradise and heard unspeakable words, which it is not lawful for a man to utter. Of such one will I glory."

The thirteenth-century Saint Anthony of Padua is another Christian figure who is said to have had an OBE. Saint Anthony was a Franciscan friar who was in demand as a preacher. One day while in the middle of preaching a sermon at a church in Limoges, he suddenly remembered that he had promised to do a Bible reading for another service at the same time in a different church in the town. Saint Anthony knelt down in silent prayer for a few minutes, then arose and continued his sermon. Meanwhile, in the other church parishioners saw Saint Anthony stride up to the lectern, read his allotted passage, and then leave again.

What makes the experience of Saint Anthony different from that of most other OBEs is that he was seen by independent observers in two different places at the same time. Most people who experience an OBE are seen by other people only in the one place, though they may report moving around or being somewhere else.

CLOSE TO DEATH

During World War I Ernest Hemingway was serving in the trenches when a German shell exploded nearby and a splinter of shrapnel plunged into his body. Hemingway reported that after the immediate pain, he felt calm and tranquil, free from pain or feeling except for a general sensation of lightness. He felt himself floating into the air and out of his body, "rather like you would pull a silk handkerchief out of a pocket by one corner." After spending a few seconds floating above the battlefield, Hemingway felt drawn irresistibly back to his body, whereupon the pain recurred. He opened his eyes to see his comrades administering first aid to him. Hemingway later decided that he had been killed and his soul left his body. The swift action of his fellow soldiers had brought him back from the dead, dragging his soul back to the body.

On a similar note, Lord Geddes, a highly regarded Scottish doctor in the early 1930s, once had a seizure and collapsed in his study. Geddes felt his body go limp and made relentless efforts to reach the phone to call for help when he realized that he was not actually seeing the phone from where he lay slumped in his chair but from above, near the ceiling of the room. No sooner had he realized this than Geddes found himself floating above his house and over the garden. There he met an invisible being that he could not define, other than to say that the entity was benevolent and powerful. The being explained that Geddes was free of his body and could move on to wherever he wished.

Geddes then saw a friend enter his study, grab the phone, and call a doctor. The doctor arrived and administered an injection. Geddes was promptly pulled back to his body, much against his will. He then felt himself losing consciousness. When he came to some hours later, Geddes learned that events had unfolded exactly as he had seen them when apparently out of his body.

Another inexplicable experience involves an African farmer who was run over by a truck on a remote road outside Moshi in Tanzania. "I suddenly found that I was watching the scene from several yards up in the air," he wrote later. "I watched as I was

---

The Study of OBE

The modern study of the OBE can be traced back to the work of Professor Dean Shiels of the University of Wisconsin. In 1976 he produced a study that collected accounts and stories about OBEs from around the world. Shiels did not himself investigate any of the cases he documented but did establish the phenomenon as a potentially real event. What had before been scattered references to odd events now had a definite name and a description.

Shiels's study suggested that more detailed studies and investigations might reveal more about OBEs. The University of Virginia, for instance, has conducted a survey of students and residents in Charlottesville. Of the 1,000 people questioned, 180 declared that they had, at some time or another, felt detached from their bodies. Most of these experiences fell short of a true OBE, but they do indicate that some sort of phenomenon is taking place that has gradations of intensity.

thrown about and as my friend came over to examine my body. I also saw the lorry drive off. I remember thinking that I looked a terrible mess lying there on the road and could well be dead." He then blacked out and came to in the hospital a couple of days later.

"Eternity is not something that happens after you are dead. It's going on all the time." —CHARLOTTE PERKINS GILMAN, AUTHOR

These OBEs, and others like them, share many common features. The person, under enormous physical stress from either injury or illness, suffers unconsciousness. Those nearby observe nothing unusual. The unconscious person experiences the feeling of leaving his or her body and reports witnessing the scene from a different vantage point, usually at least a few feet up in the air.

The key problem with OBEs is obtaining independent evidence of what actually occurs. Those experiencing the OBE seem to possess knowledge of what occurred while they were unconscious, but scientifically that proves little. Although apparently senseless, the person may still be absorbing sounds and even sights of the world around them. Some people rationalize this by claiming that the subconscious mind can still retain information when a person sleeps or faints—though quite why this floating phenomenon recurs so often is unclear.

ONE STEP FURTHER

Although many OBEs occur when a person is close to death, or at least seriously injured, the true near-death experience is on an altogether different scale. A typical NDE begins as an OBE, though the percipient is often aware that he or she is dying and going on a journey. The experience progresses, and the person feels that he or she is traveling along a tunnel or through a cavern out of this world toward another. This other world is often visible as a brightly lit room or a field at the far end of a tunnel.

Most NDEs end at this juncture, and the percipient returns to the physical body. Some people report that they snap back to their body, while others say that they are told by some entity that it is not yet their time to travel and that they need to return home. A few NDEs reportedly progress further, and the percipients exit from the tunnel to enter the new world of light. There they are met by a human figure—sometimes a friend or relative who has died recently. This figure welcomes the person and sometimes passes on a message, before firmly turning the percipient away and sending him or her back to their bodies.

Individuals who have undergone an NDE generally report a loss of all fear of death. They often believe their experience to have spiritual or religious significance, which they interpret according to their own culture, despite the fact that the experience itself is independent of that culture. Christians, for instance, do not meet Christ, and Hindus do not meet Hindu deities. Some claim the experience represents information buried deep in the human psyche that surfaces only under the stress of apparent death. Others truly believe these experiences reflect a preview of the afterlife.

An eighteenth-century illustration depicting the moment a soul leaves a dying person. The way the soul is depicted floating upward is typical of the way that many near-death experiences are reported.

Reincarnation and Past Lives

The conundrum of what occurs after death has puzzled religions, mystics, and philosophers for millennia. Many ideas have been put forth, but the essential mystery remains. Is the human soul somehow separate from the body that houses it, as most religions hold, and if so, can it survive the death of that body? Just as important, where does it go next?

Bare Bones

- Reincarnation teaches that the soul not only survives death but is subsequently reborn into another physical body.

- This belief is central to both Buddhism and Hinduism, but many other people also believe it to be true.

- In recent years several cases note people recalling their past lives in some detail while under hypnosis.

Some religions maintain that the soul is reborn into another body. Hindus, Jains, Sikhs, and Buddhists all hold that reincarnation—in varying forms—is a fact. The old Germanic pagan religion and the traditional beliefs of the Inuit also support reincarnation, as do others. The precise way in which reincarnation happens, and the theological reasons for it, vary from religion to religion. Buddhists, for instance, believe that the soul is on a journey through many lives in a quest to achieve spiritual enlightenment.

LOOKING FOR PROOF

While scholars in the East have generally accepted reincarnation, Western investigators have demanded proof. Until recently this research centered around young children claiming to be reincarnated. These children generally begin to recall events from previous lives at about three years old but have forgotten these details by the age of around seven. Many cases occur in the East, and most of these claims are blindly accepted by those around them but not investigated unless explored by westerners with an interest in reincarnation.

One example dates back to 1930, when a four-year-old girl from Delhi, Shanti Deva, announced that she had once lived in the village of Muttra. She claimed she had been a woman named Ludgi who died giving birth to her fourth child. When taken to Muttra, Shanti recognized the family home where a mother named Ludgi had died in childbirth a few years earlier. Shanti also recognized several people in the village, telling them things that had been known only to themselves and the now deceased Ludgi.

The British authorities of colonial India viewed such events as odd and interesting but made no real attempt at a systematic investigation—not until 1967, when Dr. Ian Stevenson began a systematic study of such phenomena.

Much of Dr. Stevenson's evidence is open to dispute because he did not personally investigate every case and, in some instances, accepted information reported by witnesses some years after an incident occurred. In such cases recollections of a past life could represent nothing more than a childhood fantasy or a deliberate falsification. Stevenson, however, always drew a clear distinction between his own investigations and evidence and stories that he had collected second- or third-hand.

One compelling case that Stevenson himself investigated involved a young boy from a Druze village in Lebanon, who

U.S. general George Patton was a firm believer in reincarnation, and thought that in a previous life he had been the ancient military commander Hannibal. Hannibal's greatest victory at Cannae in 216 B.C. had involved a maneuver known as the double envelopment, also one of Patton's favored military tactics.

claimed he had been reincarnated. Stevenson did not arrange the trip in advance, giving the family in question no advance notice of his arrival or intentions. On arrival Stevenson found the boy, Imad Elawar, and questioned the five-year-old closely. He noted 57 statements made by Imad about his former life. Stevenson then drove to the village where Imad claimed to have been a farmer in his earlier life. Of the 57 statements, about 30 were quickly established as true, and none could be proved false.

PROMINENT BELIEVERS

Although the West has displayed only a limited interest in the idea of reincarnation, some have become firm believers. Motor magnate, Henry Ford, for example, commented:

> I adopted the theory of reincarnation when I was 26. Religion offered nothing to the point. Even work could not give me complete satisfaction. Work is futile if we cannot utilize the experience we collect in one life in the next. When I discovered reincarnation it was as if I had found a universal plan; I realized that there was a chance to work out my ideas. Time was no longer limited...Genius is experience. Some seem to think that it is a gift or talent, but it is the fruit of long experience in many lives. Some are older souls than others, and so they know more. The discovery of reincarnation put my mind at ease. If you preserve a record of this conversation, write it so that it puts men's minds at ease. I would like to communicate to others the calmness that the long view of life gives to us.

Ford believed that one of his previous incarnations was a soldier killed at the Battle of Gettysburg, the climactic battle of the American Civil War, fought in 1863. Another firm believer in reincarnation was U.S. World War II general George Patton, who expressed the belief that he was the reincarnation of the ancient Carthaginian commander Hannibal.

HYPNOTIC REGRESSION

In recent years reincarnation interest and research has centered on hypnotic regressions to past lives. It has been known since the early twentieth century that some people, when asked under hypnosis to travel back in time, will spontaneously relate that they once lived in some remote historical period. Such cases have only been studied on a systematic basis since the 1970s. However, the work began in 1956 with Emile Franckel, who was employed by NBC to produce a series of TV shows in Los Angeles, and it has continued with many others, such as Colorado businessman Morey Bernstein and the British researcher Arnall Bloxham. It was Bloxham's tape recordings of his hypnotic sessions that brought the phenomenon to the wider public in the 1980s.

Some of the results of this sort of hypnotic regression are impressive. In the 1960s Joanne MacIver was hypnotized by her father, and while in this state, she claimed she was Susan Ganier, a farm girl born in St. Vincent, Ontario, in 1835. MacIver related many incidents from Ganier's life and recalled numerous details about rural nineteenth-century Canada. Hypnotist Jess Stearn set out to verify these details. He soon found that a Susan Ganier had lived in St. Vincent at the time stated, and he located records of many of the people mentioned by MacIver. He even found an 85-year-old man who recalled Susan Ganier, then an old woman, living nearby when he was a child. He also dug a hole where MacIver claimed there was a well, only to find a well that had been filled in 100 years earlier and totally forgotten about. The vast majority of past lives recalled under hypnosis are as mundane as that of Susan Ganier. This makes the claims easier to believe than claims of past royalty or notoriety, but it also makes it frustratingly difficult to check them against historical data. When a person cannot be identified from records, it may mean either that this person never existed or that the records were poorly kept.

Skeptics believe that these apparent past lives represent details from long-forgotten history lessons or books read long ago and that hypnotized individuals may unconsciously combine this information with their own imaginations, living out a fantasy that appeals to them on a subconscious level. Other people maintain, however, that hypnotic sessions indeed extract memories of a previous existence and therefore prove the concept of reincarnation.

The Case of Bridey Murphy

In 1952 and 1953 Wisconsin housewife Virginia Tighe recounted under hypnosis details of a previous life as Bridey Murphy, an Irish woman from Cork born around 1796 who married and then moved to Belfast. Tighe spoke with a faint Irish accent when recalling the life of Murphy, giving numerous details about Bridey's life and about conditions in Ireland at the time.

Journalist William J. Barker subsequently checked these accounts. He found that some of the most obscure information given by Tighe about coinage, dancing, and music was true, and even that shops in Dublin had been owned and run by men named by Tighe. On the other hand, the church she claimed to have attended never existed. Most frustrating was the fact that all records of births and marriages from Cork in this period have been lost.

It was later found that an old Irish woman had lived near Mrs. Tighe when she was a young girl, and there has been speculation that she picked up the details of nineteenth-century Irish life from her. On the other hand, no evidence exists to suggest that the two ever met. Even if they had, many people find the level of detail in Bridey Murphy's story impressive.

Prophecies and Predictions

Predicting the future has long held a fascination for humankind. After all, if the outcome of a horse race could be known in advance, a veritable fortune could be won. If it were known that a train was to crash, an early death could clearly be averted by not getting aboard.

Bare Bones

- Throughout history man has been fascinated by the possibility of predicting the future, despite all the dilemmas that this could produce.

- One of the most famous prophets of the past was Nostradamus, who made a substantial amount of money from his apparent ability to predict the future.

- Unfortunately, the majority of prophecies are only recognizable after they have been fulfilled. They rarely provide enough detail to prevent the tragedies they foretell from occurring.

NOSTRADAMUS

Among the most famous prophecies of the past are those made by Nostradamus, the pseudonym of scholar and doctor Michel de Nostradame de St. Remy. Born into a prosperous Jewish family in 1503, Nostradamus converted to Christianity while still a boy. As an adult, he produced a vast quantity of prophetic writings, grew his hair and beard long to better look the part, and earned substantial cash by his writings. It was claimed that in the course of his wanderings, while in Rome he saw three Franciscan monks herding cattle. Nostradamus then flung himself to the ground in front of one of them, convinced that he was the pope in disguise. The young monk was no such thing but was Felice Peretti, who eventually became Pope Sextus V.

Officially, he did not predict the future, since he was wary of offending the tribunal of the Inquisition, which could inflict savage punishments on heretics. Most often Nostradamus wrote in verses, which mixed Latin, Greek, and French. This made his predictions difficult to translate and even more tricky to interpret.

One prediction that quickly got Nostradamus into trouble was:

> The young lion will overcome the older one on the field of combat
> in a single battle, Inside a cage of gold his eyes will be put out,
> Two wounds made one,
> He dies a cruel death.

Four years after this verse was published, King Henri II of France died during a joust when a lance that pierced his gilded visor put out his eyes and crushed his skull. Some thought that Nostradamus had not only foretold but also caused the king's death by this verse. Fortunately for him, the queen, Catherine de Medici, did not hold him accountable.

Another verse that seems to have been accurate was this one:

The rejected one will at last reach the throne,

Her enemies found to be traitors,

More than ever shall her age be triumphant

At seventy she will go to death in the third year of the century.

These lines seems to fit Queen Elizabeth I of England, who was rejected by her father, hated by Catholic nobles, but ascended the throne in 1558 and died at 70 years of age in the year 1603.

Accurate or not, the information still proves useless from a practical point of view. The verse does not mention England or Elizabeth—only with hindsight can it be deemed accurate. Many of Nostradamus's writings are similarly vague and ill defined.

TRAGEDY FORESEEN

In more recent times one man who tried to take positive action after receiving what he felt was a precognitive vision was a 23-year-old office manager from Cincinnati, Ohio, named David Booth. For seven consecutive nights in May 1979, Booth had an identical dream. He saw a three-engine jetliner carrying the insignia of American Airlines take off, roll over, and crash into flames. On May 22 he phoned the Federal Aviation Authority to warn them of impending disaster. The call was logged, but no action was taken. Four days later a three-engine American Airlines DC10 jet crashed upon takeoff from Chicago's O'Hare Airport, killing 273 people. In hindsight the vision had been horribly prophetic.

Spanish hotel worker Jaime Castell had another ominous premonition, in 1979. Castell heard a voice that told him that he would soon die. Convinced that this would prove true, he took out a life insurance policy on himself for a huge sum of money. Three weeks later he was killed when a car coming in the opposite direction on a two-way road went out of control, flipped over the central barrier, and landed on top of Castell's vehicle. The insurance company paid the insurance to his then pregnant wife.

The Kennedy Predictions

The controversial American psychic Jeane Dixon allegedly managed to predict the assassinations of both President John F. Kennedy and his brother Robert Kennedy, though in neither case was her prediction detailed enough for preventive action to be taken.

In 1952 Dixon went to Saint Matthew's Cathedral in Washington to pray. As she knelt, she had a vision of the White House with the numbers 1 9 6 0 floating over it. A voice told her that the president inaugurate that year would be murdered before he could stand for reelection.

In 1968 Dixon was speaking at the Ambassador Hotel, Los Angeles, and invited questions from the floor. One person asked if Robert Kennedy would become President. "No," replied Dixon, "he won't, and it will be because of something that happens in this hotel." One week later Robert Kennedy was shot in the Ambassador Hotel, Los Angeles.

Not all predictions are immediately recognized for what they are. In 1898 author Morgan Robertson wrote a novel called *Futility,* set against the backdrop of a maritime tragedy. The ship in the novel was named SS *Titan* and was a huge liner that sank after hitting an iceberg. In the story most of the passengers drowned because the ship did not have enough lifeboats, and a ship hurrying to the rescue did not arrive in time.

In 1912 a ship named SS *Titanic*, the largest ship afloat, sank on her maiden voyage after hitting an iceberg. Many of the 2,250 people on board drowned because the ship did not have enough lifeboats, and a ship hurrying to the rescue did not arrive in time. Ironically, the publisher of the *Titan* story died on the *Titanic*.

STUDYING PREDICTIONS

Those who have studied cases of predictions and prophecies have tried all sorts of experiments. The Mind Science Foundation of San Antonio, Texas, conducted one of the best-known experiments in 1979. When the researchers there learned that the Skylab space station had begun its final descent to Earth, they contacted more than 200 people who claimed to have precognitive powers and asked them to predict where and when Skylab would crash to Earth. Nobody predicted correctly.

This came as little surprise to those who research predictions. Even those who claim the powers of prophecy say that they cannot control their gift. They may know with absolute certainty that a particular thing will happen, but they cannot present a prediction on demand. It is as if some outside agency whispers into their ears at random. Moreover, the majority of predictions that turn out accurate are lacking the vital details that would make the prediction useful. Booth's vision of the crashing DC10 turned out to be accurate, but he had no way of knowing where or when it would happen, and so nothing could be done to prevent it.

One other fact has emerged from the study of predictions in recent years. The vast majority of accurate predictions are made less than 10 days before the event happens. And around half are made within 48 hours.

A poster advertising the sister ships *Titanic* and *Olympic*, the pride of the White Star Line. The tragic sinking of the *Titanic* seems to have been foretold in a novel written 14 years earlier that contained many eerie statements that later came true in the real-life sinking of 1912.

Déjà Vu: All Strangely Familiar

Déjà vu is a French term that translates roughly as "already seen." It refers to a vague feeling of familiarity, of having already been to a place or having already experienced a certain chain of events. The feeling is instantaneous, occurring as events are unfolding.

Bare Bones

- Déjà vu is the name given to the vague feeling of familiarity that people sometimes experience in new places or circumstances.

- Often these feelings can be explained by the fact that the percipient has experienced those events, or something very similar, before.

- Déjà vécu is slightly different and describes an intense feeling of déjà vu, often accompanied by feelings of foreboding or dread.

SEEN IT ALL BEFORE

This widely reported feeling is one of the most common of all paranormal experiences. The problem with déjà vu is that it is a subjective phenomenon that cannot be objectively proved. At its most mundane it involves the feeling that one has read a book or seen a television program before. Of course, often one *has* read that particular book or seen that show on a previous occasion, and the fact simply has been forgotten. Only when the percipient begins to read or watch is he or she reminded that this is the second time around.

STRANGE FOREBODING

True déjà vu, however, is rather different. Researchers sometimes label this experience déjà vécu, meaning already lived, to distinguish it from its more mundane counterpart. Déjà vécu involves an intense feeling, often accompanied by thoughts of foreboding or a presentiment that something unpleasant is about to happen. In a few cases the percipient does predict by a few seconds what will occur next, though this is unusual. The key feature of déjà vécu, as opposed to prediction or prophecy, is that it is an immediate and inarticulate feeling of familiarity that unfolds as a place is visited or events happen.

Those investigating déjà vécu in recent years have drawn some general conclusions, but there is disagreement about what causes it. Déjà vécu usually lasts less than 10 seconds before the feeling passes, and the phenomenon is reported overwhelmingly by young adults between the ages of 16 and 30. It appears to be more common among people suffering from stress and anxiety problems.

STORAGE PROBLEMS

One scientific explanation for déjà vécu, which avoids any sort of paranormal process, involves the way the human mind distinguishes between short-term and long-term memory. Events from the last few minutes are stored in a short-term memory where they can be instantly accessed by the conscious mind. However, once an activity is complete or a person has moved on to a new location, the more recent events are moved to a longer-term memory store from which they can generally be retrieved only by a conscious effort. If, however, a recent event is mistakenly pushed off to the longer-term memory store, it may be brought back to the conscious mind as if being retrieved from an event that happened a long time previously rather than in the past few seconds. Thus, a room in which the percipient is standing will seem to be remembered from some previous occasion when it is, in fact, being recalled from two seconds beforehand.

Another scientific explanation involves a possible mismatch between the optical nerves of the percipient. If one optical nerve carries messages from its eye to the brain a fraction of a second later than the other, then the brain will receive images in a slightly skewed time frame rather than simultaneously. The brain will try to compensate for the difference, with the resulting disorientation being experienced as déjà vécu.

Both these theories, and others like them, suffer from the fact that they have proved impossible to test in a laboratory setting. People do not tend to suffer déjà vécu when conveniently wired to scientific instruments measuring brain activity, so these hypotheses remain nothing more than attractive reasoning.

Paranormal theories are also consulted to explain the phenomenon. The most widely accepted of these is that the feeling results from a prediction that has been incompletely or improperly remembered. If a person receives a precognition that they will visit a particular place but then the conscious mind forgets the vision, it will nevertheless remain stored in the unconscious mind. When the prediction subsequently comes true, it will be recalled as the experience of déjà vécu.

Jamais Vu

The opposite phenomenon to déjà vu occurs when people experience familiar places or people as if they are seen for the first time. This is known as jamais vu, or never seen. The experience is more rare than déjà vu and can prove extremely disorientating for those who undergo it.

Dr. Chris Moulin of the University of Leeds, England, found that he could induce feelings of jamais vu by instructing volunteers to conduct a simple task repetitively. For instance, when volunteers were asked to write the word "door" constantly for 60 seconds, several of them found themselves having to stop because they began to doubt either that door was what they were supposed to be writing or even, in a few cases, that door was a real word in English.

Intuition: A Gut Feeling

Intuition describes the phenomenon at work when a person knows something without any discernable way in which they could have acquired that information. People who regularly experience intuition describe it as "knowing in my head" to distinguish it from a fact that they have been told or have experienced it using their five senses.

Bare Bones

- Many different types of intuition involve knowing information with no obvious source.

- People who claim that they are highly intuitive often fail to perform under test conditions.

- Skeptics suggest that people who claim to be using intuition to receive information actually pick up clues subconsciously from their environment and make deductions from them.

- Another suggestion is that such information may actually be received telepathically from the object of the intuition.

As with déjà vu, intuition comes in many varieties. The range of the phenomenon has convinced some researchers that it is not, in fact, one phenomenon but several. There is not, as yet, any clearly defined set of terms to describe these. Others prefer to see intuition as one single phenomenon experienced in a variety of ways. Also, many believe that a high number of reported instances of intuition can be explained in a nonparanormal way.

"I JUST KNOW"

Widely experienced forms of intuition go by a variety of common names. Women's intuition is perhaps the best known of these, though copper's nose is another. Both refer specifically to having unexplained knowledge about a person who has only recently been met. This form of intuition is usually described in fairly similar terms by the percipient. It is as if the piece of knowledge has just popped into his or her brain. Those receiving an intuitive piece of knowledge do not, as a rule, hear a voice or see a vision. They are generally at a loss to explain how they acquired the knowledge—they just know it.

READING THE CLUES

Researchers have experimented with intuition to no avail. People who claim to be adept at it generally score much lower in laboratory tests than in the real world. Interestingly, they do not make many wrong calls, but claim that the gift seems to have deserted them. A policeman who is adept at stopping suspects who have drugs on them, for instance, will often seem to lose the gift entirely

under test conditions. More than likely the percipient is actually engaging in highly effective subconscious reasoning but perceives the results as paranormal, simply because they seem to be unexplained. Although research in this area is limited, it is thought that body language is the main factor at work.

To return to the example of copper's nose, a policeman who often succeeds at identifying suspects carrying drugs may actually be relying on subtle changes in behavior. The officer may not be aware of the small visual signals that he is seeing, but his subconscious mind assembles the disparate clues, recognizing patterns that have been seen before and reaching a conclusion about the likely explanation. The resulting deduction will then pop into the police officer's mind as a fully formed conclusion. Skeptics argue that all forms of intuition rely on this basic framework.

Packets of illegal drugs discovered by police officers searching a house used by drug dealers. Some policemen believe they can identify the guilty party by using a form of intuition known as "copper's nose."

READING MINDS

There remain, however, some instances that defy this explanation. Some people who experience intuition will know a fact or facts about a person that could not be deduced from body language or previously known information that has been forgotten. This leads some researchers to suggest that what is manifesting as intuition is, in these cases, a form of mind reading. This simply explains one paranormal experience by saying that it is, in fact, a different one, leaving the phenomenon as yet another unsolved mystery.

Interpreting Dreams

Dreams have long held a fascination for those who experience them regularly. Some dreams are remarkably vivid, others rather hazy and ill defined. Some dreams contain people and places known to the dreamer, while others involve strangers in unfamiliar surroundings. Some dreams are pleasant and enjoyable, and others are disturbing and terrifying. It is no wonder that throughout human history, people have sought to find meaning in dreams.

Bare Bones

- The biblical story of Joseph shows that man has sought meaning in dreams for many thousands of years.

- Dreams are often highly symbolic, with some symbols offering significance to the individual dreamer and some having a wider significance.

- The most studied form of dreaming is lucid dreaming, when an individual is aware that he or she is dreaming during the dream and may therefore be able to influence the outcome.

BIBLICAL DREAMS

Many people in the Western world are familiar with the Bible story of Joseph, who interpreted the dream of the pharaoh of Egypt. The pharaoh dreamed that seven fat cows came up out of the Nile, followed by seven thin cows, which ate up the fat cows. Joseph said that the fat cows signified that for seven years the floodwaters of the Nile would irrigate the fields of Egypt to produce bumper crops, but that in the following seven years the waters would not flood as usual, resulting in famine. Thus warned, the pharaoh built enormous granaries in which to store the crops produced in the first seven years, then used these stores to ease the famine of the next seven years.

EVERYDAY DREAMING

The vast majority of dreams are caused by the resting mind sorting out the experiences of the day, trying to make sense of anything that was puzzling at the time and generally preparing itself for the day ahead. The dreams generated by this process may be bizarre, surreal, or random, but they are not considered to be paranormal in any meaningful sense.

Dreams are often heavily influenced by symbolism. Much of this symbolism pertains to the person having the dream and relates to his or her own individual circumstances or personal background. Some symbols, however, seem to have a more general application, and whole books have been written interpreting the symbolic meaning of different dreams. Bright lights are generally linked to intelligence, while flying symbolizes a release from anxiety or worry. These dreams can be useful to psychologists seeking to understand the mind of a patient but have little to do with the paranormal.

LUCID DREAMING

There are some dreams, however that stand out dramatically. These types of dreams have been actively studied and subjected to discussion by investigators. The most studied form is probably lucid dreaming. This occurs when the percipient knows that he or she is dreaming while the dream is occurring. Some people who experience lucid dreams on a regular basis—and most people do not—have found that they can control the content and the way in which events unfold within the dream. Dutch scientist Dr. Fredrik van Eeden first noted the existence of lucid dreams in 1892.

In the 1970s Dr. Keith Hearne of Hull University discovered a way to induce lucid

> "Dreams are today's answers to tomorrow's questions." —EDGAR CAYCE, PSYCHIC

dreams artificially. A small electrode was attached to the wrist of a volunteer, who was then allowed to fall asleep. When REM sleep was noticed, a small electric shock was applied through the electrode. This shock alerted the sleeper to the fact that he was dreaming, turning a normal dream into a lucid dream. The technique does not always work, but it is effective enough to have become the basis of much recent lucid dream research.

DREAMING THE TRUTH

Other dreams seem akin to ESP in that they reveal knowledge to the percipient that could not have been acquired by any normal means. One of the earliest and most famous cases of this kind led to a notorious murder trial, which was later turned into a famous stage melodrama entitled *Maria in the Red Barn*.

In the spring of 1827, Maria Marten, a mole catcher's daughter from the village of Polstead in Suffolk, England, fell pregnant by

Sleep Patterns

Most people experience the same pattern of sleep each night. When first falling asleep, a person enters what is known as Stage 1 sleep. This is a light sleep during which brain activity continues much as it did when awake. A person can be roused from this stage fairly easily.

After 20 minutes or so the sleeper enters Stage 2, when brain activity slows somewhat. In Stage 3, 30 minutes later, the brain slows further and the limbs relax. In Stage 4 the brain becomes even more sluggish, and the limbs are floppy. Rousing a sleeper from Stage 4 is difficult.

After about an hour and a half of sleep, the sleeper jumps suddenly back from Stage 4 to Stage 1. He will then remain quite still, while his eyes flick back and forth rapidly under the lids. This is the stage called Rapid Eye Movement (REM) sleep. It is in this stage that dreaming occurs. REM lasts about 15 minutes, after which the cycle repeats itself.

William Corder, the rather wayward son of a wealthy local farmer. Corder agreed to marry Maria but said that he would have to carefully choose the time when he would tell his family the news. Meanwhile, Maria's condition was starting to show, so Corder said that he would arrange for Maria to stay with friends in Great Yarmouth while she had her baby. The wedding, he said, would take place in the autumn after she returned. On May 18 Maria left her home to meet Corder.

As the weeks passed, Maria's mother, Ann, was plagued by a dream that repeated itself every three or four nights. In the dream, Ann Marten saw Maria inside a red barn that stood on Corder's land. Ann became convinced that something bad had happened to her daughter in the red barn. When Corder suddenly left the village, Maria's father, Thomas, took up his wife's worries. He went to the red barn, spotted some disturbed earth, and dug down to discover Maria's body. The search was then on for Corder, who was later found living under an assumed name and working as a schoolmaster in London. He was found guilty of murder and hanged in August 1828.

DREAM MESSAGES

Rather more prosaic were the experiences of novelist Upton Sinclair and his wife, Mary Craig. In the 1920s the couple claims that they realized that Craig often had dreams that related to what her husband had been doing that day, even when he was away on business and had not spoken to her. They later found that Upton could deliberately send a simple message to Craig while she was asleep—the message manifesting itself as an image in her dream. Upton later included the information of the various events in a book. Scientists at the time, however, did not lend any legitimacy to the couple's claims.

Since then, investigators into the paranormal have subjected lucid dreamers to various experiments into ESP and telepathy. The Maimonides Medical Center in New York undertook a series of experiments over a 15-year period into lucid dreams and telepathy. The majority of these tests involved a waking person studying a picture and attempting to send its contents to a sleeper by means of telepathy. The results were mixed, though some of the people participating in the tests proved to be better than others. One pair achieved results that beat the odds of chance by around 1,000 to 1.

The results were mirrored by similar experiments carried out in England by Joseph Friedman, a lecturer in parapsychology at the University of London. Friedman divided his team into pairs and urged them to write down any dreams that seemed to involve the other person. Some of the results were striking. In one account a man dreamed of having a picnic with his dream partner in a forest surrounded by men dressed as miners. That very night, the partner was eating a meal with friends in the town of Colliers Wood.

Various experiments conducted since have produced broadly similar results. However, the heavy symbolism of dreams makes the results tricky to interpret. Skeptics choose to see the similarities as coincidence rather than as evidence of ESP or telepathy.

The content of dreams is often highly symbolic. The presence of bright lights or shimmering patterns is often linked to intelligence or to the development of new ideas.

History and Uses of Hypnosis

Hypnosis is a trancelike condition that outwardly and superficially resembles sleep but is quite different in both its causes and effects. When a subject is under hypnosis, they are more open to suggestion and instruction than when fully awake. It is this aspect of hypnotism that is exploited most often by stage acts, but which can also be put to use for medical purposes. The subject at no time loses the ability to reassert their own will over the suggestions or instruction put to them; it is simply that they are far more open under hypnosis than at other times.

Bare Bones

- Hypnosis is a trancelike state that has been used for many years for religious purposes.

- Franz Anton Mesmer sparked modern interest in hypnotism with his studies of animal magnetism in the 1770s.

- Mesmer used hypnosis for medical purposes and this practice continues even today.

- Hypnotism is also used in stage acts and for the investigation of past lives and abductions.

Although hypnotism is a controversial subject, it is not paranormal. It has, however, been put to various paranormal uses, and many claims linked to the paranormal have been made for it. It is interesting to note that around 10 percent of people seem to be immune to hypnosis.

EARLY FORMS OF HYPNOSIS

The early history of hypnotism is shrouded in mystery, largely because it was often linked to deities, spirits, magic, and so forth. Those who knew how to hypnotize people usually did so for religious reasons and tended not to write down anything about what occurred. Researchers have found glimpses of hypnotic practices in some ancient accounts. The ancient Greeks, for instance, took their sick to the temples of the healing god Asclepius, where priests put them into a divine sleep, which some consider to have been a form of hypnosis.

There is some evidence, mostly circumstantial and secondhand, that the witches and wizards of medieval Europe practiced hypnotism. Some accounts of the powers of these people read like examples of hypnotic suggestion. For instance, Pigtail Bridger, a famous wizard of early nineteenth-century England, could paralyze people with a glance—a trick he normally performed at fairs or on folk whom he disliked. The unfortunate victim was unable to move until Bridger told them, "Get off with thee." Although educated people seldom took such stories seriously, they were recorded as examples of the credulity of rural folk and allow a glimpse into the nature of the power of witches and wizards.

FRANZ MESMER

Scientific interest in hypnotism is generally traced back to around 1770, when the Austrian doctor Franz Mesmer began to investigate what he called "animal magnetism." This concept was quickly dubbed mesmerism in his honor. Mesmer used his hypnotic gifts for medical purposes. He hypnotized people and then instructed them to feel no pain while undergoing operations or other procedures. More remarkably, he could stanch bleeding from wounds by hypnotizing patients, then waving a wooden stick over the wound while informing the patient that the bleeding would cease. Mesmer himself claimed that the manipulation of magnets explained his powers for putting subjects into a trance. Mesmerism was regarded as a rather quaint phenomenon by mainstream scientists and remained a minority interest for a number of years.

MEDICAL USES OF HYPNOSIS

In the 1840s Dr. James Braid, a Scottish-born physician living in Manchester, England, adopted Mesmer's ideas. Braid realized that it was the ritual that induced the trance, not the magnets. He favored enticing a subject to concentrate on a rhythmically moving object—such as the stereotypical swinging watch. Braid realized that the trance was sleeplike in some ways, so he adopted the term hypnosis from the ancient Greek for sleep. Other British doctors followed Braid in using hypnosis for pain relief, but the invention of more reliable chemical anesthetics led to its decline.

Meanwhile, French neurologist Jean-Marie Charcot espoused hypnotism as part of his treatment of hysterics and other patients suffering from mental illness, and it seemed extremely promising. When Sigmund Freud turned against it, however, hypnotism lost favor, though it has been gaining ground again in medical circles since the 1960s.

Franz Anton Mesmer was an Austrian doctor of modest background. In 1772 he announced he had discovered a new force that he called "animal magnetism," but which is now recognized as hypnotism. He used hypnotism in his work for many years, until 1785 when a panel of scientists declared that animal magnetism did not exist, forcing him into retirement.

Hypnotic Progression

The practice of hypnotic regression—the use of hypnosis to recover lost memories—is well known, but hypnotic progression is less popular. Frenchman and psychic researcher Albert de Rochas conducted some of the most comprehensive work in this field during the early twentieth century.

He hypnotically progressed 10 subjects to see what their future lives would contain. The results were varied but not inherently unlikely. The women all predicted that they would have fairly uneventful lives, which tended to be unhappy or violent.

Interestingly, one woman claimed to die, exist for a while in a dim and nebulous limbo, and then be reborn as a baby girl named Lili.

The results of these sessions were published in 1911, and in the years that followed, de Rochas kept in touch with his subjects to see if their hypnotic progressions proved true. They did not. Notably, none of the women predicted the Great War that broke out in 1914, which had a profound impact on all their lives.

Hypnosis can be successful in a limited range of conditions. Dissociative disorders, phobias, habit change, depression, and post-traumatic syndromes are known to be susceptible to hypnotherapy. Some have voiced concerns about the rapidly spreading use of hypnotism. Certain people can experience intense emotions while in a hypnotic trance, and those emotions can persist for some time after the trance has ended. Inexperienced hypnotherapists may miss the warning signs and therefore subject their patients to unnecessary days of fear, depression, or anxiety.

More poignant is the problem of false memories. These are memories of events that never happened but which become lodged in the subject's mind as a result of carelessly worded questions by the hypnotist. This has caused some people to believe that they were molested as a child or have been the victims of other crimes or abuse.

HYPNOSIS ON STAGE

Outside of the medical profession, people use hypnotism for a variety of purposes. The best known is stage hypnotism. The show hypnotist will typically call for volunteers from the audience. The invitation is usually delivered in terms that entice the more suggestible people to volunteer.

Once the volunteers are on the stage, the hypnotist will talk to them for a while, looking for signs that indicate which individuals are most likely to react well to hypnotism. These few will then be put into a trance, during which they are given suggestions by the hypnotist that lead to comical situations for the entertainment of the audience. These usually involve the subject being told to perform a ridiculous action, such as barking like a dog or standing on a chair, when they hear a particular word or phrase. The hypnotist is usually careful to ensure that the suggestions do not last longer than the show.

INVESTIGATING THE PARANORMAL

Investigators into the paranormal have often researched the fact that many people recall details and facts under hypnosis that their conscious mind has forgotten. Care is needed when this sort of work is undertaken, because it is easy for a hypnotist unwittingly to plant an idea in the mind of a subject. Leading questions must be avoided, but even when these are absent, it can be easy for the inexperienced to encourage a subject toward a particular line of thought. Subjects can unknowingly let loose their imagination under hypnosis, further skewing the truth.

A reliable and responsible hypnotist, however, is a powerful tool for investigators into the paranormal—for example, the case of Betty and Barney Hill in the 1960s, who were able to recall the details of their abduction by aliens under hypnosis. Many ufologists rely on hypnosis to break through the memory lapses that they believe afflict many witnesses of UFO activity. Ufologists use this evidence to compare information regarding alien abductions.

Hypnotic regression to unlock forgotten memories has also played an increasing role in the investigation of reincarnation and the idea of previous lives. Extrasensory perception, telepathy, and other apparently paranormal phenomenon have all been investigated using hypnosis. However, since so much about hypnosis itself remains controversial or unexplained, the evidence it has produced remains inconclusive.

A woman undergoes surgery while under hypnosis to numb the pain. This type of pain relief was one of the earliest medical uses of hypnosis, but it has generally been replaced by chemical drugs that are more consistent in their effects.

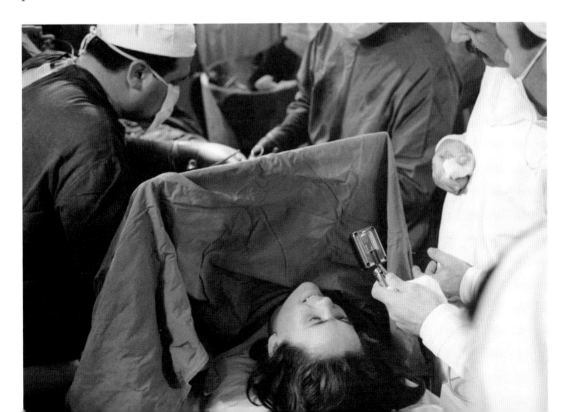

Altered States

In its broadest meaning, an altered state of mind can include any mental state other than that experienced normally when awake. The phrase could embrace sleep, drowsiness, shock, and fever. Generally, it is used to mean any mental condition that the average person would not be expected to encounter in the course of a normal day or week. Most researchers do not consider symptoms related to mental illness to be an altered state, though some diagnoses may clearly show similarities.

Bare Bones

- An altered state is any state of mind different than that normally experienced when awake.

- Specific brain-wave patterns can apparently be attributed to different altered states.

- Altered states may be experienced accidentally, after trauma to the body or shock, or brought on deliberately through physical and mental practices such as yoga and meditation.

- Taking drugs can also induce an altered state.

BRAIN-WAVE MONITORING

The use of electronic equipment to monitor brain activity has led some researchers to try to ascribe different types of altered states to the various readings obtained from brain-wave monitors. The results obtained and deductions made have proved controversial, though they can serve as a useful guide to a whole mass of difficult terminology.

In normal circumstances a person who is awake has brain waves ranging from 9 to 13 hertz. This is generally known as the alpha state. Those engaged in meditation can achieve rates at the lower end of this scale, while those engaged in frantic mental activity produce readings toward the upper end, sometimes straying into the beta state above 13 hertz. Sleep and hypnotic trances generally lie in the theta state, when brain waves are in the 5 to 8 hertz range. Below theta comes the delta state, with readings of 1.5 to 4 hertz. These low readings are found in those experiencing the deepest trances, including mediums who claim to be under the control of spirit guides.

BRING IT ON

An altered state can come about accidentally through events that involve oxygen deprivation, heavy blood loss, or traumatic shock. It can also be experienced after deliberate acts of sensory deprivation, such as floating in an isolation tank. Some practices, such as yoga, may also lead to an altered state. More controversially, altered states may be reached by taking various drugs. Alcohol produces a mild form of altered state, while other drugs—such as LSD, DXM, 2C-I, peyote, marijuana, mescaline, MDMA, and psychedelic mushrooms—produce far more dramatic and intense reactions.

MEDITATION

One of the milder forms of altered state is obtained through meditation. This involves the deliberate and total concentration of the mind on one thought or object. Typically, the practitioner sits quietly in a place with as few distractions as possible. The meditator then concentrates all his or her mental faculties on a simple chant, prayer, or object. Ideally, the mind gradually becomes closed to outside stimuli until it turns inward, becoming disassociated from the real, material world and free to wander within.

In recent years meditation has become widespread and hugely popular even among those who would not consider themselves spiritual. Meditation is seen as a way to relieve tension, anxiety, stress, and depression without drugs. Many people also meditate as a way to relax or take a break.

TRANCE

Beyond the state of meditation is the trance. The condition experienced during hypnosis may be considered the archetypal trance. The state has been defined as a mental state in which physical action is possible without mental effort. It was discovered as early as the time of Alexander the Great that soldiers tire less quickly if they march in unison to the beat of a percussion instrument, such as a drum. Under the stress of combat and long marches without rest, some soldiers fell into a form of trance comparable to sleeping while they continued to march. Some people suggest that one of the attractions of modern electronic dance bands is the way the music, when played repetitively and accompanied by rhythmic dance, may induce a similar trancelike condition.

A number of preliterate societies encouraged trance states as part of religious or cultural ceremonies. The tribes of the North

Altered States and the Law

Most legal codes have long recognized that a person suffering from an altered state is not fully responsible for their actions, at least in a legal sense. Those suffering from mental illness have long been sentenced to treatment or imprisonment rather than face execution, amputation, or whipping.

In recent years the recognition that temporary or even mild altered states may impair responsibility has been accepted by most law codes. Perhaps because of this recognition, drugs that induce altered states are generally banned in most countries.

Legal attitudes toward cannabis have softened recently in some countries, while others have even decided to permit mind-altering drugs traditionally used in indigenous religious ceremonies. However, the move has not always been toward tolerance. The Netherlands largely decriminalized the use of certain hallucinogenic fungi but then banned them again after some unfortunately violent incidents. Many of these drugs have the potential to cause long-term psychological damage if not used carefully. The debate over the legal status of these drugs will likely persist for years to come.

The chemical diagram for mescaline, one of the most powerful psychedelic drugs in use today. The drug has a place in the belief systems of some of the first nations of Central America.

Intentionally induced altered states are a traditional part of the spiritual life of many indigenous cultures. It is best to keep out of the way of this Brazilian *paje,* or shaman, when he wanders, machete in hand, his brain disordered with hallucinations.

American plains famously induced trances among the warriors who performed the sun dance, which involved considerable physical pain and sleep deprivation to gain a vision from the gods.

HALLUCINATIONS

Hallucinations can be visual in nature but may also involve smells, sounds, tastes, and touches—or any combination of the senses. The key identifier is that the percipient believes the hallucination to be real, unlike visions or dreams. Although the mechanisms that create hallucinations are not properly understood, they tend to occur under well-defined circumstances. An alcoholic may experience hallucinations after the sudden cessation of drinking, and an epileptic may have a hallucination a day or two after a particularly severe attack.

More recently recognized are hypnagogic hallucinations. These strike on the cusp between sleep and waking. They can take many forms, but among the most common is the sighting of a human figure. These hypnagogic hallucinations were to blame for several reported ghost sightings in the past. It has been suggested that these hallucinations occur when the part of the brain that creates dreams continues to function after it would normally have ceased.

CHEMICALLY INDUCED ALTERED STATES

More controversial are drug-induced altered states. Psychoactive drugs are generally divided into psychedelic, dissociatives, and deliriants. The psychedelics include LSD, peyote, and mescaline. They distort the inputs to the conscious mind in a way that can lead to enhanced color perception or to the feeling that a mundane phrase has enormous spiritual significance. Dissociative drugs, on the other hand, block inputs to the conscious mind. These drugs include PCP and certain types of fungi. They induce a dreamlike trance during which hallucinations are common. Deliriants are not usually taken for recreational purposes, because they overstimulate the inputs to the conscious mind, inducing all-encompassing hallucinations, feelings of paranoia, and intense emotions, which can be long lasting and severe.

Coincidence and Synchronicity

Many people experience coincidences in their lives. An old friend calls just after a person had been thinking of phoning him or her. Or a news item on television resembles a story in a book a person is reading. However, such mundane coincidences pale in comparison to some of the more startling examples.

TRAGIC COINCIDENCES

One outstanding case concerns two murders that took place in the small English village of Erdington in Warwickshire. On May 27, 1817, a local farm woman named Mary Ashford went to a dance with a friend at the village hotel. Her friends noticed that she spent most of her time with a bricklayer named Abraham Thornton, who was new to the area. Mary left the dance with her friend, her friend's boyfriend, and Thornton. The group split up, and Mary was last seen at about 4:00 A.M. walking home alone. At 6:30 A.M. a local man spotted a bloodstained dress beside the road in Penn's Mill Lane. He alerted the local constable, and a search was organized. Mary's body was found later that day. She had been raped and strangled. Suspicion at once fell on Thornton, who was arrested and tried for murder. Thornton was able to prove he had been with a friend from 3:30 A.M. on and thus was acquitted.

On May 27, 1974, Barbara Forrest of Erdington went to a dance with a friend at the village hotel. She left the dance alone to walk home but never made it. She was raped and strangled some time around 4:00 A.M. Her body was found just off Penn's Mill Lane. Suspicion at once fell on a work colleague, named Michael Thornton, who seemed to have an interest in the girl. He was charged with murder but was able to prove that he was with a friend at the time of the murder and was acquitted. The similarities between the two killings are striking.

Another string of coincidences with tragic results followed the sports car owned by Hollywood star James Dean. In September 1955 the car crashed, killing Dean. Mechanics later repaired the

car body to be used as a gruesome show, but it fell off its display mount twice, once breaking the legs of a viewer and the second time breaking the hip of a passerby. Meanwhile, the engine was sold to a man who was killed driving the car in which it was mounted. The driveshaft was similarly reused, and again the vehicle in which it was installed was involved in a fatal accident. In 1959 the car broke apart into 11 pieces for no apparent reason.

The wreck of the car in which Hollywood actor James Dean was killed in 1955. Parts of the car were later reused in other vehicles, which were all involved in a string of fatal accidents.

NAMESAKES

On July 28, 1900, King Umberto I of Italy traveled to Monza to attend an athletics meeting. On the way he stopped at a restaurant called Umberto's, which was run by a man named Umberto. The king had a chat with the restaurateur and was amazed to find that

The Goblin Universe

In the 1970s the writer and paranormal investigator Ted Holiday developed the idea of the Goblin Universe, which has since been developed further by others.

Holiday wrote, "Truth is an actor who dons one mask after another, then vanishes through a secret door in the stage scenery when we reach out to grab him. All he leaves behind is a sardonic chuckle, which we record, take away, analyze, and debate. But we never see his face."

The concept of the Goblin Universe suggests that coincidences, reincarnation, ghosts, yetis, and UFOs are all linked at a level beyond human understanding. Holiday himself hinted that he thought some vastly powerful creator with a sense of humor was responsible, though others have avoided this quasi-religious explanation while still subscribing to the idea that all paranormal experiences had some sort of underlying linkage.

they shared not only a name but also the same birthday and that both had married women named Margherita. Moreover, the restaurant had opened on the day that the king had been crowned, and both men had been born in Milan. Impressed and amused, King Umberto invited the restaurateur to join him in the royal box at the next day's events.

The restaurateur did not appear the next day, so King Umberto sent a messenger to see if there had been some misunderstanding. The aide returned with the sad news that the restaurateur had died that morning when his hunting rifle had accidentally gone off. As King Umberto left the sports meeting, he was shot by an anarchist and died instantly.

LOST AND FOUND

Most coincidences are less fatal, but no less dramatic. In the 1950s the Chicago newspaper reporter Irv Kupcient was visiting various cities in Europe. In London he stayed at the Savoy Hotel and, while unpacking, found in a drawer some papers that belonged to Harry Hannin of the Harlem Globetrotters. Kupcient sent the papers to Hannin in New York. When he got back to work in Chicago, Kupcient found a package addressed to him and post-marked Paris. In it he found a tie that he had lost and a letter from Harry Hannin explaining that he had found the tie when unpacking in a hotel in Paris.

Equally striking was the story concerning the book *The Girl from Petrovka* by George Feifer. Actor Anthony Hopkins was asked to play a role in a film based on the book, and he went to London to buy a copy of the novel. Hopkins couldn't find the book anywhere, so he gave up and decided to go home. Boarding the train, Hopkins found, discarded on a seat, a copy of the very book he was looking for. Weeks later Hopkins met Feifer to discuss the project. Feifer told Hopkins that he was struggling because the copy of the book in which he had been scribbling notes had been lost when he was in London a few weeks earlier. Hopkins pulled out the book he had found: It was the missing annotated copy.

In May 1944 the London *Telegraph* newspaper daily crossword puzzle was brought to the attention of the men planning the invasion of Normandy by Allied troops. The answers to the crossword included the words Overlord, Mulberry, Omaha, Utah, and Neptune—all code words linked to top-secret aspects of the invasion. Fearing that a German spy was sending secret messages via the crossword, the secret services pounced on the *Telegraph* offices. They found that an English schoolteacher named Leonard Dawe had compiled the crossword, had been doing the job for 20 years, and had no connections to Germany or Nazism.

UNLIKELY BUT NOT UNNATURAL

Those who look for a nonparanormal explanation for such coincidences usually rely on the law of probabilities. Put simply, this states that no matter how improbable something might be, so long as it is possible, it may one day occur. Thus, from time to time even the most improbable things must happen. For instance, the odds of being dealt a hand in the card game bridge that contains all 13 cards of the same suit are approximately 635 billion to one. Yet this happened to Vera Nettick of New Jersey, who promptly won the game. There is no supernatural force at work here, the skeptics argue, but humans are inevitably struck by these events and ignore the vast number of utterly probable non-coincidences that occur every day.

Others, however, look for more meaning than mere chance. In the 1970s Wolfgang Pauli and Carl Jung published their book *Synchronicity, an Acausal Connecting Principle.* These two Nobel prizewinners suggested that particularly unlikely coincidences, which they termed synchronicities, were visible manifestations of some hidden physical law that was as true and immutable as the recognized laws of physics but had simply not yet been detected by scientists. Exactly what this undiscovered law might be, they could not say, as it has not yet been discovered. It was, they argued, some organizing principle that was trying to bring order and regimentation to our chaotic universe.

King Umberto of Italy discovered that his life was bizarrely linked to that of a humble restaurant owner of the same name, same birthday, and ultimately, same day of death.

"Coincidence is the word we use when we can't see the levers and pulleys." —EMMA BULL, AUTHOR

Angel Visions

Angels are the messengers of God in the Christian, Islamic, and Jewish religions. In fact, the word angel means messenger, though in the written texts of all three religions, the angels have a variety of other tasks and are more properly considered to be the servants of the supreme deity, ready to do his will whatever that may be.

Bare Bones

- Angels are heavenly creatures thought to bring messages from God or offer assistance to humans in times of crisis.

- The earliest angel visions are described in Christian, Islamic, and Jewish sacred writings.

- The conventional appearance of angels, with wings and a halo, comes from early pagan descriptions of spirits and does not correspond to how angels are described in original sources.

- True angels may be difficult to distinguish from humans and are reportedly sometimes mistaken for them.

Many people believe that there are a vast number of angels residing in heaven with God. These angels perform various divine tasks on behalf of God, only some of which involve coming to Earth where they encounter humans. Each angel is considered to have a

The cover from a piece of sheet music published in 1914. The image of the angel is typical of the way that firsthand reports were embellished.

name and individual identity, though few of these have ever been revealed to humans. There is also a hierarchy of angels, with some clearly senior to others. Various people at different times have hypothesized about the number of angels and the way they are organized, but this is little more than guesswork.

BIBLICAL CREATURES

The angels that appear to humans in the Bible are not always well described. They seem to have a basic human appearance but are highly attractive. Those who see them do not always immediately recognize these beings as angels.

For instance, in Chapter 19 of Genesis, a pair of angels visit Lot at his home in Sodom. As soon as Lot sees them, he realizes that they are angels and falls down before them, welcoming them to his house. The rest of the citizens of Sodom, however, thought the angels were men and caused a riot outside Lot's house demanding that he hand over the two good-looking strangers. Lot refused, and was rewarded by the angels by being spared when they subsequently destroy Sodom.

When struggling to distinguish angels from men, early Christian artists borrowed a pagan convention from the artists of ancient Rome that showed any spiritual entity as having wings. By the fourth century it had become usual to add wings to human figures to indicate that they were angels. This iconography was firmly established by around A.D. 900 and remains the dominant image. This has had interesting results. When angels are reported in the modern world, they are often not recognized at first. Unlike the angels in books, they do not have wings, conforming instead to descriptions in the Bible and other holy works. Conversely, those who claim to have seen angels complete with wings are often shown to be suffering from hallucinations or to be untrustworthy for other reasons.

ANGELIC SIGHTINGS

A typical, though much misreported, case occurred in 1914. In August of that year, the Germans invaded Belgium, marching

Zoroastrianism

The Zoroastrian faith also holds that the supreme deity Ahura Mazda has divine messengers that visit humanity. Like the angels of the Christian, Jewish, and Islamic faiths, those of Zoroastrianism have names and identities as well as being organized into a hierarchy.

At the top of the hierarchy are the six Amesha Spenta, each of which embodies a particular virtue such as wisdom or righteousness. These Amesha Spenta are often considered to be emanations of Ahura Mazda rather than distinct entities. They assisted Ahura Mazda in the creation of the universe.

Assisting the Amesha Spenta are 23 Yazatas, each of which embodies a concept such as light, fortune, or honesty. There are a vast number of other Yazatas who are entrusted by Ahura Mazda with a variety of other tasks.

southwest. On their way, they met a small unit of the British army at the Belgian town of Mons. Heavily outnumbered, the British began an epic retreat, but as the men fell back, many units got lost, muddled, or broken up. Among these was one company of the Coldstream Guards, which became detached from the regiment. Around midnight on September 1, the officers of the company realized that they were hopelessly lost and ordered their men to dig in to wait for dawn. By 2:00 A.M. the unit had become aware of numerous men marching nearby, all of them speaking German. The company was surrounded.

Then, just before 3:00 A.M., one of the guardsmen saw a lantern moving about in the field some 50 yards (45 m) away. The light drew closer, and soon all the men were staring at it, wondering who would be wandering about in a battle with a lantern. The light then stopped and became brighter. By the light of the lantern— though nobody could actually see a lantern—the men saw a female form in a long pale gown. She was beckoning the men. The guardsmen saw their captain walking toward the figure, so they followed. The glowing figure led the men to a road, then pointed along it, waved, and vanished. The men hurried along the road and by dawn had found a British patrol.

The story spread quickly. The men involved were divided about what had happened. Some believed an angel helped them, while others felt that the figure had simply been a local woman who looked a bit odd. The story was scooped, inflated, and embellished by the press. Within a few weeks the story was in the British newspapers, illustrated by drawings showing the Angel of Mons as a typical angel complete with sandals and wings—quite unlike the figure the men actually reported seeing.

Catherine Labouré, a French nun, saw a rather different angel in her convent on the night of July 18, 1830. "I saw a boy child of about six years old," Labouré wrote later, "...dressed all in white. From him came rays of light that lit the room." The luminous figure in the form of a young boy behaved much as angels are reported to do, though he did not conform to the stereotypical appearance of an angel.

Joseph Smith, founder of the
Mormon religion, receives a
revelation from the angel Moroni.
The figure of Moroni shown in this
illustration is as Smith described him,
lacking the wings conventionally
added to angels in art.

Rather more conventional was the angel seen outside a Coptic
Church at Zeitoun in Egypt in 1968. This figure took the form of a
man in a long robe and hovered in midair over the church. In 1971
the township of Pontiac, South Carolina, was the venue for an
equally dramatic sighting. The mobile home of Frank Harley was
suddenly illuminated one night by a bright light. Looking out his
window, Harley saw a blazing cross floating in the air, accompanied by a figure in a long white gown. The vision was repeated several times and was seen by many people.

The amount of angel literature available is growing exponen-
tially. The Internet provides an ideal forum for sharing angel stories, and if the many Web sites are to be believed, these heavenly
friends are kept busy on Earth offering protection and guidance.

Miraculous Cures

A miracle is an event that has no clear cause or explanation compatible with the usually accepted laws of physics. In its strictest sense, a miracle is distinguished from a paranormal event by being due to a religious presence or person. So a miraculous cure or immunity would be attributable to a deity or saint. In a looser sense, however, a miraculous cure might be one caused by some unknown paranormal force. What is often termed psychic doctoring is unconventional medical practice attributed to paranormal or sacred powers.

Bare Bones

- Miraculous cures are those that can be attributed to saints and deities or, more loosely, to psychic healers who claim their powers come from other, paranormal, sources.

- Many miraculous cures have been recorded at Lourdes in France, one of the most famous sites of Christian pilgrimage.

- Some claim that psychic surgery can also produce miraculous results, but this practice has been largely discredited.

Many holy leaders have been credited with performing miracles, and among them miraculous cures are perhaps the most striking. Jesus is recorded as curing a great many people. In Mark, Chapter 8, he cured a leper with swift, almost casual, ease: "And Jesus put forth his hand and touched him saying 'I will cure thee. Be thou clean.' And immediately his leprosy was cleansed."

MIRACLES AT LOURDES

Christians have firmly believed in miraculous cures since the time of Jesus. Many saints have been credited with miraculous cures over the years, and a number of shrines still claim to cure those who seek them out. Of these the most famous is Lourdes, in France. More than 300 cures have apparently taken place at Lourdes and have been recognized as being miraculous by the Lourdes Medical Bureau, which investigates claims of cures.

On average about 40 cures are reported to the Lourdes Medical Bureau each year, but some 90 percent of these have natural and logical explanations. The remaining cases are investigated, and the few that progress past that process are submitted to a panel of 20 leading medical specialists from various religious backgrounds, who thoroughly investigate not only the cure but also the original illness. If two-thirds of the panel agree that the cure is genuine, the case is then forwarded to the Church to make a final declaration, or not, of miraculous intervention.

Of the cases declared miraculous, the more impressive include Jeanne Fretel, a student nurse afflicted with tubercular peritonitis for seven years. Taken to Lourdes in 1948, she was completely cured despite being in a coma at the time and unable to pray. In 1952 the Swiss man Léo Schwager was cured of multiple sclerosis. The Italian Vittorio Micheli had a cancer of the bone in his hip that made his legs unable to function. After visiting Lourdes in 1963, he could stagger a few steps and by 1964 the cancer was gone.

SECULAR HEALERS

Faith healers are those who claim they can cure disease and alleviate suffering through spiritual or paranormal means. The results achieved by some faith healers are dramatic. Rose Gladden apparently cured a 54-year-old woman of recurrent pains in the back and legs, which had been present for 33 years. Reportedly, healer George Chapman cured Frenchman Joseph Tanguy of a brain tumor.

The power at work in faith healing is not entirely clear. Often even practitioners cannot explain the phenomenon. Many people reason that the placebo effect may explain the results. This is a well-known feature of medical research. When drugs are being tested, patients who are not given the new drug but are told that they are can sometimes show signs of recovery. It seems that if the mind genuinely believes that it is being given an effective treatment, then it can somehow make the body better by sheer willpower.

Altogether different is the practice of psychic surgery. Although an element of placebo effect or faith healing may play a role in its successes, the practice itself has been widely discredited. The U.S. Federal Trade Commission has declared that "psychic surgery is nothing but a total hoax" and has banned travel agencies promoting psychic surgery tours.

In 1858 in the French town of Lourdes, a local peasant girl named Bernadette Soubirous claimed to have seen the Virgin Mary no less than 18 times in the space of six months. The town is now a famous place of pilgrimage, and many miraculous cures have allegedly taken place there.

"Miracles are not contrary to nature, but only contrary to what we know about nature." —SAINT AUGUSTINE, BISHOP OF HIPPO

Spontaneous Human Combustion

Spontaneous human combustion (SHC) occurs when a human body becomes consumed by fire without any apparent cause or source. Typically the surroundings where the corpse is found are untouched by the fire, which adds to the mystery.

Early Cases

One of the earliest cases of SHC to survive the realms of folklore and fiction was the death of retired doctor John Irving Bentley at Coudersport, Pennsylvania, in 1965.

According to a report by investigator Larry Arnold in 1974, a neighbor called the police after smelling burning and being unable to get someone to answer Bentley's door. The police broke in to find a pile of ashes in the bathroom, from which poked Bentley's leg, intact from above the knee down. The rest of the body had been consumed by fire, though the bathroom was untouched except for a burn mark or two on the floor. The death was officially reported as asphyxiation, presumably because that is the most usual cause of death in a house fire. The coroner made no efforts to explain the more bizarre features of the case.

Another, even earlier, case comes from Whitley Bay, England. In 1908 retired teacher Margaret Dewar went to waken her sister, Wilhelmina, only to find the lady's body burned to ashes from the chest down in her bed. There was no other sign of fire in the room. Given the great heat needed to burn a human body, it was surprising that the bed and even the sheets were intact except where they touched the body. This time the coroner reported the case as an accidental fire and left it at that.

Typical Features

In recent years a greater willingness has grown toward investigating these strange deaths. Certain features of SHC have emerged as being typical. First, the victim dies quickly. Bodies are often found sitting in chairs or lying in beds in poses that suggest the people made no attempt to escape the fires. Other remains are found on the ground in a pattern consistent with the

SHC in Literature

The great nineteenth-century author Charles Dickens delighted in lifting unusual or bizarre events from the newspapers and weaving them into his stories. In the novel Bleak House, Dickens uses SHC as a dramatic way to dispose of the villainous Krook. Krook is last seen retiring to his room, but when he does not reappear, William Guppy and Tony Weevle investigate. They find the evil man reduced to a pile of ashes, while a black soot coats the ceiling of the room and a thick yellow film covers the objects near the body. Dickens uses the event to illustrate a moral point, saying that the fire was, "inborn, inbred, engendered by the corrupt humours of the vicious body itself." Real cases of SHC do not prove Dickens's theory that only the wicked fall victim to the phenomenon.

The gruesome remains of Dr. John Irving Bentley.

victim collapsing as if struck dead on the spot, the body being burned afterward. Second, the parts of the body affected are usually reduced completely to ashes, while unaffected parts are left intact. The separation between the two is clear and sudden. This is inconsistent with an external fire, which would typically scorch or partially burn some remaining parts of a body. Third, the fire rarely affects objects close to the body; even papers or highly flammable items such as clothing are not even scorched. Fourth, a thick, black, oily soot often coats the room in which the body is found. Most victims live alone and are elderly or in some form of ill health. Obviously this is no ordinary fire.

Hot Theories

One hypothesis blames some form of human electrical disturbance. A few researchers have theorized that the electrical system within the body malfunctions, causing sudden death followed by high temperatures that trigger the fire. Ball lightning has also been suggested as a culprit, but since scientists don't know for certain how ball lightning forms or behaves, it is difficult to know if conditions were conducive to the phenomenon on the days when SHC has occurred.

The wick effect has also been hypothesized. This holds that once a fire has started on a dead body, the clothing and the melting human fat will act like a candle. This will maintain a small but hot flame that could, it is said, consume much of a human body over a period of 12 hours or so. The suggestion has its merits, but there is usually no obvious source of an initial fire.

Some have suggested that if a massive buildup of static electricity occurs and then a person suffers a massive heart attack and collapses, the static may be discharged as a flash when the body hits the ground, and this could trigger the wick-effect fire. This would require extremely dry air, plus particular types of footwear, and these conditions are not always present in documented cases.

Cases of SHC are rare, so it may be that they are the result of some equally rare combination of natural events that has not yet been discovered. Given the fatal nature of the phenomenon, experiments are not possible.

UFOs and Unexplained Disappearances

For decades people have been reporting strange flying objects moving through the skies over Earth. Some of these objects are seen in association with humanoid life forms, which appear to be crew from the flying craft. When these reports first hit the headlines, they were dubbed flying saucers, but they are now usually termed UFOs, for unidentified flying objects.

Bare Bones

- In 1947 Kenneth Arnold spotted some unusual saucer-shaped flying objects, sparking a wave of public interest in UFOs.

- The USAF Project Blue Book, which investigated sightings, was closed in 1970, but many claim that the U.S. military is still covertly investigating UFOs.

- In 1964 a sighting of alien crew next to a UFO ignited interest in the occupants of these craft.

- Some people have claimed that aliens have abducted them and subjected them to medical tests.

Although people have been seeing odd things in the sky for centuries, the modern era of UFOs began on June 24, 1947. On that day, businessman Kenneth Arnold was flying from a meeting in Chehalis, Washington State, back to his home in Oregon. As he flew over the Cascade Mountains, Arnold spotted a formation of unusual aircraft a few miles away that were on a course toward the front of his own airplane.

The craft Arnold saw were crescent-shaped, with wide, sweeping wings but no clear fuselage. They were polished and silver-colored, which reflected the sunlight with intensity. There were nine of them, flying in a military-style echelon. The motion of the objects was unusual in that instead of flying in a straight line, they followed an undulating path. Arnold later likened this to "how a saucer would move if you skipped it over water," and so gave rise to the term "flying saucers." This type of motion is now frequently associated with UFO sightings. Arnold estimated their speed at around 1,300 miles per hour (2,092 km/h).

After he landed, Arnold began to worry that the strange craft might be top-secret military aircraft from the Soviet Union. He reported the sighting to the FBI and to a local newspaper, which ran the story. The public's imagination was gripped. Soon dozens, then hundreds, of other people came forward to report sightings of bizarre flying objects. Some of these reports predated Arnold's sighting by many years.

This photograph was faked using a model UFO, but most UFOs conform to the shape shown here: they are round, domed, and have a flange or rim around the outer edge.

In 1950 retired U.S. Marines officer Donald Keyhoe published a book entitled *Flying Saucers Are Real*. In this he reported the results of his research and conversations with military personnel about the flying-saucer issue. Keyhoe advanced the theory that the U.S. military knew more than they told the public. He also stated his belief that flying saucers were alien spacecraft, bringing intelligent beings from another planet to study humanity. These two theories have underpinned much of the research work that has since been done on UFOs.

PROJECT BLUE BOOK

In fact the U.S. military did know a lot more than they revealed in public. The U.S. Air Force (USAF) ran an investigation

A sign at Roswell, New Mexico, illustrates the continuing interest in UFO activity and alien contact, for which the place gained a reputation following mysterious events that took place here in 1947.

codenamed Project Blue Book throughout the 1950s and 1960s. A top-secret team collected reports of UFOs, investigated them thoroughly, and made recommendations to the air force regarding how to respond.

Project Blue Book concluded that most UFO reports were sightings of normal objects seen in unusual circumstances. Although it acknowledged that some witnesses clearly saw something truly extraordinary, Blue Book pronounced that the strange craft were not a military threat to the United States. As a result, the U.S. military and government lost all official interest. Blue Book was wound down and finally closed in January 1970, and from that time forward, the many reports made by the public were filed without investigation.

THE ROSWELL SAUCER CRASH

At least that was the official story. Rumors persisted that a top-secret team, based at Wright-Patterson Air Force Base in Ohio, continued to study UFOs. In the late 1980s the rumors began to coalesce around events that occurred at Roswell, New Mexico, in July 1947.

On the evening of July 4, something crashed on semidesert grazing land outside the town. At the time, the USAF declared it was a weather balloon but years later changed its story to state that the object had been a highly secret spy device launched to study Soviet air space. Whether or not this explained the elaborate cleanup and the security clampdown that occurred after the incident is still hotly debated. Many UFO investigators believe that the odd events surrounding the affair indicate that what crashed was really a UFO, complete with an alien crew. It is thought that the USAF has been studying the UFO ever since. Other investigators think that if this were the case, some direct evidence would, after more than 60 years, have emerged.

DRAMATIC SIGHTINGS

Even without tales of crashed saucers, the reports of UFOs and their crews are dramatic. Discounting reports that likely constitute planets, aircraft, or satellites seen in unusual circumstances, a clear pattern emerges to these sightings.

UFOs tend to be reported at between 30 and 100 feet (10 and 30 m) in size. They are often rounded in outline, though not always circular, with a smooth and seamless outer layer, which may or may not have features such as windows or lights, but rarely has any insignia or writing. The objects can move quickly, changing direction with a rapidity that would kill any human inside them. Generally, however, they move slowly and usually with a bobbing or undulating motion. They are often drawn toward large metal objects, such as cars or aircraft, seeming to follow them or circle around them.

UFOs encountered at close range are often said to radiate heat or bright light, and more than one witness has ended up in the hospital suffering from sunburnlike symptoms. Many UFOs have a disruptive effect on electrical systems, causing car engines to stop or radios to collapse into static.

Close Encounters

UFO investigators use ufologist J. Allen Hynek's system of classification for sightings.

1 **Daylight Disks.** These are flying objects seen during the day at such a distance that little or no detail can be deciphered.

2 **Nocturnal Lights.** Like Daylight Disks, these are objects seen at a distance. They are, however, seen at night, when their lights are clearly noticeable.

3 **Radar-Visual Contacts.** This category covers those Daylight Disks or Nocturnal Lights, where the object seen is also tracked by radar.

4 **Close Encounters of the First Kind, or CE1.** This category covers UFOs seen in detail and for some period of time.

5 **Close Encounters of the Second Kind, or CE2.** This includes those close encounters where the object has some kind of impact on its surroundings. This might include leaving marks in the soil, or on vegetation, or simply causing tree branches to sway as it passes.

6 **Close Encounters of the Third Kind, or CE3.** CE3s include all sightings when apparently intelligent entities—usually interpreted as crew members—are seen in association with a UFO.

ALIENS SIGHTED

Mistaken sightings of aircraft or satellites cannot explain the thousands of reports of UFO crews that have been made. For many years reports of crew members came from isolated farmers or prospectors, and nobody took them seriously. Then, in 1964, an impeccable witness came forward to claim that he had seen humanoids next to a landed UFO.

Police officer Lonnie Zamora was an experienced and highly regarded officer. On April 24 he abandoned pursuit of a speeding motorist when he saw what he took to be an explosion in the desert near Socorro, New Mexico. Zamora saw an oval object descending toward the ground, emitting a jet of flame but no smoke. Making his way over the desert, Zamora lost sight of the object for a few minutes. As he crested a ridge, he saw the object on the ground. Next to it stood two humanoid figures about 4 feet (1.2 m) tall. They were dressed in light-colored overalls and wore helmets of some kind.

Zamora radioed his base to report a crashed aircraft, though he added that it seemed strange. Returning to the ridge, Zamora heard a sound as if a door had slammed shut. The object at once began to emit flames and climb into the sky. Zamora dived for cover as the object flew overhead. A second policeman arrived just in time to watch the object disappear. The two men inspected the landing sight and found marks apparently left by rectangular landing gear.

The Socorro incident transformed the entire UFO debate. No longer was the emphasis on flying objects; now investigators were more interested in the humanoid entities related to them.

THE VARIOUS CHARACTERS

Since 1964 hundreds of sightings of beings associated with UFOs have been made. Although some of these are unlikely, most fit into one of several general categories. By far the most numerous are the Greys. These beings are around 3 feet (0.9 m) tall with large egg-shaped heads, black eyes, and no visible ears. Their arms tend to be long and slender, ending in hands that have one finger much longer than the others. Reportedly, Greys can be aggressive toward humans. A few witnesses report seeing tall Greys who seem to be in charge.

Nordics are basically human in appearance but are taller than normal and have long blond hair. They often hold conversations with humans using Earth languages and are generally friendly.

Tricksters fall somewhere between the other two. They are basically human but rarely stand more than 4 feet (1.2 m) tall. They wear a wide variety of costumes and headgear and almost invariably behave in a mischievous manner. They may temporarily paralyze a human, steal mundane objects from their pockets, or simply leap out of hiding to scare someone.

TAKEN

In recent years the terrifying experience of abduction has been reported more often. The phenomenon began with scattered reports in the 1950s and 1960s, but by the 1970s they were apparently becoming more common. Several people who had seen a UFO found that they had apparently blacked out and were unable to remember a period of time—usually around an hour—after the experience. When regressed under hypnosis, these witnesses often recalled being taken forcibly into the UFO and subjected to painful tests, apparently of a medical nature. The beings conducting these tests are almost invariably Greys.

RESEARCH CONCLUSIONS

Some researchers hold that the UFO phenomenon should really be divided into two or more unrelated areas. UFOs are often seen without humanoid crews, and humanoid crews without their UFOs. The majority of UFOs may be accounted for by some odd natural phenomenon, while most encounters with aliens can be explained in terms of waking dreams and other recognized psychological events.

Or it may be that aliens really are visiting planet Earth to undertake terrifyingly brutal medical tests on human beings and other creatures. So far, no one knows.

UFOs in the Spotlight

As interest in UFOs and aliens was reaching a peak through the early 1950s, Hollywood stepped up to feed the public's imagination with a raft of alien invasion-themed movies, including such classics of the genre as *The Day the Earth Stood Still* (1951), *Invaders from Mars* (1953), *Earth vs. the Flying Saucers* (1956), and *I Married a Monster from Outer Space* (1958).

One of the most famous was George Pal's 1953 film adaptation of H. G. Wells's novella *The War of the Worlds*. Published in 1898, Wells's story was one of the earliest and most successful depictions of an alien invasion of Earth, and it spawned many adaptations over the years.

It wasn't until Steven Spielberg's hugely successful 1977 movie *Close Encounters of the Third Kind* that the possibility of a more peaceful encounter with aliens was depicted. Spielberg continued this trend with another feelgood movie: *E.T. the Extra-Terrestrial* in 1982. More recent treatments of the topic include Roland Emmerich's *Independence Day* (1996), Tim Burton's 1996 parody *Mars Attacks*, and Spielberg's 2005 remake of *War of the Worlds*.

Terrestrial and Aquatic Monsters

Stories about fantastic, often monstrous animals living in remote regions of the world have fascinated audiences for centuries. Ancient writings contain many stories about dragons, unicorns, centaurs, and mermaids. Most of these creatures were figments of the imagination, but sightings are still being reported of creatures that remain unknown to science. Some appear monstrous, while others are perfectly credible but unproved.

Bare Bones

- The scientific name given to the study of animals that have not yet been proved to exist is cryptozoology. Such animals are known as cryptids.

- Famous examples of cryptids include Bigfoot, the yeti, and the Loch Ness Monster.

- A lesser-known but equally controversial example is the De Loys' American Ape.

- Occasionally, cryptids are proved to exist and pass into the realms of scientifically accepted animals, but unfortunately this sometimes happens only after the creature itself has become extinct.

The study of animals that have not been proved scientifically to exist is known as cryptozoology, the study of hidden animals. Many dedicated scientists risk ridicule by collecting evidence for the existence of unknown animals. Occasionally one is proved to exist, moving from the borders of cryptozoology into the mainstream. One such was the Okapi, a nineteenth-century rumor that in 1901 was finally recognized as a real animal.

The problems cryptozoologists face are illustrated by the case of de Loys' Ape. Shot and photographed by geologist Francois de Loys in the Venezuelan jungle in 1920, its existence is hotly debated to this day. Many scientists believe that the ape was a hoax fabricated by de Loys with a spider monkey corpse. An apparent second sighting in the 1980s has done nothing to cool the debate.

BIGFOOT

De Loys' American Ape is not the only cryptid in the Americas. There is more evidence for the existence of Bigfoot. This is another ape, though it is usually taken to be more hominid than anthropoid because it walks upright on its hind legs and shows clear signs of intelligence. Reports of Bigfoot have been made from the more remote frontier regions of North America since the 1830s but have excited scientists only since the 1950s.

Bigfoot is named for the enormous footprints that have been found. These are typically twice as long as those of a human and lack the manlike hourglass shape in favor of a straight-sided form. The toes are in a straight horizontal line, not an arched row as on the human foot. The creature itself is said to stand about 8 to 9 feet (2.4–2.7 m) tall, though some larger ones have been sighted. It is covered in shaggy fur that varies in color from almost black to reddish brown. Most reports show Bigfoot eating berries or leaves, with only a few claiming to have seen one feasting on small animals. The Bigfoot is normally sighted either on its own or in small groups that appear to be families.

"I shall not commit the fashionable stupidity of regarding everything I cannot explain as a fraud." —CARL JUNG, PSYCHOLOGIST

An alleged photograph of a Sasquatch or Bigfoot taken by researcher and explorer C. Thomas Biscardi in 1981. This photo has not been accepted as genuine by all researchers, though it does give a very clear idea of the probable appearance of this elusive creature.

Lost Opportunity

In 1658 the French admiral Etienne de Flacourt returned from Madagascar and wrote a book about his adventures. In it he told of a seemingly fantastic bird called the Vouroupatra that lived in the swampy forests of the island. It stood, Flacourt said, over 8 feet (2.4 m) tall and laid eggs eight times bigger than those of an ostrich. Nobody believed him.

In 1832 French naturalist Victor Sganzin saw such an egg for himself in Madagascar but was unable to get it back home. The locals said a rare, gigantic forest bird had laid it there. Nobody believed Sganzin.

In 1866 Alfred Grandidier found the skeleton of a bird 8 feet 9 inches (2.6 m) tall. The locals told him that the giant birds had been around in their parents' days but were no longer seen. The skeleton was named Aepyornis. By 1900 the swamp forests had been largely drained. The bird was extinct. If only somebody had believed Flacourt or Sganzin, they might have found a living Aepyornis.

Investigators have amassed thousands of footprint casts, and there are hundreds of eyewitness reports, some of them from highly respectable and credible individuals. Collections of droppings and what appear to be sleeping nests have also been found. A few photos and pieces of movie film claim to show Bigfoot. The clearest of these is the so-called Patterson footage, shot in Bluff Creek, California, in 1967.

The film shows a female Bigfoot walking away briskly, peering over its shoulder toward the camera at one point, then disappearing into woodland. Patterson says that he then chased the creature, but by the time he entered the woodland, it was bounding away at high speed up the hill and was soon out of sight. The film has been subjected to intense scrutiny. It is generally agreed that it shows a humanoid figure about 7 feet (2.1 m) tall walking at about 5 miles per hour (8 km/h). Beyond that there is little agreement. Skeptics say that it shows a man in a fur suit, but others argue that the gait of the creature is nonhuman and could not be faked.

In Canada, Bigfoot is more commonly called Sasquatch (a native word for wild man or hairy man). Dozens of alleged sightings have occurred there. Indeed, the mysterious creature is so popular with Canadians that Sasquatch Provincial Park, near the town of Harrison Hot Springs, British Columbia, is named for it, and one of the mascots for the 2010 Winter Olympics in Vancouver is a furry little beast named Quatchi.

Most Canadian Sasquatch sightings have taken place in the British Colombia woods, lending credence to the theory that Bigfoots roam the woods of the Pacific Northwest. However, other sightings, including recent ones, have occurred in neighboring Alberta and as far east as Saskatchewan and Manitoba.

Two Canadians have claimed they were kidnapped by Bigfoots, the best known being lumberjack Albert Ostman, who said a Sasquatch picked him up in his sleep one night in 1924 near Toba Inlet, B.C., and carried him a great distance to a camp where a family of Sasquatches was living. Canada has also been the site of some of the more notorious Sasquatch hoaxes, beginning with the "Jacko" affair of 1884, in which a creature described as "half man, half beast" was reportedly captured near the town of Yale, B.C., by a group of trainmen and kept for days in the local jail.

THE YETI AND THE NANDI

The other famous cryptid ape is the yeti of the Himalayas. Unlike Bigfoot, the yeti is described as being more apelike than hominid. It is said to move on its four legs, using the knuckles of its hand to support it. There have been many sightings of the yeti over the years, but there is no firm evidence that it exists.

Nor is there any real evidence to support the existence of the nandi, a massive bearlike animal reported from East Africa. The nandi, also called the chemosit, is reported to have a thickset body that slopes from the shoulders down to the hips with no visible tail. It has fur that is thicker and longer over its shoulders than elsewhere, and is a dark or sandy brown color with spots or splotches of a darker color. The beast has a pointed snout and ferocious claws.

THE LOCH NESS MONSTER

Of all the cryptids, few are as famous as the Loch Ness Monster. This creature, which allegedly inhabits the Scottish lake that gives it its name, is said to be about 40 feet (12 m) long and to resemble a prehistoric plesiosaur. Despite its fame, evidence for this creature is slim. All the photos accepted as genuine show an object that could have a variety of explanations. Also, there is not enough food in the lake to sustain a breeding population of creatures this big, though it is possible that the monster is not native to the lake but is a sea creature that has drifted upriver.

Canada is also home to a famous lake "monster." Sightings of an aquatic beast with the head of a horse and the body of a serpent in British Columbia's Lake Okanagan date back to the nineteenth century. In 1926 belief in the beast, nicknamed Ogopogo, was strong enough to compel the provincial government to equip the newly built lake ferry with "monster repelling devices."

Large creatures unknown to science could very likely exist, but which ones are real and which are imaginary is hard to decipher, until somebody captures one.

This famous photograph of the Loch Ness Monster was taken in the 1970s. It appears to show the head and neck of an unknown beast, but skeptics argue that what it shows is either part of a floating log or a deliberately constructed hoax.

Ancient Monuments

Scattered around the world are many monuments built by human hands in centuries past, which stand with little evidence as to who built them, when, or why. Some of these impress by their sheer size, others by the complexity of their design or the ingenious nature of their construction. Modern archaeology and science has done much to unravel the mysteries of these ancient monuments, but many still remain enigmatic and mysterious.

Bare Bones

- There are many ancient monuments around the world whose origins and purpose remain shrouded in mystery.

- Some examples of these monuments include the stone circles of Western Europe, including Stonehenge in England; the Great Pyramid of Giza, in Egypt; and the North American Indian Mounds, such as those found at Effigy Mounds National Park in Iowa.

STONEHENGE

More has probably been written about Stonehenge than about any other site. This monument in England takes the form of concentric circles of standing stones erected within a henge: a circular earthen bank and ditch with a single entrance. The sheer size of the stones makes this the most impressive of the stone circles in Western Europe. The outer ring of stones originally had a complete circle of lintel stones carefully balanced on top, a unique feature, while the central stones are arranged in a horseshoe and are likewise topped by lintels.

Stonehenge has posed a mystery since medieval times, but it has been studied only since the seventeenth century. It was soon realized that some of the stones were arranged so that they aligned on important astronomical events such as midsummer sunrise, midwinter sunset, and various movements of the moon. In 1905 the modern society that seeks to re-create the ancient druidic priestly caste of Celtic Britain began holding ceremonies and rites at Stonehenge in the belief that it was a pre-Roman Celtic temple. These celebrations became hugely popular, and by 2007 the midsummer festival had been moved outside the henge itself, because the huge numbers of people attending threatened to damage the monument.

"Mystery creates wonder, and wonder is the basis of man's desire to understand." —NEIL ARMSTRONG, ASTRONAUT

Meanwhile, archaeologists discovered that the monument had nothing to do with the druids, since it had been abandoned for more than 1,000 years before they came to Britain. Stonehenge was traced back to 3100 B.C., when it consisted of an earthen henge enclosing a circle of upright wooden posts. The site was gradually added to and altered until about 1900 B.C.

No more building work was undertaken, but finds from the site show that it remained in use until at least 1600 B.C. and perhaps until 900 B.C. Thereafter, it was abandoned: Presumably, the gods whose worship had called it into being were no longer venerated—perhaps because the Celts and their druids had arrived.

THE GREAT PYRAMID

The Great Pyramid of Giza in Egypt is perhaps even more famous than Stonehenge. This vast monument was built around 2560 B.C. to serve as the tomb for the great pharaoh Khufu, sometimes known as Cheops, of the Fourth dynasty. Although it was not the first pyramid built as a tomb in ancient Egypt, nor the last, it is certainly the largest and the most elaborate, sitting at the center of a great necropolis of tombs for nobles and royalty.

The great standing stones of Stonehenge in Wiltshire, England, have been in place for over 3,800 years. The stones are aligned on a number of important astronomical events, such as midwinter sunset and midsummer sunrise.

The Great Pyramid of Giza, Egypt, is a massive construction composed largely of sandstone blocks. It contains a network of corridors and chambers, the purpose of which is not clear. Some believe that there is an undiscovered secret chamber near its center.

The Great Pyramid was originally built to be 480 feet (146 m) tall and 755 feet (230 m) square. It is composed of solid blocks of limestone but was originally faced with polished granite to reflect the sun and was topped by a gilded point. It is estimated that the construction took 20 years, with a workforce of around 30,000 men. The geometry involved in the alignment and construction of the pyramid is so precise it has led some to speculate that it could not have been built without nonhuman aid.

Inside the pyramid are three chambers linked by passages and galleries. The main burial chamber is about 16 by 32 feet (4.8 x 9.7 m) and has a height of around 20 feet (6.1 m). Inside this is a broken sarcophagus. The pharaoh's body is missing. Some believe that the Great Pyramid has not yet revealed its secrets. It may be that the real burial chamber has not yet been found. Certainly other Egyptian tombs are mazes of passageways and hidden chambers. The pyramid has tiny corridors too small for humans to travel along. Small robots have been sent along these, only to find that they end in closed doors that are impossible to open. Other tiny corridors are open and point to astronomical points in the sky that line up with certain stars. Their purpose is unknown.

NORTH AMERICAN INDIAN MOUNDS

Scattered across North America are a number of mysterious large earthen mounds. The most striking of the mounds are those that are built in the shape of stylized animals, such as Serpent Mound in southern Ohio and the bear- and bird-shaped mounds at Effigy Mounds National Monument in northeastern Iowa, though most are simple shapes such as squares or ovals. When the first European settlers started arriving in the area, the mounds were already abandoned. The local tribes had nothing to do with them and could pass on little more than rumors and folklore concerning their origins and use. Many mounds have been lost to European farming methods and buildings, but hundreds still remain.

The Europeans refused to believe that the local tribes or their ancestors could have built the mounds, so they looked for other explanations. One of the earliest ideas, put forward around 1820, was that Vikings built the mounds. Later it was suggested that Mesopotamians, Egyptians, or Israelites might have been responsible. Not until 1894 did a report by Cyrus Thomas of the Bureau of American Ethnology conclude that the mounds were built by Native Americans. It is now thought that the mounds date from various cultures from about 1000 B.C. to A.D. 1500. They were used as temple platforms and burial mounds and were usually linked to ceremonial activity.

Atlantis

One site that has excited the interest and imagination of people for centuries, without ever being found, is Atlantis.

According to the ancient Greek philosopher Plato, the records of Atlantis were preserved in Egyptian temples. Plato wrote down what he knew, which was that Atlantis was a large island west of Gibraltar that had been the seat of a mighty empire some 9,000 years earlier. This vast empire had warred against both the Egyptians and Greeks but had been overthrown by earthquakes and tsunami in a single day and night of disaster. The Atlantic Ocean was named for this sunken island.

Scholars and geographers have argued about Atlantis's location, and even if it ever existed. In fact, if the date were to be changed to 900 years before Plato's time and the location shifted closer to Egypt, the story makes more sense. The island of Crete was, at this time, the center of the powerful Minoan civilization that did war with Egypt and Greece. A massive volcanic eruption ruined the Minoan cities and wiped out whole populations, leaving the culture fatally weakened. Without the original Egyptian records, now lost forever, the truth may never be known.

Science
& Psychic
Phenomena

Science has unlocked many golden secrets, from the Big Bang, which brought the universe into being, to the genetic code, the origin of life itself. But the human brain is the most complex structure known and has yet to reveal all its mysteries, including, perhaps, the greatest: Do psychic phenomena truly exist? For more than 150 years some of the finest minds have sought answers to that question. This chapter reveals discoveries to date, including theories, techniques, and experiments. It discusses the various organizations and scientists involved and investigates that mysterious life force called the aura, as well as other paranormal phenomena. Finally, this chapter explores whether or not all creatures, even the tiniest, may have some form of psychic ability.

Scientific Theories of the Psychic Realm: Fact or Fantasy?

Many psychic researchers believe that phenomena such as extrasensory perception (ESP) exemplify natural sensory abilities, although these types of events remain unexplained by science. Just as bats use ultrasound to avoid obstacles, and pigeons navigate via the Earth's magnetic field, why shouldn't humans, with their much larger brains, have psychic powers?

Bare Bones

- Since 1889 scientists have been investigating the involvement of extremely low frequency electromagnetic fields in telepathic transmission.

- Skeptics claim that statistics prove coincidences to be unlikely but perfectly natural events. Some researchers believe they are signs of a universal pattern that people don't yet understand.

- Some scientists believe that the existence of dimensions that have not yet been discovered may explain some psychic phenomena.

Professor Gary Schwartz of the Laboratory for Advances in Consciousness and Health at the University of Arizona believes in the existence of a psychic realm into which sensitive people may tune. Schwartz has worked with many psychics, including Chris Robinson, who dreamed about 9/11. Schwartz suggests that if the mind is in a highly receptive state, it may become attuned to psychic powers. Sleep may be one such state.

If this is so, what is the nature of this psychic realm? In 1889 British physicist Sir Joseph Thompson suggested that extremely low frequency (ELF) electromagnetic fields could be the "physical mechanism of telepathy." In the 1960s a Russian professor, Ippolit M. Kogan, even proposed transmitting telepathic messages using ELF signals.

Dr. Michael Persinger, a psychologist at Laurentian University in Sudbury, Ontario, and others adopted this theme, claiming their research supports the theory that psychic events may be driven by low electromagnetic frequencies. The Earth's magnetic field (magnetosphere) normally vibrates at around 8–12 cycles per second (cps), a frequency to which the brain's temporal lobes are highly sensitive. These brain regions are involved with vision, hearing, language, memory, and one's sense of self in space and time. Brain waves of 8–12 cps are associated with meditation and, it is claimed, telepathy. Perhaps psychics tune into brain-wave patterns imprinted on the magnetosphere.

Professor Harold Puthoff of Stanford University, who has studied Zero Point Energy for 30 years, believes it connects "we and all the matter of the universe…to the furthest reaches of the cosmos" and provides both a medium for psychic phenomena and an inexhaustible source of power for space travel.

Persinger found that reports of psi phenomena are more common when sunspot and electrical storm activity are low and the magnetosphere is calm. Laser physicist and parapsychologist Dr. Harold Puthoff of Stanford University goes further. He believes the universe itself may act as a medium for psi phenomena via a background field of electromagnetism called Zero Point Energy. This concept of an all-pervading energy field, once dismissed by scientists, is now gaining ground among theoretical physicists.

PSYCHICAL OR STATISTICAL?

This might explain telepathy and telekinesis, but what about precognition, which defies time? Evidence for precognition is based mainly on experiments that present better-than-chance results. Skeptics call these results statistical quirks. If you keep tossing a coin, it will land on heads 50 percent of the time. But occasionally it may land on heads 20 times in a row. Such statistical clusters seem significant but are mere random events.

So not psychical, just statistical—in other words, coincidence. Certainly, remarkable coincidences do occur. A 1950 edition of *Life* magazine reported the story of a normally punctual choir, whose 15 members were all late for a 7:20 P.M. practice at their church in Beatrice, Nebraska. They had—in total—10 different reasons for not reaching the venue on time. This was just as well, because at 7:25 P.M. a gas explosion caused the church to blow up. This story was cited by U.S. mathematician Warren Weaver in his book *Lady Luck: The Theory of Probability* as an example of statistical clustering.

COINCIDENCE—OR SOMETHING MORE?

U.S. psychologist Rex Stanford suggests that coincidences show an ability to influence events subconsciously. He cites the example of a couple visiting a city for the first time that wanted to eat a vegetarian meal at an Indian restaurant but didn't know where to go. They stopped at a small diner. A group of people at the next table began discussing the best places for vegetarian Indian meals. Stanford calls this a psi-mediated instrumental response (PMIR). A common example is thinking about a person you haven't heard from in years when—out of the blue—they telephone you. The Irish call this phenomenon the bells.

> "We persevere. The answer will come eventually." —TONY CORNELL, PARANORMAL INVESTIGATOR

Some of the world's greatest thinkers have claimed coincidences are signs of a universal pattern that people don't yet understand. Austrian biologist Dr. Paul Kammerer collected examples of coincidences and published them in 1919 as *The Law of Seriality (Das Gesetz der Serie)*. He said they showed unknown forces at work, which brought together—in time and space—people, objects, and events that were "cosmically linked."

Theoretical physicist Wolfgang Pauli and psychologist Carl Jung expanded on Kammerer's ideas, suggesting that coincidences indicate a universal principle that acts independently of known laws of physics. Jung coined the term synchronicity to describe meaningful coincidences, which he grouped with telepathy and precognition as evidence of a mysterious force trying to impose order on chaotic human life. Jung published his thoughts in *Synchronicity: An Acausal Connecting Principal*.

MULTIPLE DIMENSIONS

Psychic researchers say skeptics are blinded by outdated views of classical science and that theoretical physics holds the key. Lithuanian-born German mathematician Herman Minkowski, a major influence on his most famous pupil, physicist Albert Einstein, introduced the concept of "space-time" in which "space...and time...fade away" to be replaced by a "union of the two" (*see box* "The View beyond Flatland").

U.S.-born quantum physicist P6rofessor David Bohm suggested a quantum world of "unbroken wholeness" with every particle connected to every other particle, and psychic phenomena revealing connections that our three-dimensional view can't explain. The late British mathematical physicist Dr. Adrian Dobbs, of Cambridge University, proposed that time exists in two dimensions—one of which predicts the "probabilities of future outcomes." He claims that knowledge of future events is carried via particles called "psitrons" that travel faster than light. M-theory—which Professor Ed Witten, of the Institute for Advanced Study in Princeton, New Jersey, says stands for "magic, mystery, or matrix, according to taste"—predicts 22 dimensions.

In 2007 Professor David Deutsch and coworkers at Oxford University in England published new evidence in support of the "many worlds" theory—a universe of branching parallel dimensions—proposed by Princeton graduate Hugh Everett 50 years ago. If an event can have more than one outcome, reality splits into separate dimensions, where each outcome is played out.

According to biologist Dr. Lyall Watson, time itself holds the key:

> If [time] is indeed continuous, then any alteration in its properties anywhere will be instantly noticeable everywhere [and] phenomena such as telepathy or any other communication that seems...independent of distance will be easier to understand.

The View beyond Flatland

It is not easy to understand multidimensional space, let alone how it might explain psychic phenomena like ESP. In our daily lives people are aware of only three dimensions, so four-dimensional "space-time" (length, width, height, and time) boggles the mind.

The nineteenth-century fantasy *Flatland, A Romance of Many Dimensions* may help. Rev. Edwin Abbott wrote the novella and—with remarkable prescience—dedicated it to "the secrets of four, five or even six dimensions."

Flatland is a two-dimensional world populated by simple geometric figures. Unknown to the inhabitants, it folds over so that Flatlanders far apart in two-dimensional space may suddenly become closer together via the three-dimensional reality they know nothing about. At such times they may catch a glimpse of each other across the void.

The concept of space–time suggests that time (the fourth dimension) also "folds" back on itself. People and events that, in our reality, are distant in time and space would then be closer in space-time. Perhaps psychics are able to glimpse future events across this four-dimensional void.

Scientific Techniques: Probing the Paranormal

Research into psychic phenomena takes many forms, including in-depth studies of psychic individuals, analysis of scientific data, and investigations into the mental processes and natural forces that may underlie paranormal events. But laboratory experiments remain the most important field of inquiry. However, psychic investigators face some fundamental problems.

Bare Bones

- Psychic phenomena are hard to study in the laboratory because they are unpredictable and difficult to control.

- Scientists use tools such as Zener cards, the Ganzfeld, and more recently, random number generators to help them to explore psychic abilities.

- Researchers are currently working on a project to collect precognitive impressions from large numbers of people so they can analyze them and seek patterns that may predict future events.

Psychic ability such as ESP can rarely be switched on at will. Indeed, psychics argue that waiting for categorical proof of a psychic event to occur under laboratory conditions is like waiting for lightning to strike. Yet no one doubts lightning exists. Spontaneous psi can occur without warning, or subjects may go through sensitive periods, when psychic activity occurs regularly, followed by a drought period when such events are rare.

Personality also plays a part. A supportive approach by researchers can support psychic activity, whereas a cynical attitude tends to inhibit it. Outgoing people are more likely to show psychic ability, whereas introverts are less likely to. Psychic investigators must consider these factors while ensuring their research is objective and produces repeatable, statistically valid results.

TELEPATHY IS ON THE CARDS

Perhaps the best-known psychic research technique involves the use of Zener cards. Dr. J. B. Rhine, formerly of Duke University, developed these cards (*see box* "Pioneer of U.S. Parapsychology," *page 128*) together with his colleague, Swiss psychologist Dr. Karl Zener, for whom they were named. There are 25 Zener cards in a deck. Each card shows one of five symbols: a cross, a circle, a square, a star, or three wavy lines. These shapes were chosen because they are easy to recognize and hard to confuse.

In a typical experiment one person (the sender) selects cards in turn and tries to transmit mental pictures to a second person (the receiver) in another room (often a separate building). The receiver names the cards, and a researcher records the answers. The order given is compared with the order of the cards selected. Zener cards can be used to test precognitive abilities, too. In this case the receiver must correctly predict the order of cards before they are selected.

Anyone can correctly guess 5 cards out of 25, on average, simply by chance. A nonpsychic may occasionally guess correctly at a higher frequency, but over time correct answers return to chance levels. To show evidence of psychic effects, subjects perform an extended series of tests and must select correct cards at a frequency higher than achievable by chance alone—a level known as statistically significant. Traditional cards have now largely been replaced by computerized systems. Subjects choose card images on a monitor by pressing buttons, and hits and misses are recorded digitally.

STUDYING DREAM ESP

Subjects often seem more receptive to telepathic influences when dreaming. Studies into dream telepathy have been conducted since 1961 at the Dream Laboratory, at Maimonides Medical Center, State University of New York. The laboratory, founded by psychiatrist Dr. Montague Ullman, investigates all aspects of the dream state, including possible psychic ability.

Researchers look at art prints, or picture postcards, and transmit these thought images to subjects sleeping in the laboratory, while an electroencephalogram (EEG) monitors the sleepers' brain-wave patterns. Dreams are most likely to occur during periods when the eyes flicker, called rapid eye movement (REM) sleep. At such times a subject's brain-wave pattern appears different from other sleep periods *(see box* "Sleep Patterns," *page 84).* Once REM brain-wave patterns appear, subjects are woken up and asked to describe their dream. An independent observer then compares their dream impressions with the transmitted image.

A dreamlike mental state can also be induced with a form of sensory deprivation called the Ganzfeld (or whole field) State, developed by psychologist Dr. Carl Sargent at Cambridge University, England. Subjects lie on a bed listening to white noise—a featureless form of radio static. Their eyes are covered with half Ping-Pong balls, and a soft pink light is shone onto them. Blocking out extraneous sound and visual stimuli helps subjects become mentally attuned.

A sender looks at an image, such as a photo, video clip, or art print. The receiver says out loud what image or "mentation" is being received, while experimenters record these impressions. Alternatively, the receiver is shown the selected image along with three dummies and must select the correct one. Chance alone would give a success rate of 25 percent, so a significantly higher score suggests psychic factors are involved.

PLAYING THE NUMBERS GAME

Parapsychologists must accumulate large volumes of data to weed out statistical quirks and produce results that are consistently above chance. They must rule out confounding variables that may distort results, including experimenter error, unintentional bias, or fraud. One solution is to use automated techniques.

Starting in the 1960s, German physicist Helmut Schmidt developed a random number generator (RNG) while working at Boeing's research laboratories in Seattle, Washington. His RNG used the unpredictable release of electrons from radioactive strontium–90, as detected by an electron particle counter. This RNG switched on one of four colored lights whenever an electron was released, creating an entirely random sequence.

Using ESP to predict the sequence, subjects had to press a button to indicate which light they thought would come on next. Electronic counters recorded hits and misses. According to studies published in *New Scientist* and the *Journal of Parapsychology*, results by nonpsychics were at chance level, 25 percent, whereas those individuals who claimed to have psychic powers performed significantly better than this.

Schmidt also developed a binary system that randomly selected ones or zeros and switched on a sequence of lights arranged in a circle, either to the left or to the right. Chance dictated that the lights would move in one direction or the other 50 percent of the time, on average. Psychic subjects had to influence the lights to go in one direction more often than the other. Again, results obtained were above chance level.

Schmidt's work influenced physicist Professor Robert Jahn, an expert on jet propulsion, who was based at Princeton University, New Jersey. Professor Jahn set up Princeton Engineering Anomalies Research (PEAR), with developmental psychologist Brenda Dunne. They developed random event generators (REGs) based on electronic white noise. A typical REG produced

Dr. Joseph Banks Rhine and his wife, Dr. Louisa Rhine, devoted their lives to making psychic research a legitimate branch of science in the United States. Rhine established the term parapsychology to denote the study of psi phenomena and invented many of the psi research protocols used today.

random numbers just above or below 100, the equivalent of flipping an electronic coin. Psychic subjects had to attempt to make the machine produce more higher numbers (heads) or lower numbers (tails). Random event generators (REGs) produce huge volumes of data so that any difference due to psychic effects emerges from chance levels.

A study of the large amounts of data produced by REGs over many years (called meta-analysis) conducted by parapsychologists Dr. Dean Radin and Dr. Roger Nelson has concluded that the detectable difference is a statistically significant 51 percent. This suggests an observable and inexplicable effect but has not been enough to persuade the wider science community that psi exists. The PEAR facility at Princeton finally closed in February 2007 after 28 years. Jahn, age 76, told the *New York Times*, "If people don't believe us after all the results we've produced, then they never will."

> "I am convinced that discoveries of far-reaching importance remain waiting along these shadowy and discredited paths." —JOHN LOGIE BAIRD, ENGINEER

DETECTING PSI GLOBALLY

Nelson has applied the REG concept to field research using portable devices dubbed Field REGs. These detect the collective consciousness field generated when groups of people are mentally in tune, such as at mass entertainment and sporting events and religious gatherings. The emotional high points of these meetings are then compared to the Field REG to see if a significant deviation occurred at those times.

Nelson has detected significant responses during moments of group emotion, with the strongest effects occurring at highly charged religious meetings. By comparison, business meetings and other gatherings, with minimal emotional involvement, cause little deviation. Radin, Nelson's colleague, used Field REGs to monitor the collective response of millions of TV viewers watching the trial of O. J. Simpson and the Oscars in 1995, and the 1996 Summer Olympics in Atlanta, Georgia, with similar results.

The study has been expanded to monitor global collective consciousness using a worldwide network of Field REGs. The Global Consciousness Project has been collecting and processing Field REG data, recording collective responses to every major global event—including 9/11—since 1998.

FUTUROLOGY—PUTTING ESP TO WORK

The next phase of ESP research may use the widespread potential of the Internet to collect psychic data. Information from people with precognitive skills could be processed to identify patterns, giving advance warning of potential catastrophes—like 9/11. Steps can then be taken to avert the crisis. This may seem like science fiction, but people with close links to the Pentagon believe it is achievable.

Futurologist John L. Petersen is president and founder of The Arlington Institute—a "non-profit research institute" and "global agent for change"—based in the U.S. Air Force Association Building, in Arlington, Virginia. Petersen worked for several U.S. defense departments, including that of the Secretary of State for Defense and the National Security Council. Psychic reports he has reviewed, as well as psychic subjects he has met, have led him to believe that there is "far more to this reality than conventional mainline science…admits."

He is developing a Web-based program—WHETHEReport—to connect precognitive dreamers all over the world and store their impressions in a database. Pattern recognition software then creates a map of future global events. In a 2007 TV interview he said:

> Before every major event, whether 9/11 or the tsunami, common people have anomalous dreams. These [dreams] are qualitatively different and [the dreamers] know they mean something. It is clear this precognizant capability and process exists and if we can learn how to interpret it… it would have profound implications for being able to anticipate big events.

Famous Experiments: Milestones in Psychic Research

Throughout the 1800s psychical research focused mainly on proving there was life after death. Over time the emphasis changed to investigating the mind itself as a source of psychic power. But the Victorian "table-rapping" image has proved difficult to shake off, and many mainstream scientists remain skeptical. Claims of poor experimental design and falsified results have not helped. Nevertheless, for more than a century psi researchers have continued to investigate the paranormal under scientific conditions, consistently producing results above chance level that seem to fly in the face of orthodox thinking.

Bare Bones

- Emphasis in scientific research has shifted from the early interest in proving life after death to investigating the power of the mind.

- A series of experiments took place throughout the 1960s that aimed to test whether or not the physiological response of a person sensitive to psychic influences could be used to send messages.

- Other famous experiments have tested whether or not psi works in outer space and whether or not lucid dreamers can receive premonitions in dreams.

DRAWING ON PSYCHIC POWER

In the 1930s Maryland-born novelist Upton Sinclair performed ESP experiments with his apparently psychic second wife, Mary Craig. Sinclair drew a picture, and Mary, in an adjoining room, would try to duplicate it. Sinclair's artistic skills were limited, and his wife often successfully reproduced the image he had drawn without recognizing what it was. She thought his picture of an erupting volcano was a beetle, for example. Observers relying on her verbal description alone would have called this a failure, yet the two images were remarkably similar.

In his book *Mental Radio: Does It Work, and How?*, Sinclair describes 290 tests, of which 23 percent were hits, 24 percent misses, and 53 percent partially successful. The preface to his book was written by physicist Albert Einstein who, while skeptical of his conclusions, said Sinclair's "good faith and dependability are not to be doubted."

Psychologist Professor William McDougall was so impressed he started a parapsychology unit at Duke University, North Carolina, with Dr. J. B. Rhine. Professor McDougall conducted his own experiments with Mary Craig, but with less success.

EXTRASENSORY SIGNAL TRAFFIC

French psychologist René Warcollier was the first to perform long-distance telepathy experiments—between France and the United States. Participants transmitted mental images of drawings to receptive subjects who recorded their impressions as "form, [or] part of form, with subconscious understanding." Warcollier's experiments, published in *Experimental Telepathy* and *Mind to Mind—Studies in Consciousness*, set protocols for paranormal research that influenced later psychic investigators.

In 1957 Czech physician Dr. Stepán Figar found that just thinking about someone sensitive to psychic influences produced a detectable increase in their blood volume, as indicated by a plethysmograph machine, which measures changes in volume within an organ or throughout the body. He used this technique to study telepathy.

British-born electrochemist E. Douglas Dean, formerly of Newark College of Engineering, New Jersey, saw practical ways of using Figar's findings. Dean, who was interested in psychical research, wondered if these physiological changes might be employed to send Morse code messages. In 1960, working with two engineering colleagues, Robert Taetzsch and John Mihalasky, he put it to the test.

A sender and receiver who had a suitable emotional tie were chosen. The sender's thought message caused a change in the receiver's blood volume, as detected by plethysmograph. A strong response counted as a Morse dot, while no response was a dash. In this way the team sent messages between college rooms, then between buildings, and finally 1,200 miles (2,000 km), from New York to Florida. Dean's research suggested that up to 25 percent of people might show this kind of sensitivity.

In 1965 two ophthalmologists at Jefferson Medical College in Philadelphia, Thomas Duane and Thomas Behrendt, published a study in *Science* showing a psychic link between two test subjects—identical twins. When one twin began to meditate, an alpha brain-wave pattern (also associated with telepathy) showed on an electroencephalogram (EEG), which records brain activity.

In February 1971, astronaut Dr. Ed Mitchell attempted an ambitious telepathy test on board *Apollo XIV*. He was so profoundly affected by his space trip and moon landing that a year later he founded the Institute for Noetic Sciences in Petaluma, California, to study psi and human consciousness (noetics).

The late Jerry Garcia and his rock band Grateful Dead took part in a 1971 dream telepathy experiment with psychic Malcolm Bessent. An image of a levitating yoga figure with colored spiral chakras and a halo of light was projected onto a screen for audience members to transmit psychically. Bessent dreamed of a man "suspended...in midair," with an "energy box" and a "spinal column."

Simultaneously, this pattern appeared on the EEG of the other twin, who was in a different room.

Two years later Russian scientists combined the two techniques to attempt Dean's Morse record. The jawbreaking "Bio-information Section of the A. S. Popov All-Union Scientific and Technical Society of Radio Technology and Electrical Communications" was founded in Moscow to investigate psychic phenomena. Its director, Professor Ippolit M. Kogan, used two gifted subjects, biophysicist Yuri Kamensky and Moscow actor Karl Nikolaiev. The pair had already demonstrated telepathic ability by scoring a 60 percent hit rate in tests using Zener cards.

For the code experiment Kamensky was in Siberia and Nikolaiev in Moscow, 2,000 miles (3,200 km) away. Kamensky, the sender, imagined he and Nikolaiev, the receiver, were fighting, injecting as much emotion as possible. He sent his thoughts in 15- or 45-second bursts, representing Morse code dots or dashes. As Nikolaiev reacted to these outbursts, changes in his brain pattern and physiology showed up on an EEG and blood pressure monitor. The message came through loud and clear—*dash dash* (M), *dot dot* (I), *dash dash dot* (G)—MIG—Russian for instant.

PSI IN OUTER SPACE

Astronaut Dr. Edgar Mitchell, who has long been interested in the mind's psychic potential, conducted an ESP experiment aboard *Apollo XIV* while flying to and from the moon. Over four nights in February 1971, Mitchell randomly copied a series of numbers on a sheet of paper, each one relating to a Zener card. These numbers were compared with impressions formed by psychics in four U.S. cities. Mitchell said the results obtained were significant, quoting probabilities of getting the same result by chance as 3,000 to 1.

Many aspects of the experiment have since been questioned. Unknown to the receivers on Earth, the launch was delayed by 40 minutes. In addition, Mitchell performed the experiment only on four occasions—fewer than planned. This made it more difficult to match Mitchell's selections with those of the psychics on Earth.

According to James Randi, whose foundation works to debunk claims of paranormal ability, the significance of the result stemmed from the fact that the psychics had actually scored an unusually *low* success rate, at odds of 3,000 to 1 compared with chance alone. Randi claims this made the experiment a failure.

TELEPATHY? IN YOUR DREAMS...

Subjects are said to be particularly receptive to telepathy during lucid dreaming—when they know they're asleep and are able to influence the contents of their dreams. The Dream Laboratory at Maimonides Medical Center in Brooklyn, New York, conducts experiments into lucid dreaming.

One of the center's most ambitious experiments was into dream telepathy, conducted by researchers including Dr. Stanley Krippner and Dr. Montague Ullman. It involved a two-thousand-strong audience at a six-day rock concert performed by the band Grateful Dead at Capitol Theater in Port Chester, New York, in 1971. Each night, an image was projected onto a screen behind the stage, and audience members sent it telepathically to British lucid dreamer Malcolm Bessent, asleep in the Dream Laboratory. The image, chosen at random, changed each night. Malcolm was said to have scored four hits out of six.

James Randi—Skeptic or Cynic?

Canadian-born James Randi, a stage magician and TV broadcaster, takes an uncompromising stance toward claims of psychic powers. Seen as a skeptic by supporters and a cynic by opponents, he claims he set up the James Randi Educational Foundation in Fort Lauderdale, Florida, to promote critical thinking about the paranormal.

The organization offers a One Million Dollar Paranormal Challenge for successfully demonstrating psi powers "under satisfactory observing conditions." Until April 2007 the competition was open to anyone. Now those claiming paranormal powers must have a media presence—that is, have been featured in published or broadcast material—and have the backing of an academic before being eligible to participate.

The competition has been criticized for lack of independent judging and for allegedly setting the criteria too high for a realistic chance of success. Randi says that both parties agree on the test protocol in advance and the evidence either "does or does not demonstrate psychic power," hence no judging is necessary. Of the 1,000 applications received to date, 54 have reached preliminary testing stage—but none further.

The Parapsychological Association: Daring to Go One Step Beyond

When Galileo Galilei announced that the Earth orbited the sun, he based his claim on planetary observations any astronomer could make. But it went against established wisdom and contemporaries distanced themselves from his "heretical" notions. Parapsychological Association (P.A.) members say they are in a similar situation today. Like Galileo, their research could be further explored by mainstream scientists, yet it is often outright rejected.

Bare Bones

- The Parapsychological Association is a professional body founded in 1957 by psychologist Dr. J. B. Rhine.

- The P.A. provides a public forum where open-minded scientists and academics can debate psychic phenomena.

- The association has 250 members from all scientific fields. They have differing views on the origins and significance of psi phenomena, but are united by a desire to develop scientific protocols to study the nature of psi, assess current theories, and explore and develop new ones.

The P.A. is a professional body founded in 1957 by botanist-turned-psychologist Dr. J. B. Rhine, a pioneer of paranormal research who coined the term extrasensory perception (ESP). Rhine and his wife, Louisa, began the first large-scale scientific investigation into ESP in 1927 at the psychology department at Duke University, North Carolina.

Rhine's first set of results, published in 1934, caused controversy. Many scientists rejected his findings, claiming they were a statistical quirk. Three years later, following a study into his methods, the American Institute of Mathematical Statistics declared Rhine's research valid. In 1955, in *Science,* the journal of the American Association for the Advancement of Science (A.A.A.S.), G. R. Price, a medical researcher, accused Rhine of fraud. This led to a protracted argument between the two men that ended only when Price publicly withdrew his allegations.

CONVINCING THE SKEPTICS

Rhine even challenged one critic, psychologist Bernard Frank Riess, a fellow of Barnard College, New York, to conduct an ESP experiment for himself. Riess accepted, using a young female psychic. Her success rate—70 percent correct answers—converted Riess from skeptic to supporter. Riess later told the American

Psychological Association that the "only error that may have crept in is a possibility of deception, and the only person who could have done the deceiving is myself since the subject at no time knew how well she was doing nor had any idea of cards, which were being turned by myself."

Such incidents proved the need for a public forum where open-minded scientists and academics could debate psychic (psi) phenomena, and so the P.A. was born. Now based in Petaluma, California, P.A. members stress that the para in *para*psychology means alongside—not outside. Writing in the electronic journal *Dynamical Psychology*, renowned researcher Dr. Stanley Krippner points out that parapsychology-pioneered research into aspects of human behavior is "now part of mainstream psychology," including hypnosis, multiple personalities, lucid dreaming, and out-of-body experiences.

The grave of Charles Hoy Fort (1874–1932), Amercian writer and researcher into anomalous phenomena. Fort was deeply skeptical of mainsteam science and was an early investigator into events that were denied or ignored by the scientific establishment of the time. In contrast members of the P.A. often come from within the scientific community and work toward acceptance of their work into the mainstream.

Four-time president of the Parapsychological Association, Dr. Dean Radin has conducted wide-ranging research into psi phenomena and is credited with helping to raise public consciousness of psychic research through his best-selling books, including the award-winning *The Conscious Universe* and *Entangled Minds*.

MISSION IMPOSSIBLE?

Clairvoyance, precognition, psychic healing, psychokinesis, remote viewing, and telepathy—"Cinderella" topics, as far as mainstream science is concerned—are fair game for P.A. members. The P.A.'s mission statement is that:

> If new principles of physics, biology, or psychology do underlie psi experiences, then our current knowledge of human nature and the world… is incomplete—and will remain so, until the scientific community makes a sustained effort to understand these experiences.

Psi experiments are conducted in the laboratory and in the field—homes and workplaces of people exhibiting psychic traits. Members also review past research and analyze new data.

The 250 members of the P.A. are not scientific outsiders but hail from physics, biology, medicine, social science, and psychology. They are united by a wish to develop scientific protocols to study the origins and nature of psi, assess current theories, and explore and develop new ones. P.A. members represent a broad range of disciplines and opinions and

"I too much value the pursuit of truth...to avoid inquiry because it appears to clash with prevailing opinions."

—SIR WILLIAM CROOKES, CHEMIST AND PHYSICIST

there is no consensus as to whether psi phenomena originate in the mind, nature, or physics. As Krippner makes clear, "The essential touchstones for parapsychologists include the need to stress the speculative nature of the field, to be candid about its controversial status, and not go beyond what is warranted by the evidence."

Their mission statement also stresses the need to promote scholarship and scientific inquiry and to disseminate information to scientists and public alike. To this end the P.A. organizes annual conferences in North America and Europe to brief members on current findings, encourages an exchange of views, and publishes its proceedings. The 50th Annual Parapsychological Association Convention, held in 2007 in Halifax, Nova Scotia, attracted delegates from all over the world.

PUBLIC PARTICIPATION

Dean Radin, former president of the P.A., notes that:

> Science is good at studying a lot of things, but not everything. Through science [P.A. members] are able to demonstrate that [psi] effects are real. There's plenty of personal interest among scientists in the U.S., but it's not very safe to talk about this from an academic standpoint. There's a taboo.

To break the taboo, the P.A. integrates psi research with mainstream science by sponsoring events through organizations such as the American Association for the Advancement of Science (A.A.A.S.) to which the P.A. has been affiliated since 1969. The public can take part in online research through the P.A.'s Web site. Ongoing studies include one conducted by the Boundary Institute of Saratoga, California, which allows participants to discover their psi abilities, plus the Dice Game—online research into precognition, conducted by the Pacific Neuropsychiatric Institute, at Seattle, Washington State.

Members of the P.A. publish their work in various science publications, including the *Journal of Parapsychology*, *Journal of the American Society for Psychical Research*, *European Journal of Parapsychology*, and *International Journal of Parapsychology*.

Psychic Feedback

The Parapsychology Association promotes a Psi Explorer CD-ROM, developed by Dr. Mario Varvoglis and his team, that uses "psychic feedback" to help people develop psi abilities.

Just as patients with high blood pressure can lower it by focusing on a blood pressure meter—a process called biofeedback—so psi feedback is designed to help people develop their psi powers.

In the accompanying literature, Varvoglis explains that "the most interesting insights will come not...from the specialists and the laboratories, but from the many, many individuals who explore their mental potentials on their own— using their own personal psi labs."

The Koestler Unit

It is probably in the United Kingdom that parapsychology, the scientific study of the paranormal, most robustly survives within academic contexts. That is largely because of the legacy of Arthur Koestler, the author of the celebrated novel *Darkness at Noon*.

Bare Bones

- The Koestler Unit based at the University of Edinburgh is a research department devoted to the study of parapsychology.

- Arthur Koestler and his wife Cynthia left almost their entire estate for the establishment of a chair of parapsychology at a British university.

- The first occupant of the chair was the U.S. parapsychologist Robert Morris, who held the position from 1985 until his unexpected death in 2004.

Koestler was born in 1905 in Hungary, though he later became a British citizen. He studied science and psychology and became an international journalist. In 1937, while covering the Spanish Civil War, he was captured by Franco's Nationalist forces and imprisoned under sentence of death. During his incarceration Koestler had an experience that changed his attitude toward ESP, about which he had once been skeptical. A passage from a Thomas Mann novel, *The Buddenbrooks* (1902), regarding Arthur Schopenhauer's essay "On Death and its Relation to the Indestructibility of our Essential Being," popped into Koestler's head and brought him great peace of mind. So much so that after being set free, he wrote to Mann to thank him. Mann replied that he had not looked at the essay for many years, but a few days previously he had suddenly felt impelled to read it. As he went to fetch the book, the doorbell rang. It was the postman delivering Koestler's letter.

The study of coincidence formed the topic of Koestler's main work on parapsychology, *The Roots of Coincidence* (1972). In this Koestler attempted to find a basis for paranormal events in coincidence—synchronicity—whose roots he sought in the Alice-in-Wonderland subatomic world of quantum physics.

THE KOESTLER LEGACY

When Koestler and his wife died in 1983, they left almost their entire estate for the endowment of a chair of parapsychology at a British university, specifying that the money be used for "parapsychology and parapsychology alone." Edinburgh University assumed the task and U.S. parapsychologist Robert Morris

Arthur Koestler, prominent author and journalist, died in a suicide pact with his wife, Cynthia, in 1983 after suffering declining health. They left a substantial legacy that they stipulated must be used for the endowment of a chair of parapsychology. This resulted in the establishement of the Koestler Unit.

became the first Koestler Professor at the Koestler Parapsychology Unit (KPU). "I see parapsychology as an interdisciplinary problem area," Morris stated. He felt that parapsychology had to include other disciplines, such as physics, sociology, and neurophysiology.

The work (and even the layout) of the KPU was designed to minimize procedural flaws—even stage magicians were consulted to guard against trickery. Between 1993 and 2003, six out of nine major parapsychological experiments produced statistically significant results. Then, in 2004, Morris died suddenly at the age of 62.

MOVING FORWARD

Calls went out for a successor to Morris, but it was announced in 2007 that new funding had been obtained to establish the Robert Morris Chair, while the Koestler Chair would remain unfilled for the foreseeable future. So the KPU continues, but not quite in its previous form. Koestler's legacy survives in additional ways, however, because Morris had quietly produced numerous Ph.D. students in parapsychology, 12 of whom now hold permanent academic positions in university departments where they continue to pursue their research.

Electronic Voice Phenomena

The term electronic voice phenomena (EVP) refers to inexplicable voices heard on electronic equipment. At first, these voices were detected in the background hiss or white noise of audiotapes and in the static hiss of untuned radios. In recent years, the phenomena have been noted on telephones left off the hook, cell phones, digital recording devices, computers, and just about any type of electronic audio equipment. A visual version of EVP has also been claimed, with mystery images reported in the staticlike snow of untuned TV sets.

The First Voices

The story of EVP began in 1959, when Swedish artist and filmmaker Friedrich Jürgenson heard faint human voices on tape recordings he made of birdsong in the countryside. Intrigued, he made further recordings of silent locations—faint voices could still be detected. He published a book, *Voices from Space*, in 1964. Experimenting further, Jürgenson detected a voice that he was sure belonged to his dead mother because it called him by a private nickname. This convinced the Swede he was picking up voices of the dead, and in 1967 he published his book *Radio-link with the Dead*.

Americans Attila von Szalay and Raymond Bayless had been conducting similar experiments a little before Jürgenson, but it was the Swede who elevated interest in EVP, largely because a Swedish-based Latvian psychologist, Konstantin Raudive, continued Jürgenson's work. Raudive made more than 100,000 recordings. Like Jürgenson, Raudive became convinced the voices were from spirits of the dead. So in 1968 he published a book claiming successful electronic communication with the dead; this had considerable impact when it was translated into English as *Breakthrough* in 1971, and EVP was initially referred to as Raudive voices.

Listening in

The basic EVP technique is to use a tape recorder with no microphone, and factory-fresh audiocassettes running in the machine. Researchers feel that

EVP in the Spotlight

The concept of EVP has proved a useful dramatic device in film and television productions. The 1982 movie Poltergeist *showed a group of terrifying spirits using the static on a television set to communicate with a five-year-old girl. In the psychological thriller* The Sixth Sense *(1999) Bruce Willis's character, psychologist Dr. Malcolm Crowe, hears the voices of the dead in the background of a tape of one of his therapy sessions. The 2005 movie* White Noise *takes the concept one step further. Michael Keaton plays Jonathan Rivers, a grieving architect who, while initially skeptical, discovers he can contact his dead wife through EVP and becomes obsessed with the phenomenon, with dangerous consequences.*

In recent years some investigators have claimed to see supernatural images in the static of untuned television sets. The term instrumental transcommunication or ITC has been coined to include both this phenomenon and EVP.

some ambient noise is required, such as tape hiss or the hum produced by amplified circuits, because the disembodied spirit trying to communicate has to manipulate the sound produced by the equipment.

Most voices are faint, speaking in a fluid rapid rhythm and usually on the borderline of comprehensibility, uttering fragmentary phrases such as "This is G!" or "Save me!" It is claimed that it is possible to ask the voices questions and receive answers.

Explanations

The most common belief among EVP enthusiasts is that the voices are from the dead, but other suggestions are that they are from extraterrestrials;

thought forms from the operator's own subconscious; or even the results of unconscious psychokinesis, in which the operator changes the distribution of magnetic material on tapes.

Skeptics take a different view. They say the human brain is designed to seek patterns in sensory data and that voices are simply being read into unstructured sound. Just as people see pictures that aren't there in the Rorschach inkblot test, so too they hear voices in white noise. Some attribute the phenomenon to the occurrence of stray radio interference, anomalies such as signal capture errors and processing in what is usually fairly crude electronic equipment, and occasionally even downright hoaxes.

ESP: The Gift of Second Sight?

The term extrasensory perception (ESP) describes the ability to obtain knowledge of people and events by means other than the conventional senses of sight, hearing, touch, taste, and smell. Parapsychologists divide ESP into specific abilities, such as telepathy, clairvoyance, and precognition, but ESP can be hard to categorize.

Bare Bones

- Extrasensory perception (ESP), is the general term used to describe psi events that are analogous to sensory functions.

- It is usually divided into specific abilities, such as telepathy, clairvoyance, and precognition, but the boundaries between these different abilities are not always clear.

- Duke University, North Carolina, and the Institute for Noetic Sciences in Petaluma, California, are both parapsychology centers that conduct research into ESP.

A MEETING OF MINDS

Dr. Stanley Krippner became interested in psychic phenomena following an experience he had as a 14-year-old. As young Stanley lay in bed thinking about asking his Uncle Max for money, he bolted upright and thought, Uncle Max can't help me, because he's dead! At that moment "I heard the telephone ring. My mother answered the phone and then began sobbing as my cousin told her that Uncle Max had unexpectedly been taken ill, was rushed to hospital, and had just died."

One night in June 1978, Dr. Mario Varvoglis was asleep in his Brooklyn apartment when he heard his mother's panic-stricken voice calling his name. He awoke with a feeling of dread—as if the ceiling were about to fall on him. Eventually falling asleep, he was awoken again, this time by a friend calling from Varvoglis's hometown of Thessaloniki in Northern Greece, where his mother still lived. An earthquake had rocked the region. The link between events in Greece and the nightmare were clear to Varvoglis.

Both men have since devoted their lives to studying psychic phenomena. Krippner has conducted pioneering work into dream telepathy and is the author of many books on psychic phenomena. Varvoglis is director of the Institut Métaphysique International, in France, where he develops computer technology to enable the public to explore their psychic potential.

FORENSIC ESP

People claiming psychic ability often take part in scientific research at parapsychology centers, including Duke University,

North Carolina, and the Institute for Noetic Sciences in Petaluma, California. Sometimes psychics get involved in forensic science too, by helping police find missing people and solve crimes. Perhaps the best-known crime-fighting psychic today is medium Allison DuBois. The part played by Patricia Arquette in the prime-time TV show *Medium* is based on her.

In contrast, members of the U.S. Psi Squad keep a low profile. The late Bevy Jaegers of St. Louis, Missouri, founded this team of psychic detectives in 1971. According to a survey conducted by *Skeptical Inquirer*, only a third of the 50 U.S. police departments polled claimed to have used psychics. Most said the information was too generalized to be helpful. But U.S. Psi Squad's current director, Lance Daniel, says many agencies use their services, including the FBI and Interpol, but, he told *St. Louis Magazine*, they don't own up, because they "don't want the public to lose confidence in them."

In the UK, police have had mixed results from psychics, as illustrated by the case of the serial killer dubbed the Yorkshire Ripper. A bogus tape sent by a man who had a distinctive regional accent misled some psychics, including renowned medium Doris Stokes, into thinking the killer was from Sunderland. Kent psychic Nella Jones wasn't fooled. In her book *Ghost of a Chance: The Life Story of a Psychic Detective* (1982), Nella recounts telling reporter Shirley Davenport that the killer was called Peter and lived in a big house (No. 6) in an elevated area of Bradford, Yorkshire. He drove a truck with the company name—beginning with C—on the side. In 1980 Nella told Shirley, "He'll kill again— on November 17." Nella turned out to be right in every respect.

THE FUTURE IS NOW

Disasters are invariably followed by people claiming to have had visualizations and dreams regarding these events in advance. Many reports are impossible to verify, because no prior record was made. But in one remarkable case a British man claiming precognitive dreams was taking part in psychic research in the United States when his premonition came tragically true.

Psychic Crime Fighters

Beverly "Bevy" Jaegers, of St. Louis, Missouri, who died in 2001, was the founder of the U.S. Psi Squad. Bevy believed ESP was not a gift for those with "God's thumbprint on their forehead" but a skill to be acquired.

In 1971 a high-profile criminal case put Bevy in the spotlight. Police were holding Anthony Damico in connection with the disappearance of wealthy 36-year-old housewife Sally Lucas. Damico was found asleep in Lucas's car, but with no body and little evidence it was likely he would not be charged. Sitting in Sally's car, Bevy reported impressions including horses' heads, a small bridge, the letters C and CC, a creek bed, a poker, an airport, an empty church, and pillar mailboxes.

Sally's body was found the next day near the Spirit of St. Louis Airport. She lay in a dry creek by a small bridge at the junction of Routes C and CC. Nearby were Poker Flats ranch, Assembly of God church, now abandoned, and a row of pillar mailboxes. Damico was later convicted of Sally's murder.

In 2001 Chris Robinson was taking part in dream precognition studies at the Laboratory for Advances in Consciousness and Health, University of Arizona, run by psychologist Professor Gary Schwartz. Robinson had to dream the mystery location he would be taken to next day. But what happened partway through the test shook the professor. On August 11 Robinson had a nightmare. The next morning, he told Schwartz, "I don't even want to talk about what I saw last night. Planes were crashing into tall buildings," he said. "Thousands of people were dying." Robinson continued to have the nightmare regularly over the following month until, on September 11, terrorists flew two airliners into the Twin Towers of Manhattan's World Trade Center.

Before the disaster unfolded, the professor had taken little notice of Robinson's dream, since it was not part of the test. But in an interview in 2007 for the Channel 5 TV show *The Man Who Dreams the Future*, Schwartz said the incident left him "personally traumatized...that someone I knew, who came to me for help, was getting information that...could have potentially prevented [the attack]."

One morning in October 1966, nine-year-old Eryl Mai Jones told her mother she'd dreamed her school vanished. "Something black came down all over it," she said. That day, Eryl's school, and much of her South Wales village of Aberfan, was engulfed by a mountain of coal waste from a nearby mine, with the loss of 140 lives—including Eryl. The Aberfan tragedy led British psychiatrist Dr. John Barker to publish a request for anyone who had predicted the disaster to contact him. Of 76 replies, 24 had sufficient corroboration to be worth investigating. Barker published his findings in 1967 in the *Journal of the Society for Psychical Research*. One respondent said she'd seen an old village school in a valley, an avalanche of coal, and rescuers. Members of her church confirmed that she had told them about it the day before the disaster.

In 1967 Barker set up the British Premonitions Bureau so the public could record precognitive experiences. A year later the Central Premonitions Agency was established in New York. The online Central Premonitions Registry has since replaced both.

In the aftermath of 9/11, hundreds claimed they had dreamed about the attack beforehand. Most claims were unsubstantiated because the subjects failed to mention their premonition until afterward. An exception was Chris Robinson, who was taking part in a scientific study into psychic dreaming when he foresaw those terrible events.

Aura Definition and Recognition: Visualizing the Life Force

The aura is the radiant cloud of energy said to emanate from all life forms. Usually invisible, many who boast psychic or mystic powers claim to see it or sense its presence. The aura is not a true light but a subtle energy or life force that psychics respond to on a deeper level. They say its multilayered form represents our physical, emotional, and spiritual natures.

Bare Bones

- The aura is a field of radiant energy that is said to emanate from all life forms, but can be seen only by those who are psychically sensitive.

- It has seven layers, all of different colors, that relate to different aspects of our physical, emotional, and spiritual nature and well-being.

- Over the years scientists have researched several different devices that may allow ordinary people to see the aura, from dye-filled goggles to a Gas Discharge Visualization Device.

Belief in the aura dates back to ancient forms of worship, including Native American shamanism. In 1960 Peruvian-born author Carlos Castaneda met a Yaqui Indian *nagual*, or mystic guide, from Central America who described how he saw the aura as a "fibrous luminous sphere." The *nagual* said the aura connects humans in this reality with other dimensions. This enables *naguals* to travel through time and space in their quest for knowledge.

Asian healing traditions often use the life force of the aura. In Chinese medicine it is called *qi* and travels around the body along channels called meridians. Ayurveda, an even older form of knowledge, originated in India more than 5,000 years ago and includes yogic teaching. The Ayurvedic life force, or *prana*, is concentrated at brightly colored circles of energy called *chakras*.

Changes in the aura (or *qi* or *prana*) mirror changes in the body's energy systems, revealing imbalances in physical, emotional, and spiritual well-being. The aura may change size, shape, or color in response to illness, injury, or powerful emotions, such as depression or joy. Many healers regard the aura as an essential tool for diagnosing illness.

WESTERN BELIEF IN THE AURA

The concept of the aura as a life force was introduced to North America by the Theosophical movement, which translated and interpreted ancient texts on Ayurveda, Buddhism, and Chinese medicine for a Western audience. English clergyman, Charles W. Leadbeater, wrote two books, *Man Visible and Invisible* and *The Chakras,* which were a major influence in the field.

Leadbeater described the aura as having seven layers, with those closest to the body reflecting the physical and emotional selves, and the outer layers representing the spiritual nature. Each auric layer has a specific function and a color that reflects part of the spectrum—red, orange, yellow, green, blue and indigo/violet—merging to form a golden white light.

> "The aura given out by a person or object is as much a part of them as their flesh." —LUCIAN FREUD, ARTIST

- First is the red etheric layer, concerned with physical well-being.
- Second is the orange emotional layer, reflecting temperament and mood.
- Third is the yellow mental layer, which represents ideas, hopes, and plans.
- Fourth is the green astral layer, which connects earthly and spiritual selves.
- Fifth is the blue etheric layer, marking the inner boundary of the spiritual self.
- Sixth is the indigo/violet celestial body, communicating with the spiritual dimension.
- Seventh is the golden white ketheric layer—the region of spiritual purity.

Psychics who detect auras say happiness generates bright colors but depression turns it black. Children have bright auras that darken as they reach adulthood. People fixated with earthly matters such as power and wealth reflect reds and oranges from the lower auric layers. Healers have greener shades, while spiritual people display purple hues.

Absence of aura indicates death. The celebrated American psychic and healer Edgar Cayce claims to have witnessed this. "One day the appearance of a woman in our neighborhood struck me as odd, though I could not for the moment see anything strange about her," Cayce reported. "When I got home, it suddenly struck me that she had no colors about her. Within a few weeks this woman had died." Cayce claimed to have seen auras as a boy, regarding it at the time as "a natural action of nature" and not realizing it was uncommon.

SCIENTIFIC EVIDENCE

Many scientists have speculated on whether or not the aura is a form of light invisible to all but a gifted few. The light people normally see includes only a small part of the full spectrum of electromagnetic radiation emitted by the sun. The term visible spectrum (0.4–0.7 micrometers) refers to what humans can see—many creatures see a wider range.

Rattlesnakes detect long infrared wavelengths below the visible spectrum to see prey at night. Humans sense infrared as heat, but to see it, they need special cameras that reveal living creatures as

Psychic and healer Edgar Cayce (1877–1945), of Hopkinsville, Kentucky, believed that the ability to read auras was quite normal and a skill that "all people will someday possess." The Edgar Cayce Association for Research and Enlightenment, established in his name, now has centers in 27 countries, including the United States and Canada.

warm or reddish images against a colder, bluish background. A more sophisticated technique, thermography, detects subtle temperature differences emitted by different regions of the body and displays them in color on a monitor. Bees are sensitive to short ultraviolet (UV) wavelengths, above the visible spectrum, and see vivid flower patterns invisible to humans. Humans normally only notice UV light when it causes suntan or sunburn. One theory is that gifted people may detect infrared or UV wavelengths visually.

The first scientist to investigate this was Dr. Walter J. Kilner of St. Thomas' Hospital, London. In 1911 he made a lens from two pieces of glass with a layer of blue dicyanin dye between them. Kilner claimed to see his patients surrounded by a 6-inch (15-cm) aura of vaporous energy, the shape and color of which reflected a patient's health. Regular viewing with the lens helped sensitize his eyes to these subtle emanations, he said, and enhanced his ability to diagnose illness.

> "Some things have to be believed to be seen." —RALPH HODGSON, POET

He published his findings in *The Human Atmosphere* (1911). Kilner believed that 95 percent of the population could learn to see the aura. He suggested viewing subjects in low light, because the aura radiating from them could be lost in bright surroundings. Another approach was to view subjects silhouetted in a doorway.

Kilner thought the aura was caused by emanations of UV light. Tests on his lens, performed in the 1960s by Arthur J. Ellison, a psychical researcher and professor of engineering at City University, London, showed that the lens let through some visible light in the violet and red range. Only the central part of the visible spectrum was blocked completely.

In 1937 biologist Oscar Bagnall of Canterbury University, England, made a pair of goggles with hollow lenses filled with the dye pinacyanol. The aura appeared to him to have a hazy outer layer and a brighter inner core. He saw rays of light streaming from the body, especially from the fingers or nose. Periodically, he said, he could see a brighter ray reaching out like a searchlight

Colorful pictures of the head seemingly surrounded by an energy field, as taken by "aura cameras," are a popular attraction at New Age mind/body/spirit festivals. However, many psychics who claim to see the aura unaided say these images bear no relation to the "real thing."

before disappearing. Bagnall said the aura was unaffected by air currents but changed shape when an electromagnet was applied.

Parapsychologist Dr. Charles T. Tart established guidelines for investigating the aura. He noted that a psychic claiming to give auric readings may use other clues—such as a subject's clothing, complexion, posture, or voice—and not the aura at all.

He invented the doorway test to prove a psychic's authenticity. The target stands at the edge of a doorway, partially hidden from view, so only the aura around their body projects beyond the frame. Periodically, the target moves away. A psychic, viewing from the other side, has to say whether the target is there or not. The Australian Institute of Parapsychological Research claims that all psychics tested so far, including British healer Matthew Manning, have failed this test.

One study, reported in the *Journal of the American Society for Psychical Research* in 1997, used an experimental group of 10 psychics and a control group of 9 nonpsychics. After more than 36 sessions of 40 tests per session, the two groups scored a statistically insignificant 381 hits, with nonpsychics performing slightly better than psychics (196 hits to 185).

Tart expressed mixed views of Kilner and Bagnall's tinted glasses. They may have "mistaken the malfunctioning of their visual system for something…in the environment," he said. But he conceded that this doesn't explain all reported effects, such as changes caused by an electromagnet, which "shouldn't affect [the aura's] transmission characteristics."

The body produces weak electromagnetism. This is the principle behind magnetoencephalography (MEG), where an array of sensitive detectors placed around the head records changes in the magnetic field caused by brain activity. Researchers don't know whether or not the aura involves electromagnetism, but this would help explain the images produced by devices used to photograph it.

IMAGING THE AURA

In 1891 Croatian-born U.S. inventor Nicola Tesla built a device said to reveal the aura as a glowing sphere, based on the Tesla coil, a powerful electromagnet that produces high-voltage electricity. This was incorporated into the imaging machine developed by Semyon Kirlian, a Russian engineer who had attended talks given by Tesla. Kirlian photographs show objects surrounded by a halo of light.

Newer aura imaging devices are more complex. The Gas Discharge Visualization (GDV) device, invented by Russian physicist Konstantin Korotkov, detects electrostatic discharge from the skin. It aimed to standardize the Kirlian method and avoid variables such as moisture, dirt, and pressure that critics had said made Kirlian's device unreliable.

In the 1980s U.S. inventor Guy Coggins developed Aura Imaging Photography. This converts radio waves transmitted "through the subject's electromagnetic field" into computer-generated images displayed on a TV, computer screen, or film. Other types of imaging emulate an aura by measuring skin resistance and converting this into a halo effect inside the camera.

Whether such devices produce aura or artifact is debated. Television psychics Jane and Craig Hamilton-Parker are unimpressed. They say aura camera images bear no resemblance to the aura they detect psychically.

Kirlian Photography

Kirlian photography creates spectacular images of objects surrounded by a corona (or halo) of bright light. Also called aura, radiation-field, or corona discharge photography, Kirlian photography has found a place in both orthodox and alternative medicine, and even agriculture. Yet the interpretation of these Kirlian images remains controversial.

Bare Bones

- Kirlian photography is a technique invented by Russian Semyon Kirlian in 1939 that produces photographs of living things surrounded by a bright halo of colored light.

- Some claim that these photographs reveal the aura that previously only psychically gifted people were able to see.

- It has been claimed that Kirlian photographs can be used in medical diagnosis.

- Skeptics argue that what Kirlian photographs show is merely an electromagnetic effect of no scientific significance.

Some claim Kirlian photographs reveal the psychic aura that only those gifted with special powers, such as healers and mystics, were previously able to see. Skeptics say it is a simple electrochemical effect of no significance. So who is right?

A SHOCKING REVELATION

The story begins in 1939 when a Russian engineer made a discovery that amazed and divided the scientific community. Semyon Kirlian noticed that when patients received treatment on a d'Arsonval electrotherapy machine, a bright spark appeared. He wondered what sort of image this might produce on photographic paper. While repairing a machine in the hospital's laboratory, Kirlian decided to find out. He replaced the standard glass electrodes with riskier metal ones and developed an image of his hand surrounded by streamers of bright light.

For the next 20 years Kirlian and his wife, Valentina, researched high-voltage imaging in a homemade laboratory at their apartment in the Ukraine. The machine they built comprised a high-voltage Tesla coil attached to a metal plate and insulated by glass. Light-sensitive paper was placed on the glass, and the object to be photographed rested on the paper. The resulting image showed the object surrounded by a jagged halo of light.

Soviet scientist Dr. Victor Inyushin of Kazakh University, Russia, thought the corona was a bioplasmic energy field of ions, free protons, and free electrons, given off by all life forms. According to Inyushin, bioplasma is maintained in healthy creatures by a balance of positive and negative particles produced by cells. Injury or sickness disrupts this balance, and this is reflected in the image.

Followers of Rudolf Steiner, Austrian pioneer of modern holistic therapy, claimed Kirlian images confirmed his teachings. Steiner advocated anthroposophical medicine, which is based on the belief that illness develops when a body is out of balance and unable to prevent disease or heal itself. A cornerstone of anthroposophy is belief in the life body, an energy force that forms the blueprint for the whole body. Steiner believed gifted people could see the life body as a corona the color of peach blossom. Perhaps Kirlian imaging revealed this too?

DIAGNOSTIC DEMONSTRATION

Kirlian himself unwittingly discovered that his Kirlian photography might be used to diagnose illness. While giving a demonstration, Kirlian produced an unclear image of the corona around his own hand. Yet an image of his wife's hand showed a sharp well-defined corona. Some hours later Kirlian experienced the first signs of influenza. This convinced him that his illness had been revealed by the dull image.

A U.S. laboratory then asked Kirlian to photograph two seemingly identical leaves. One gave off a sharp corona, while the other produced an indistinct image. Later Kirlian discovered that the leaves were from different plants—one healthy and the other diseased. In other experiments, Kirlian claimed a leaf's corona remained intact even if a section of leaf was removed—something now known as the phantom leaf effect—but other researchers have failed to duplicate this.

It has been claimed that Kirlian imaging reveals psychic powers, even in those who did not realize they were so gifted—the brighter the aura, the stronger the gift. British healer Matthew Manning appears to emit exceptionally long streamers of light from his fingertips in Kirlian images when using psychic powers.

THE CASE AGAINST KIRLIAN DIAGNOSIS

Some have disputed claims that Kirlian images indicate health. In the 1980s Arthur J. Ellison, former president of the Society for

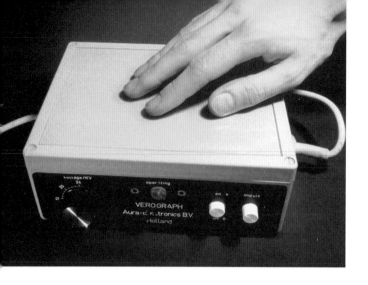

Psychical Research, and professor of electronic and electrical engineering at City University, London, suggested the corona was due to air ionization (electrical discharge) and that differences between images of healthy and unhealthy subjects were artifacts caused by bad technique, poor cleaning, or variations in moisture.

This corona discharge photography device, made by Verograph, of Holland, was small, light, battery-powered and hence portable. This made it popular with complementary health practitioners. German naturopath Peter Mandel says Kirlian Energy Emission Analysis gives precise information about the "causal chain of events" leading to energy imbalance in patients.

PRACTICAL USES FOR KIRLIAN IMAGING

Kirlian himself did not claim that his photographs had mystical, spiritual, or psychic significance. He merely believed the technique might assist in the early diagnosis of disease. New developments may prove Kirlian's theory. Leonard Konikiewicz of the Polyclinic Medical Center, Harrisburg, Pennsylvania, has used Kirlian imaging to diagnose carriers of cystic fibrosis, a genetic disease. The fingertip corona of carriers is distinctive but weaker than that of noncarriers. He also discovered that the luminosity of the image changes during the menstrual cycle of all women, becoming brighter at ovulation.

Biologist Dr. Harry Oldfield, of Charing Cross Hospital, London, suggested that Kirlian imaging might reveal an electromagnetic system that regulates all biochemical processes in the body. He developed a handheld Kirlian device to detect heart abnormalities. He and coworker Dr. Peter Kandela believed it could diagnose breast tumors, too. Dr. Kandela said the luminous discharge produced by the fingertips of women later found to have a breast tumor was "totally unlike those of healthy people."

Biochemist Glen Rein, of London University, has used the technique on biopsied (surgically sampled) tumor tissue. The glowing bioluminescence showed much greater intensity than in normal tissue. Former skeptic Dr. Malcolm Carruthers, director of clinical laboratory services at Maudsley Hospital, London, has discovered that people who are vulnerable to heart disease produce pale Kirlian palm impressions, but when given heart drugs such as beta-blockers, the resulting aura appears stronger.

Kirlian imaging has also found a home in alternative medicine. Romanian physician Dr. Ion Dumitrescu, pioneer of Kirlian electrography, found that by comparing the size and brightness of acupuncture points, he could diagnose disease. In reflexology, a therapy in which each part of the foot represents a different region of the body, a weaker aura—around the big toe, for example—indicates a disorder that can be relieved by foot massage.

Many scientists remain skeptical, however. The American Cancer Society claims there is little evidence that Kirlian photography can diagnose cancer but says the technique is harmless for most people, posing a risk only to those with a pacemaker or implanted cardiac defibrillator. But the Society is concerned that "relying on this method alone for diagnosis may delay conventional health care, with serious health consequences."

Kirlian imaging has found a place in agriculture, too. It is used in Russia to improve grain harvests. Seeds that produce strong, healthy plants emit a more powerful aura than weaker ones. In the United States the technique has been used to investigate the healing energy of superfoods such as soy. Dr. Thelma Moss, head of the Parapsychology Research Unit of the University of California at Los Angeles, was able to predict germination in soybean seeds with total accuracy. Brighter coronas were found in all foods with therapeutic properties.

Kirlian photographs give an unearthly glow to commonplace natural objects such as a leaf. Whether such images reveal the plant's aura, or life force, or this is simply an eerie artifact triggered by the leaf's moisture content is still hotly debated.

Paranormal Photography: Psychic Phenomena in the Frame

A snapshot of a paranormal event may seem like incontrovertible proof. Yet from the earliest days of photography, tricksters have faked paranormal images using techniques such as double exposure—taking two images on the same frame—or by fogging the lens with a flashlight. Modern digital cameras and image software make trickery even easier.

Bare Bones

- Attempts to capture paranormal phenomena on film are open to fraud, and strict procedures must be followed to eliminate such possibilities.

- Thoughtography is a form of paranormal photography in which images are projected from the mind onto photographic film.

- Professor Tomokichi Fukurai (1869–1952) of the psychology department at Imperial University, Tokyo, was the first person to study this phenomenon scientifically.

- In the late 1960s Ted Serios brought thoughtography back into the public eye with his colorful demonstrations.

The Society for Psychical Research (SPR) was founded in England in 1882 to investigate the paranormal by scientific means, including photography. The society has had strong links with North America from the start. U.S. psychologist Professor William James was an early associate member and founded the American Society for Psychical Research in 1885. Both societies offer useful advice for investigators through their publications: *Psychic News* in the UK and the *Journal of the American Society for Psychical Research* in the United States.

A GHOST HUNTER'S GUIDE

To satisfy science and confound skeptics, psychic investigators are advised to use strict experimental protocols to ensure any photographic evidence that they obtain is above suspicion. For example, they should ensure at least one neutral observer is present when photographs are taken or—if filming is automatic—when the equipment is set up. In addition, measures should be in place to prevent tampering with film by sealing the camera. Investigators should guard an area against unauthorized human intrusion, by:

- attaching masking tape to doors and windows.
- stretching cotton threads across pathways.
- sprinkling the floor with fluorescent powder (which glows under special lighting).

Cameras can then be arranged to fire automatically in response to sound or temperature changes, or closed-circuit TV should be put in place to monitor the scene.

Some spontaneous paranormal events are difficult to prepare for, however. Poltergeist activity—or recurrent spontaneous psychokinesis (RSPK)—is often associated with children, who cannot be kept under constant camera surveillance. But if RSPK occurs at certain times, it may be possible to have a camera ready. From 1977 to 1978, psychic investigators Maurice Grosse and Guy Lyon Playfair recorded remarkable pictures of an 11-year-old girl apparently being thrown out of her bed during RSPK activity. Such paranormal photography is not without its risks. During

> ## "If Mr. Serios did not use a trick method, all the rules of physics... must be rewritten." —JAMES RANDI, MAGICIAN

one session at the girl's north London home, a photographer was struck by a toy brick, seemingly appearing from nowhere!

THOUGHTOGRAPHY: IMAGING THE IMAGINATION

The projection of thought images onto photographic film—or photographic plates, in earlier times—is called thoughtography and was first performed by spirit mediums in North America in the late nineteenth century, but not under experimental conditions. The first attempt to give thoughtography a scientific face was made by Professor Tomokichi Fukurai of the psychology department at Imperial University, Tokyo.

Between 1910 and 1913 the professor worked with several female psychics, including Ikuko Nagao, Tetsuko Moritake, and Sadako Takahashi, and one male subject, Koichi Mita (who claimed he could see the moon's dark side). Professor Fukurai said their mental images appeared on wrapped photographic plates or etched onto surfaces.

Fukurai called this *nensha,* or spirit photography, and wrote about it in his 1913 book *Tōshi to Nensha* (*Clairvoyance and Thoughtography*). Few of his faculty colleagues accepted his claims, however, and he was asked to leave the university, later

Dr. Tomokichi Fukurai, pioneer of Japanese parapsychology, gained his doctorate in hypnotism before he moved on to spirit photography. Despite this picture by William Hope, of the Crewe Circle of Spirit Photographers, there is no evidence Fukurai claimed spiritualist powers. Hope was later outed as a fraud by ghosthunter Harry Price.

becoming president of the Psychical Institute of Japan and founding the Fukurai Institute of Psychology.

Fifty years later thoughtography was revived by parapsychologist professor Jule Eisenbud, a psychiatrist at University of Colorado Medical School, Denver, and Ted Serios, an unemployed former Chicago bellhop. Professor Eisenbud said Serios could project thought images into a Polaroid camera, which then printed the picture. Serios was aided by a gismo—a tube of black paper placed between his forehead and the camera lens. The thoughtographs—created from 1964 until 1967, when his powers finally left him—were blurred and grainy but often recognizable images, usually of U.S. city landmarks.

Serios regularly performed before invited groups. As described by Professor Eisenbud, these sessions were wild affairs, with Serios drinking heavily, often stripped to the waist. Despite the endorsement of distinguished psychical researchers including Drs. J. Gaither Pratt and Ian Stevenson, who conducted hundreds of tests with Serios and maintained they had "never seen [Serios]

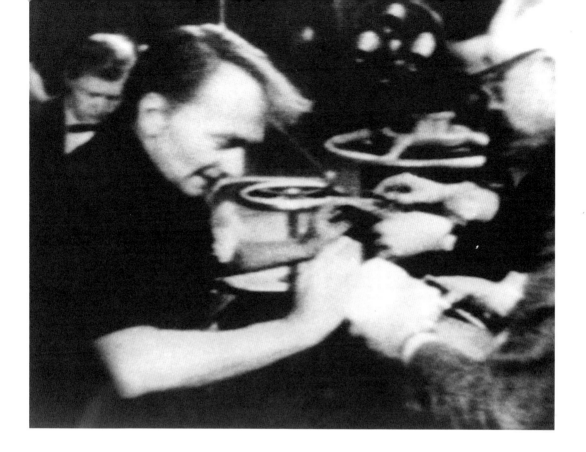

act in a suspicious way," the thought-ographs were vilified by skeptic James Randi and others. Two reporters, David Eisendrath and Charles Reynolds, even used a small homemade device to produce their own "thoughtographs," which they published in *Popular Photography* in 1967.

Eisenbud always maintained that Serios was genuine. But Nile Root, a biomedical photographer who attended a thoughtography session, claimed to have seen "a shiny object reflect from inside the paper gismo" when Serios was behaving in an erratic manner. Root suggests that Serios may have used a cheap novelty viewing device to project an image from a small portion of film transparency through the lens of the camera, using available light. This device was tiny enough for Serios to conceal and then transfer to the paper gismo when the audience was distracted by his eccentric antics. Professor Persi Diaconis, of Stanford University, a former magician who also saw Serios perform, suggests that he may have used an even simpler method—a glass marble with a photo attached to it.

Ted Serios, an unemployed former Chicago bellhop, convinced reputable academics that his thought images, which mysteriously appeared on Polaroid film, were genuine. The fact that some of his images showed aerial views or out-of-date signs (the store in one image—the Old Gold Store, in Central City, Colorado—had since changed its name) was taken as proof of their authenticity.

KGB and CIA Psi Experiments: Fighting the Psi War

In 1959 a French newspaper reported that secret telepathy experiments were being conducted between a sender aboard USS nuclear submarine *Nautilus* and psychic receivers on land. Although denied, this was the first hint that U.S. authorities might be dabbling in the paranormal. The story brought an unexpected bonus. Soviet scientists revealed that they, too, were engaged in psi research—and had been for decades. It seemed the cold war had entered a new phase—Psi Wars.

Bare Bones

- Soviet state investigation of psychic phenomena began in the 1920s and continued throughout the reign of Stalin and beyond.

- The first suggestion that U.S. authorities were investigating psi came in a French newspaper story in 1959.

- The most famous CIA-backed research into psychic phenomena took place at the Stanford Research Institute in the 1970s under various code names.

- Many people believe that covert U.S. government research into psi continues to this day.

Soviet interest in psychic phenomena dates back to 1922, when head of Leningrad University's Brain Research Institute, physiologist Vladimir Bekhterev, devised the Committee for the Study of Mental Suggestion to investigate telepathy. During the 1940s Soviet leader Joseph Stalin took an interest in psychic phenomena when he witnessed the mind-control skills of Polish stage performer Wolf Messing. Messing apparently proved his ability to the dictator by "broadcasting a mental picture" of himself as the feared security chief Beria. Stalin's security guards thought Messing was Beria, and because—like everyone else in Russia—they were frightened of Beria, they let him (Messing) through without checking his identification.

In the 1960s, with the cold war at its height, psi research received official backing from Stalin's successor Nikita Khrushchev. Professor Leonid Vasiliev, a physiologist based at Leningrad University, extended Bekhterev's research by attempting to control hypnotized subjects telepathically, described in his book *Biological Radio Communication*. By Vasiliev's death in 1966, experiments into telepathy, psychokinesis, and remote viewing were being conducted openly at centers all over the U.S.S.R. and covertly by the Committee for State Security, the

KGB. The Bio-information Section of Moscow's Popov Institute famously experimented with long-distance telepathy.

Russian scientists were keen to share their knowledge with the West. Two writers, American Lynn Schroeder and Canadian Sheila Ostrander, corresponded with Soviet scientists. In 1968 biologist and psi researcher Eduard Naumov even organized an international conference in Moscow, which was abruptly halted by the KGB. Schroeder and Ostrander, both delegates, had to flee. They published what little they had gleaned in *Psychic Discoveries Behind the Iron Curtain*.

Physicist Professor Ippolit M. Kogan, director of Popov Institute's Bio-information Section, proposed in the 1960s that telepathic messages could be broadcast via extremely low frequency (ELF) waves. In the late 1970s the U.S.S.R. began beaming mysterious radio signals in the ELF range. U.S. psychical researcher Andrija Puharich claimed this was part of Soviet psychotronic (parapsychology) research. The fear was that ELF was being used for long-distance mind control. Papers released following the collapse of the SovietUnion suggest that by the 1980s pure psi research had been sidelined in favor of ELF technology. In 1983 former spy and defector Nikolai Khokhlov was reported as saying that the Soviet mind-control program was run by the KGB with "unlimited funds."

THE UNITED STATES PLAYS CATCH-UP

In 1960 the CIA commissioned a report on ESP from the director of the Parapsychological Laboratory at Oxford University, England. This claimed evidence for psi but said it was uncontrollable. CIA interest waned, only to be revived in 1972 by a call from Dr. Russell Targ, a parapsychologist at Stanford Research Institute (SRI) in Menlo Park, California.

The Stanford Research Institute had been a center for psychical research since Thomas Stanford, younger brother of the founder, railroad baron Leland Stanford, endowed a $50,000 fund for psychic research. Targ and Dr. Harold Puthoff, a former National Security Agency (NSA) employee and laser physicist, researched

Psi and Scientology

In 1977 the FBI raided the Scientology Guardian Office premises at Fifield Manor, California, and discovered files containing detailed information relating to Pat Price's remote-viewing experiments with the CIA (*see* "The United States Plays Catch-Up"). At that time this information was top secret and should not have been divulged to anyone outside the intelligence community.

Former CIA officer Kenneth Kress said Price would "immediately go to his superior in the organization after sessions with me and divulge everything." Kress doesn't speculate further, other than to say, "As far as I know, the documents were never read by anybody who publicized them, and 'the organization' never used them."

It has been claimed that Hal Puthoff and Ingo Swann are Scientologists, too. The Church of Scientology, an organization founded by science-fiction writer L. Ron Hubbard, is committed to a belief in superhuman potential.

Scientology interest in Price and remote viewing is unknown, but according to Martin Gardner, science writer and contributor to the *Skeptical Inquirer*, and other critics, this connection left the CIA–SRI experiments too deeply flawed to retain scientific credibility.

psi phenomena—including remote viewing—at SRI. Targ wanted to alert the CIA to a film of a Soviet psychic apparently demonstrating psychokinesis, but the CIA was more interested in his remote viewing research. According to a declassified report "Parasychology in Intelligence" by former CIA project officer Kenneth Kress, published (with update) in 1999 in the *Journal of Scientific Exploration*, the CIA agreed to collaborate with SRI on a series of experiments.

Their first subjects were New York artist Ingo Swann and former police commissioner Pat Price, both gifted psychics. CIA researchers—called beacons—visited randomly chosen locations, and the psychics described what they believed the beacons could see. Investigators soon found that they could do without the beacons and gave the psychics a location's map coordinates instead. This project, dubbed Scanate or scanning by coordinate, was later called Star Gate.

In one experiment Price remotely viewed coordinates of a "possible nuclear underground testing site" (PNUTS) in Semipalatinsk, Kazakhstan. According to Targ, writing in *Remote Viewing at Stanford Research Institute: A Memoir*, Price only knew that the site was a research and development establishment yet gave an "architecturally accurate drawing of a gantry crane at the site" confirmed by spy plane. Although the researchers involved consider this a successful demonstration of psychic abilities, reports since released under Freedom of Information legislation, confirmed by Kress, suggest that, in fact, much of Price's account was vague or inaccurate.

Relations between SRI and skeptical researchers at the CIA's Office of Research and Development (ORD) soon deteriorated. "SRI contractors were claiming success while ORD advisers were saying the experiments were not meaningful because of poor experimental design," Kress noted. The CIA continued experimenting with Price alone. In another experiment, Price had to remotely view a suspected Libyan missile site. When Price died under suspicious circumstances from an apparent heart attack, CIA psi research stalled.

At the time, Kress felt the CIA experiments ended before they could be fully assessed. Some results "defy explanation," he wrote. Psychic research continued elsewhere, including at the NSA-Defense Intelligence Agency and U.S. military. Some investigative journalists, including Gus Russo, claim that much of this research is ongoing.

The former headquarters of the KGB, the Lubyanka, on Lubyanka Square in Moscow. According to defectors the KGB had a well-developed and well-financed program of research into psi phenomena throughout the cold war years and beyond.

SUPERPOWERS UNITE OVER MIND CONTROL?

In 1993 defense writer Barbara Opall claimed that following the end of the cold war, senior Russian military chiefs wanted to share their mind-control technology with the West. Writing in *Defense News*, Opall said a bilateral center for psych-technologies had been proposed. Both sides would now be in a position to "monitor and restrict the merging capabilities." This proposal is unconfirmed by official U.S. sources.

Bio-PK: Smart Flora and Fauna?

Bio-PK or biological psychokinesis means having a direct mental influence on nonhuman life-forms. A more recent term is Direct Mental Influence on Living Systems (DMILS). Humans have long believed they could influence plants by talking to them. But it took an ex-CIA interrogator to discover this psychic connection with other life forms—using a lie detector.

THE PLANT AND THE POLYGRAPH

Cleve Backster ran an interrogation school for New York police officers, including how to use a polygraph, a device that detects changes in the way the skin conducts electricity that indicate whether or not a suspect is lying. In 1966 Backster was watering a rubber plant when he thought of attaching his polygraph to one of the leaves to tell him when his plant was saturated. He got a read-out that—in humans—could only mean pleasure!

Backster then tried an interrogation technique called threat-to-well-being principle. First he tried dipping a leaf in a cup of hot coffee. No reaction. Then he thought about burning the plant—and the moment the notion sprang into his head, the polygraph pen jumped. It seemed the plant was reading his mind.

He called this psychic link primary perception and found it in plants and animals. With the help of his students, Backster tested plants as potential witnesses. One student was selected to enter a room and destroy one of two plants there. The second plant was wired up to the polygraph as each student in turn stood before the witness to be identified. Only the killer triggered a reaction.

GREEN WITH EMPATHY

Backster then rigged an experiment that would avoid human involvement by using an automatic randomizer to drop either live or dead brine shrimp into boiling water to see whether or not a plant reacted to the crustaceans' death. Backster saw a reaction when living shrimps died, but not when a dead shrimp fell into the water. Backster also experimented with microscopic life forms (micro–PK) such as mold, yeast, blood, and cells scraped from inside his mouth. His findings were published in a 1968 edition of the *International Journal of Parapsychology*.

Other scientists began to take an interest in Bio–PK. According to a 1973 report in the newspaper *Soviet Industry*, Russian psychologist V. M. Pushkin repeated Backster's experiments using a hypnotized female subject called Tanya. Pushkin said that when Tanya experienced emotions of joy or sorrow, the plant recorded similar emotions. New Jersey electronics expert Pierre Paul Sauvin went further and wired his plants to devices that would generate an audible tone to operate simple equipment, like garage doors or a model plane, by remote control.

Dr. Robert Miller, a chemist from Atlanta, Georgia, tested whether or not husband-and-wife psychics Ambrose and Olga Worrall could increase the growth of a blade of rye grass linked to precision measuring equipment. The psychics, 600 miles (965 km) away in Baltimore, focused on the grass at 9:00 P.M. each evening. According to Dr. Miller, at exactly that time, growth rose from 0.006 to 0.05 inches per hour—an increase of more than 80 percent.

Research into Bio-PK is not new. English philosopher and alchemist Sir Francis Bacon wrote in his posthumously published work *Sylva Sylvarum: Or a Natural History in Ten Centuries,* of: "the force of imagination upon beasts, birds…" Bacon also described using this force of imagination on microorganisms, such as, "the working of beer when the barm [yeast] is put in…" In recent years similar studies have been conducted by French parapsychologist Dr. Jean Barry and by a team at Tennessee University. In both cases, participants successfully used psychic means to inhibit bacteria growing in glass Petri dishes.

Professor William Braud, of the Mind Science Foundation in San Antonio, Texas, used a healer to protect blood cells placed in saltwater-filled test tubes. As the cells burst due to the salt, the test tubes slowly cleared, as detected by a spectrophotometer, which measures light changes. When healer Matthew Manning focused on some test tubes, the rate of light change was far less in those than in the other tubes, indicating that the cells were being protected.

Psychic
Techniques

Millions of people around the world share the belief that some members of the human race can see into the future or read minds. These mystics and mind readers are dubbed psychics. They claim their amazing mental powers allow them to miraculously bend spoons, perform psychic surgery, predict a person's life from tarot cards, and much more. Can any of these and other such extraordinary claims possibly be true? Or are they the consequence of self-deception or, at the worst, clever frauds?

Psi: Defining Psychic Powers

Used by parapsychologists and psychical researchers as a convenient term for related types of psychical phenomena—most notably ESP and psychokinesis—psi as a concept originated in the 1940s, when the British biologist Bertold P. Wiesner coined the term. He derived it from the letter *psi*, the twenty-third letter of the classical Greek alphabet, and *psyche*, the Greek word for mind or soul. Another Briton, the psychologist Robert H. Thouless, was the first man to actually use the word in an article he published in 1942.

Bare Bones

- Bertold P. Wiesner coined the term psi in the 1940s to refer to psychic phenomena such as ESP and psychokinesis.

- Research into psi had been going on for a long time before the term was invented, notably under the auspices of the Society for Psychical Research.

- Early researchers collected accounts of psychical activity and studied these. Nowadays investigators prefer to devise experimental trials and measure the statistical difference of success rates from chance to detect psi at work.

SPONTANEOUS EXPERIENCE

Research into psi and psychical phenomena started long before the term was defined. In late nineteenth-century Britain, the Society for Psychical Research organized the analysis of thousands of accounts of spontaneous psychic experiences, mailed to the society by correspondents. The result was a book called *Phantasms of the Living*, which detailed a full range of telepathic phenomena. The book concluded that apparitions were most likely hallucinations sparked off by the unconscious mind.

In France physiologist and Nobel prizewinner Charles Richet undertook a similar study in the 1920s, as did Camille Flammarion, a famous astronomer of the day. In North America, however, Louisa Rhine, the wife of Joseph Banks Rhine, the founding father of modern parapsychology, devised a somewhat different approach. Unlike her predecessors, she concentrated on discovering instances of psi operating in daily life, identifying common patterns between incidents, and then using the patterns as the basis for hypotheses to verify experimentally.

Over the years, psi researchers have hotly debated the merits of both approaches. To settle the argument, the Dutch parapsychologist Sybo Schouten employed computer analysis to compare the original British collection with that of Louisa Rhine and a German one at the University of Freiburg. What he found was a high degree of consistency between all three.

Although scientists and researchers have spent huge amounts of time and money on attempting to prove or disprove the existence of psychic powers, it seems the general public are altogether less exacting. Fortune-tellers and psychics the world over continue to make a healthy profit despite a lack of evidential proof of their gifts.

SURVEYS AND STATISTICS

Henry Sidgwick, a founding member of the Society for Psychical Research, undertook the first questionnaire survey in the 1890s. For his *Census of Hallucinations*, he received 17,000 replies, nearly 2,300 of which reported a hallucinatory experience.

Nowadays mainstream psi researchers rely on what is termed statistical inference to detect psi activity. The presence of psi is inferred when, after many experimental trials, the average success rate differs significantly from the chance baseline—the outcome that, on average, is the most likely. The more improbable the result, the more psi researchers feel it proves psi is involved.

Whether psi actually exists or not is heavily disputed. Skeptics say that much of the evidence for it is based only on anecdotal experiences. Many such experiences have proved impossible to replicate under laboratory conditions, which means that there is little solid scientific evidence to support their validity. Psi researchers have studied clairvoyance, for instance, for decades. Yet because it is so difficult to test and measure objectively, there is still no clear proof as to whether or not it is a genuine phenomenon. The same dilemma applies to precognition, telekinesis, telepathy, and teleportation.

Psychokinesis: Mind over Matter

Psychokinesis, telekinesis, and PK are terms used to describe the ability to move or otherwise affect the property of things using the power of the mind. This skill demonstrates the power of mind over matter and is reckoned to be one of the most rare psychic abilities.

Bare Bones

- Psychokinesis, telekinesis, and PK are all terms used to describe the ability to influence external objects or beings with the power of the mind alone.

- Uri Geller is one of the most famous modern PK practitioners. He claims to be able to bend metal with the power of his mind, but some maintain he is a fraud.

- Micro-PK describes effects that are not observable by the naked eye but have to be measured in the laboratory. Nowadays this type of PK is the preferred object of scientific study.

The term psychokinesis was coined in 1914 by U.S. author and publisher Henry Holt in his book *On the Cosmic Relations* and popularized by the pioneer parapsychologist Joseph Banks Rhine, who began experimenting with it in 1934. Telekinesis came into currency somewhat earlier; Alexander Aksakov, a Russian psychical investigator, invented it in 1890.

NOTABLE PK PRACTITIONERS

When most people think of PK, they usually associate it with large-scale macroscopic effects, such as the levitation of tables or the bending of metal objects. Indeed, one of the most celebrated modern PK practitioners, the Israeli-born psychic Uri Geller, is famous for his claims to be able to bend spoons, keys, forks, and other objects, and to stop and start watches with his mind.

Geller is the most talked-about PK practitioner of the present day, but many don't believe his claims. James Randi, a noted skeptic insists that Geller is a fraud, that he possesses no psychic powers and that, in fact, he is nothing more than an extremely clever conjurer. Many others, on the other hand, are convinced that Geller is genuine. The physicists Hal Puthoff and Russell Targ, who conducted experiments with Geller at the Stanford Research Institute in the 1970s, believe wholeheartedly that he is a truly gifted psychic—so much so that they invented the term the "Geller Effect" as a way of describing his powers.

The American psychic Ted Owens, who died in 1987, sparked just as much controversy during the 1970s and early 1980s. In the book *The PK Man*, the parapsychologist Jeffrey Mishlove accepted Owens's claims to possess extraordinary paranormal

Uri Geller pictured here in the early stages of his career. Geller is generally regarded as one of the world's leading PK practitioners. His supposed psychic power, particularly his apparent ability to stop watches and bend spoons and keys with his mind, won him global renown. However, he has as many detractors as admirers.

powers, including the ability to levitate spontaneously and to produce thunder and lightning at will. Mishlove even believed Owens's assertion that he communicated telepathically with space aliens. Most other psychic researchers, however, were skeptical.

Others who have claimed the ability to demonstrate PK powers include the Polish psychic Stanislawa Tomczyk and Russian psychic Nina Kulagina. Tomczyk first came to the attention of psychical investigators in the early 1900s, when it was reported that startling

PK in the Spotlight

Psychokinesis is featured in movies, on television, in books, and in computer games, as well as in other forms of popular culture. The 1976 Hollywood horror film *Carrie*, which was based on the Stephen King novel of the same name, was the first movie to feature an identifiable psychic as its leading character.

Sissy Spacek played the troubled high school student trying to come to terms with her psychokinetic powers. Other films portraying characters with psychokinetic powers include *The Medusa Touch* (1978) and *The Fury* (1978).

In the TV drama *Heroes*, the characters Peter Petrelli and Sylar both possess PK abilities. The same is true of Prue Halliwell and Paige Matthews, two of the witch heroines in the TV series *Charmed*, as well as The Source, the fountainhead of evil in the series.

Some psychics, notably Uri Geller, have starred in TV shows, and this has greatly contributed to winning them a worldwide audience. Geller made his first TV appearances in Britain in the 1970s. His latest TV project, in association with NBC in the United States, is to launch an international search for the next great psychic, someone who Geller deems worthy to be his successor.

outbreaks of poltergeist-like activity were occurring spontaneously around her. When she was hypnotized, she took on a personality, called Little Stasia, who, it was claimed, could levitate small objects when Tomczyk placed her hands on either side of them.

Soviet psychical researchers investigated Kulagina, a Leningrad housewife, thoroughly in the late 1960s and 1970s. She was reported to have moved a wide range of nonmagnetic objects—including watches, crystal bowls, and saltshakers—using only the power of her mind. In 1968 movies were released showing her apparently levitating objects off a table to demonstrate her psychical abilities. These movies inspired Felicia Parise, a technician at a U.S. medical laboratory, to try to emulate her Russian counterpart. She was reportedly successful. At the height of her fame in the early 1970s, the *National Enquirer* splashed a portrait of her on its front cover. She was pictured sitting at a table trying to perform psychokinesis with the headline FIRST AMERICAN TO MOVE OBJECTS WITH THE MIND!

Kulagina certainly impressed Soviet and Western scientific observers. Dr. Y. P. Terletsky, head of the theoretical physics department at Moscow University, declared, "Mrs. Kulagina displays a new and unknown form of energy." An article in *Pravda*, however, was much more skeptical. It labeled her a fake and a cheat, claiming that she performed her tricks with the help of concealed magnets and threads.

RHINE AND MICRO-PK

On the whole, however, parapsychologists researching the PK phenomenon prefer to focus on what they have christened micro-PK: the mind's influence on microscopic events. This is now the preferred laboratory approach for most PK investigations. Unlike macro-PK events, micro-PK ones are not observable—at least not by the naked eye. They rely on complicated statistical evaluation and on multiple, repeatable experiments.

Micro-PK research started in the mid-1930s, when a young gambler came to the Parapsychology Laboratory at Duke University in Durham, North Carolina, claiming that he could use willpower to influence the fall of dice. Joseph Banks Rhine, the director of the laboratory, was immediately intrigued by the claim and devised experiments to test its veracity. He found that the gambler indeed seemed to beat the odds and obtain the desired result much more frequently than would be expected by chance. He also tested other individuals' abilities to influence the way in which the dice fell.

The results of Rhine's experiments were highly influential. He concluded that PK did not seem to be connected to any physical brain process or subject to any of the accepted laws of physics. Like ESP, it seemed independent of space and time. Moreover, PK and ESP were mutually interactive—one could not occur without the other.

While Rhine and his fellow psychical researchers considered the results significant, there were problems that still had to be addressed. Dice, for instance, are tricky tools. They have to be carefully made in order to ensure that they are perfectly balanced. The slightest bias would cause the experiments to be invalidated. Some kind of perfectly random testing system was needed in

Using Random Number Generators as a means of testing for psi began in the late 1960s, when German-born physicist Helmut Schmidt pioneered the technology behind the technique. The generator produces sequences of numbers or symbols that lack any pattern. The subject of the experiment tries to predict or influence their occurrence.

order to operate reliably and according to the laws of chance. Rhine also stated his view that, for a conclusive PK test, two experimenters would have to be involved and that it was vital for the targets, hits, and misses to be recorded independently.

PK AT PRINCETON

The breakthrough came in the late 1960s, when Helmut Schmidt, a German-born physicist, devised the first electronic Random Number Generators (RNGs) for psi research purposes. First, Schmidt invented a relatively simple device, known as the electronic coin flipper, but soon constructed more sophisticated items of equipment. What they all had in common was the ability to produce truly unpredictable random numbers. The next step was to integrate the RNGs into computers so that the researchers could program the way in which feedback functioned and appeared.

The Princeton Engineering Anomalies Research Laboratory of the Department of Engineering at Princeton University emerged as the world's leading center for RNG research. Popularly known as PEAR, the laboratory was the brainchild of Robert G. Jahn, then the dean of the School of Engineering and Applied Science. He prompted the laboratory's inception in 1979 "to pursue rigorous scientific study of the interaction of human consciousness with sensitive physical devices, systems, and processes common to contemporary engineering practice." It finally closed in February 2007, after nearly 30 years of intensive research. Over that time, several hundred operators performed thousands of experiments involving many millions of trials.

Experimental procedure obviously varied, but the basics remained the same. In the simplest of the experiments, the subject sat in front of a computer screen watching a moving graphic line. This represented the output of an RNG. When the RNG produced more electronic heads than tails, the line moved up the screen; with more tails it shifted downward; in a 50:50 situation it hugged a horizontal baseline in the center of the screen. The subject attempted to move the line in the direction chosen by the computer at the start of the session. A feedback device enabled him or her to determine which mental approach seemed to work best.

Although taken individually any anomalies stemming from the experiments were usually relatively insignificant, the PEAR investigators concluded that "they compound to highly significant deviations from chance expectations." Psychokinesis, it appears, was definitely at work. Critics, on the other hand, note that such experiments are fundamentally flawed, since what the experimenters assume is that by testing mental intention, they can also measure it. In other words, they asked subjects to try to make something happen mentally and then measured the differences between chance prediction and actual outcome. The unspoken assumption, which by definition remains unproved, is that the differences, if any, are due to some sort of interaction between mind and matter.

"If Uri Geller bends spoons with divine powers, then he is doing it the hard way." —JAMES RANDI, MAGICIAN

WHITHER WILL PK GO?

Opinions as to whether or not PK exists are polarized. Parapsychologists say that the ability is real, or at the least, there is enough evidence to justify further research into the phenomenon. They base this belief on the apparent results obtained from the thousands of RNG experiments conducted around the world since the 1960s, along with eyewitness reports of spontaneous phenomena, though these are almost always unsubstantiated.

Skeptics say that there is no concrete proof that psychokinesis exists. They claim the evidence points only to fraud or the statistical manipulation or misinterpretation of scientific data. But many ordinary people are prepared to accept the possibility of its existence. A September 2006 survey in the United States showed 28 percent of male and 31 percent of female participants agreeing with the proposition that "it is possible to influence the world through the mind alone."

Sixth Sense: Knowing the Unknowable

Experiencing a hunch, a gut feeling, or an intuition is popularly held to indicate that a so-called sixth sense is at work. More strictly, though, parapsychologists and other psychical investigators use this blanket term to refer to certain specific psychic abilities. These include channeling—the supposed ability to hear the dead talk—extrasensory perception (ESP), telepathy, clairvoyance, and precognition.

Bare Bones

- In popular parlance sixth sense is used to refer to hunches and intuition. Psychical researchers apply the term to abilities such as ESP, telepathy, clairvoyance, and precognition.

- Those who use their sixth sense regularly claim it is a faculty everyone is born with but we rarely choose to develop.

- Scientists have long sought an explanation for this ability and have postulated many theories, some involving paranormal forces, others physical and psychological processes that we do not yet fully understand.

Believers in the paranormal argue that all people are born with an innate sixth sense, though few people ever consider developing it. This is because accepted culture, particularly in the West, has conditioned individuals to disregard anything that cannot be explained by rigorous scientific analysis. For this reason, most people tend to dismiss gut feelings and the like as a product of the imagination. On the other hand, psychic intuitives say that the extra sense they possess is real, and its power can be harnessed. Many researchers share their belief and maintain that ways of gaining information that bypass the conventional five senses do indeed exist.

ANTICIPATING DANGER

On at least two occasions during the London Blitz in World War II, British prime minister Winston Churchill and his staff survived almost certain death because an inner voice warned him of impending danger. Once, Churchill heard that voice telling him to stop as he was about to enter his car on the left, where his chauffeur was holding the door open for him, and to walk around to the other side. During the subsequent drive, a German bomb exploded near enough to kill Churchill had he been sitting in his usual seat. On another occasion he rose from the dinner table to warn his kitchen staff to take shelter. A few minutes later a bomb hit the kitchen.

Churchill himself could devise no satisfactory explanation for his behavior, but more recently, research conducted in 2005 at Washington University suggested a possible scientific explanation. Joshua Brown and Todd Braver, two research scientists at the university, identified a region of the brain—the anterior cingulate cortex—as acting, so they claimed, as a preemptive early warning system. They believe that this portion of the brain monitors environmental cues, weighs possible consequences, and helps people to adjust their behavior to avoid dangerous situations.

PARAPSYCHOLOGY AT WORK

Back in the 1930s Louisa E. Rhine postulated that sixth sense starts in the subconscious mind, which she held was a storehouse of memories, hopes, and fears. Another theory involved macrophages—cells present in connective tissue, lymph nodes, and bone marrow, which are tied to nerve endings. Some people thought that these could be ESP organs, sending and receiving impressions below the normal level of perception.

In 2004 Ronald Rensink, an associate professor in psychology and computer science at the University of British Columbia in Canada, devised a new theory, which he christened "mindsight." Rensink coined the word to describe the phenomenon where people can sense that a scene they are looking at has changed without being able to identify immediately what that change is. His conclusion is that sixth sense is a distinct mode of visual perception and may be something that everyone can learn to employ.

Today's leading U.S. parapsychologist, Dean Radin, is convinced that it is now possible to "demonstrate in the laboratory what at some level we've known all along. Many people literally get a gut feeling before something bad happens. Our viscera warn us of danger even if our conscious mind doesn't always get the message."

Skeptics, however, disagree. They argue that researchers into sixth sense frequently claim to have found evidence of it simply because all normal scientific explanations have been eliminated. This, they say, is a classic case of wishful thinking—of interpreting facts according to what the researchers would like to be true.

Animal Magic

Before the giant tidal waves slammed into the Sri Lankan and Indian coastlines in the disastrous 2004 tsunami, both wild and domestic animals seemed to know what was about to happen and fled to safety. Elephants stampeded and ran for higher ground. Flamingos deserted their traditional breeding areas. Zoo animals raced into their shelters and could not be lured back out, while dogs simply refused to go outdoors.

This behavior ties in with the long-held belief that animals possess their own sixth sense of what is going to occur. Wildlife experts say that animals' more acute hearing and other senses may well enable them to hear or feel the planet's vibration, signaling imminent disaster long before humans realize what is happening.

Many people take this quite seriously. In Japan, one of the world's most earthquake-prone countries, studies are under way to discover what animals hear or feel before the Earth starts to shake. The hope is that animals may eventually be employed as a new prediction tool.

Remote Viewing: A View from Afar

Remote viewing (RV), remote perception, or distant viewing are all terms for a particular type of clairvoyance or ESP. It involves the supposed ability of psychically gifted sensitives to gain information regarding distant people, events, scenes, or objects—to visualize or sense what is happening at remote locations. Some claims state that remote viewers can also see what happened in the past or what will happen in the future at distant places.

Bare Bones

- Remote viewing is the ability to see distant locations without using the conventionally accepted senses.

- Some remote viewers claim to see events that are distant in time as well as space.

- Research into remote viewing began with the work of Joseph Banks Rhine at Duke University in the 1930s.

- Both the KGB and the CIA funded research programs in the 1970s that studied the use of remote viewing for intelligence gathering.

Belief in RV (by whatever name) existed long ago. For instance, ancient Hindu religious texts refer to the ability to sense at a distance. The sixteenth-century physician and philosopher, Paracelsus, stated, "Man also possesses a power by which he may see his friends and the circumstances by which they are surrounded, although such persons may be a thousand miles away from him at that time." Instances of RV by subjects who were hypnotized by Franz Anton Mesmer began to be reported in the eighteenth century, and the phenomenon was claimed by Spiritualist mediums in the late nineteenth and early twentieth centuries.

Attempts at more quantifiable research on RV did not begin until the work of J. B. Rhine and colleagues at Duke University,

Russell Targ, physicist and author. With Hal Puthoff, he directed a program at Stanford Research Institute, California, in the 1970s and 1980s, investigating psychic abilities for the U.S. intelligence community.

North Carolina, in 1933. Under a variety of procedural controls, a subject would be sent to a building and there handle a set of the famous Zener Cards, each of which displayed one of a set of symbols. The subject would stare at the symbols at one-minute intervals. Another subject in a building 100 yards (90 m) away guessed as to which cards the distant subject selected, and in which order. Hundreds of such trials were conducted over a six-day period and the overall results were estimated at being millions to one against chance. By today's standards, though, these experiments were crude and the statistical analysis relatively simplistic.

I SPY WITH MY RV EYE...

Spurred by cold war reports that the Russians and Chinese were successfully studying RV, the U.S. government initiated similar research in the early 1970s to see if RV could be used operationally, particularly in espionage. A CIA-funded project was put into operation at Stanford Research Institute (SRI) in California, directed by physicists Hal Puthoff and Russell Targ.

The SRI's basic RV protocol was that a sender would proceed to a remote location chosen in a randomized and double-blind manner and mentally transmit a picture of the scene to a receiver, who would draw or otherwise describe images that came into his or her mind. There were hits and misses, and the odds were evaluated to give a score. The whole procedure was subject to a complex set of controls. The main variation to this basic model was the use of maps or intelligence briefings in place of a distant human sender.

The SRI program evolved under different U. S. intelligence and military agencies, and experimental protocols were fine-tuned as the project continued. In the early years operators working for SRI included Ingo Swann (a New York artist and noted psychic), Pat Price, and Joseph McMoneagle (a U.S. Army warrant officer), but Swann trained further operators. One of the first was Ed Dames, who gained a reputation for bizarre antics, conducting target sessions involving Atlantis, Mars, and extraterrestrials. It is reported that Dames's colleagues played a prank on him, sending a carefully guarded description of Santa Claus coming from the

Visions of Atlantis

Often called the sleeping prophet, Edgar Cayce found that he could respond to questions when in a trancelike sleep and yet afterward had no memory of what had transpired. Cayce gave over 14,000 such readings, amounting to nearly 50,000 pages of transcript during his lifetime.

In a trance in 1933, he said a portion of Atlantis survived on the seabed just off the island of Bimini in the Bahamas. In 1940 he predicted it would be rediscovered in 1968 or 1969. In 1968 a long line of sunken rectangular stones was spotted in the shallow waters off Bimini, and in 1969 fragments of fluted marble columns were found.

So the scene seemed set for the rediscovery of Atlantis when David Zink led two archaeological diving expeditions to the location in 1975 and 1977. But the line of stones, nicknamed the Bimini Road, turned out to be an eroded geological feature, and the fluted columns proved to be the scattered cargo of a wrecked ship transporting Grecian-style adornments for a plantation-owner's house in Florida.

A REMOTE-VIEWING MACHINE?

A device has been developed in the laboratories of Professor Michael Persinger at Laurentian University in Sudbury, Ontario, consisting of a set of solenoids, which produces a magnetic field, fitted to a headband. This device is placed around the subject's cranium. A computer switches the solenoids on and off in a complex sequence creating electromagnetic fields that swirl around the person's head.

Author Paul Devereux appreciated the device's potential for RV when he underwent a session on it. He was asked to describe any mental impressions that came to him. He didn't actually visualize anything but had the persistent sense of "something like a piece of fairground machinery in variegated colors, with a neon green predominating."

Unknown to him, his wife had been taken to another room and asked to open any one of several envelopes and write a description of the picture it contained. After the session the pictures from all the envelopes were displayed and Devereux was able to identify the one his wife had selected—an old steam locomotive painted in various colors, with a bright green cowcatcher on its front.

North Pole in his sleigh. Dames used his psychic powers to interpret this as an imminent Soviet missile attack.

These excesses did not charm those already critical of the SRI program. Debate ensued within the program as to whether or not anyone could be trained to perform RV; some thought they could, but others felt that a person had to be naturally gifted to do it reliably. Some days the RV operators did not get positive results, at other times they did. To skeptics this meant that the method did not have repeatability and so was unscientific, but the proponents of RV argued that the nature of the ability was subject to variables people did not yet understand. They published papers in scientific journals, and distinct successes were reported. (Someone closely involved in the SRI programs has even claimed accurate RV-obtained knowledge concerning American hostages in the Middle East.) Despite such successes, critics pointed to many instances of vague or incorrect results. The SRI adventure went under various names, including Grill Flame, Center Lane, Sun Streak, and, most famously of all, Stargate—now often used to refer to the entire SRI program. In 1996 the adventure came to an end.

OTHER RESEARCH

There were two other long-term RV programs that paralleled the SRI work. One was the research at the Princeton Engineering Anomalies Research (PEAR) laboratory at Princeton University, led by Robert Jahn and Brenda Dunne. Between 1976 and 1999 they produced one the largest databases of RV experimentation; in all, they conducted 653 formal trials. Like the SRI program, it went through a number of phases with changes and improvements in experimental protocols over the years. They also conducted sophisticated statistical analyses of the results. The overall composite database shows a probability against chance of approximately three parts in 10 billion.

The other important RV effort was conducted by the Mobius Group, directed by Stephen Schwartz, a former special assistant to the U.S. Chief of Naval Operations. He used a similar protocol to the SRI program but called RV distant viewing.

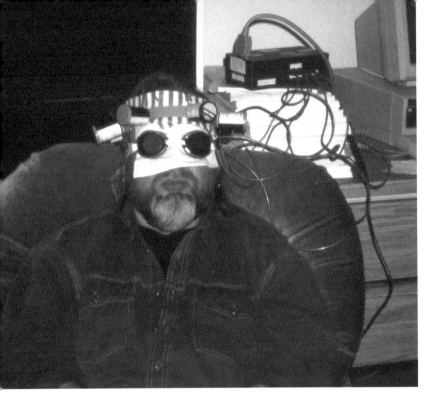

Author Paul Devereux wearing a prototype of the circumcerebral electronic device nicknamed the Octopus. He is wearing gauze and goggles to give him a darkened, even, visual field, while a headband holds solenoids attached to a computer, allowing a programmed electromagnetic field to play around the brain during the session.

Mobius was initially concerned with testing whether or not electromagnetism was somehow implicated in the mechanics of RV, and working with SRI, it used a submarine as a target because large volumes of seawater shield against any electromagnetic effect. Remote-viewing sessions by Hella Hammid and Ingo Swann correctly identified the location of the submersible in the waters off California. In another experiment, Schwartz used his RV protocol to identify the most fruitful spots at which to carry out archaeological excavations in and around Alexandria, Egypt. In another attempt the Mobius panel tried to remotely view the location of a former palace on the tip of a peninsula that had been part of the ancient city of Alexandria but was now under water. Divers found huge granite blocks at the location the panel identified, indicating the presence of a substantial drowned feature.

Although the age of major RV programs is over, research continues. In 1999 and 2001, for example, Japanese researchers measured changes in skin conductivity and brain-wave patterns in RV senders and receivers placed in cubicles screened against electromagnetism, indicating some kind of interaction. Today RV remains an enigma, neither conclusively proved nor disproved.

Telepathy: Transmitting Thoughts

Telepathy—from the classical Greek *tele*, meaning remote, and *patheia*, which translates as to be affected—is a term coined in 1882 by Frederic W. H. Myers, a British scholar, a founder of the Society for Psychical Research, and a pioneer of modern psychology. He invented it as a handy way to describe mind-to-mind communication—psychic thought transmissions from one person to another. Such people are referred to as senders and receivers.

Bare Bones

- The word telepathy was invented in 1882 by Frederic W. H. Myers to describe mind-to-mind communication.

- It is believed that telepathy is more likely to occur if the two people involved have some sort of emotional tie.

- Zener cards were designed to use in experiments to test for telepathy. They are a set of 25 cards, each with one of five designs: a star, arrow, square, circle, and three wavy lines.

Telepathy is one of the most important branches of current parapsychological research. Numerous experiments have been—and still are—conducted in an attempt to confirm the existence of the phenomenon and devise a convincing explanation for it. Parapsychologists class it as a form of extrasensory perception (ESP) or anomalous cognition. In both, information is transmitted mentally between two or more people through the power of psi.

TYPES OF TELEPATHY

Often, so it is claimed, the phenomenon involves a mental exchange between close relatives or is sparked off by a life-threatening situation involving either of the two participants. This is called spontaneous telepathic communication. The other type—intentional telepathic communication—occurs when one person is making a conscious effort to transmit information to another person, who may or may not be aware of the attempt.

Many parapsychologists believe that telepathic transmissions are often received unconsciously, never surfacing into the conscious mind, or that there can be a time lag between transmissions and their conscious receipt. Proponents of this view point to laboratory research, which they say proves that a receiver's body reacts physiologically to transmissions, even when the receiver is unaware of them. For this reason researchers now often focus on investigating the phenomenon in association with altered states of consciousness—dreams, meditation, hypnosis, and the like—in which people seem to be most receptive.

EARLY THEORIES

Speculation about whether telepathy exists or not and, if it does, how it functions dates back to early times. Democritus, the ancient Greek philosopher, developed a theory to account for the phenomenon. Centuries later the savant Franz Anton Mesmer and his fellow proponents of the healing powers of mesmerism claimed that telepathy was one of the so-called "higher phenomena" observed in the patients they magnetized. For his part the eminent Victorian scientist William Crookes postulated that telepathy relies on the transmission of radio-like brain waves.

The obvious problem with this intriguing notion is that if there were some kind of wave similar to the one that Crookes postulated, it ought to be possible to detect it radiating from people's brains. It cannot be done. Electrical activity within the brain is so weak that it can be detected only up to an inch or so away from the skull. Moreover, there would need to be a discernible transmitter and receiver in the brain to send and receive the waves. No sign of either has been discovered. Finally, the strength of such signals ought to decay with distance. It appears that it does not.

It did not take long for the psychiatrists to become involved in research. Sigmund Freud defined telepathy as a regressive, primitive human faculty that had been lost in the course of evolution, though it still possessed the ability to manifest itself under certain specific conditions. Carl Jung considered it a function of what he termed synchronicity—meaningful coincidences that cannot otherwise be explained.

Zener cards, devised by Karl Zener, an American perceptual psychologist, are used to test for evidence of precognition and telepathy. In the first instance subjects are asked to predict which card will be turned; in the second a sender tries to transmit an image of a card to a receiver in another room.

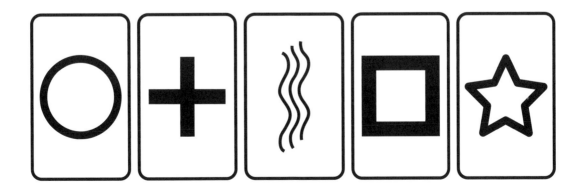

CARD GUESSING

In Victorian Britain the in-depth study of telepathy began as a consequence of the founding of the Society for Psychical Research in London by Sir William Fletcher Barrett and Henry Sedgwick. Fletcher Barrett conducted the Society's first investigation into telepathy himself. It centered on the Creery sisters, four teenage daughters of a wealthy clergyman, and their maid, who claimed to be able to communicate telepathically.

As part of his research, Fletcher Barrett devised a means of testing for telepathy that remained popular for more than a century. This was card guessing. He believed the results he obtained through his work with the Creery sisters were promising. Typically, one of the researchers would think of a name, a playing card, or a household object, and one of the girls—they ranged in age from 10 to 17—would guess what had been chosen. The answers were almost always correct.

"I have found by experience that telepathy does in fact influence dreams."

—CARL JUNG, PSYCHOLOGIST

It was Fletcher Barrett's hope that the phenomenon he was observing would prove to be real and would "necessitate a modification of that general view of the relation of mind to matter to which modern science has long been gravitating." Unfortunately for him, after six years of testing, the sisters were caught cheating. It turned out that they had been using primitive secret signs and a crude verbal code to communicate with one another.

RESEARCH IN THE UNITED STATES

Across the Atlantic, Richard Hodgson, a law professor, and astronomer Simon Newcomb set up the American Society for Psychical Research in Boston in 1885. This society also began scientific testing for telepathy. Their first experiments were simple. A sender in one room would try to transmit a two-digit number, a taste, or a visual image to a receiver in another room.

Later the approach became more sophisticated. In 1917 John Coover, who became Stanford University's first-ever Fellow in

Psychical Research, conducted four major experiments, half of which sought evidence of telepathy and half of clairvoyance. After 10,000 trials, however, Coover concluded that he could find no scientific evidence one way or the other to prove that either of the phenomena existed.

Others were not dissuaded by Coover's conclusions. Chief among them was Dr. Joseph Banks Rhine. Over the years, Rhine tested hundreds of people for telepathy and clairvoyance, using cards that Karl Zener, one of his colleagues, had specially designed for the purpose. These so-called Zener Cards consisted of a deck of 25 cards, the faces decorated with one of five symbols—a star, arrow, square, circle, or three wavy lines.

After the cards were shuffled, the sender was asked to select one at random and try to visualize the symbol on it. The receiver simultaneously attempted to determine which symbol this was. Statistically, the odds in favor of guessing the symbol correctly were one in five. Rhine held that scores repeatedly and significantly higher than this would indicate either telepathy or clairvoyance.

Over the decades Rhine's methods were continuously improved and expanded upon by parapsychologists and psychical researchers on both sides of the Atlantic. Results were mixed, and Rhine's methodology came under sustained attack for its relative lack of sophistication. The response was to diversify the approach, utilizing new technology such as the Ganzfeld (*see box* "The Ganzfeld Experiments"), as and when it became available.

DISPUTED FINDINGS

It remains the case that, in common with other psychical phenomena, telepathy is still impossible to test for systematically. Because the phenomenon is closely connected to the emotional states of both the sender and the receiver, it is extremely hard to replicate experimental results, and it is clear that other attitudinal factors can also influence a test outcome. This repeated inability to replicate results consistently and satisfactorily leads skeptics to argue that there is still no credible scientific evidence for the existence of telepathy at all.

The Ganzfeld Experiments

Probably the best-known modern research into telepathy is the on-going Ganzfeld experiments, which started in the mid-1970s. In these experiments, the subject lies comfortably listening to white noise or seashore sounds through headphones, with halved Ping-Pong balls over his or her eyes.

He or she sees nothing but a uniform white or pink field: the Ganzfeld. Meanwhile, a sender in another room views a picture or a video clip for 30 minutes. The subject is then shown four pictures or videos and asked to choose which was the target.

It is claimed that participants accomplish this far better than would be expected by chance. The Ganzfeld procedure is now fully automated. Its proponents claim that it provides reliable scientific evidence for the existence of telepathy and related psychical phenomena. Skeptics, however, argue that the experiments are still open to error and fraud.

Dowsing: Uncovering What Is Hidden

According to believers in the power of the paranormal, dowsing is one of the oldest intuitive talents that humanity possesses. This form of divination attempts to find hidden things. The Bible records how Moses used a divining rod to find water for his people during the flight from Egypt. In ancient Egypt dowsers were depicted on cartouches holding their rods and wearing elaborate headdresses fitted with what are believed to be dowsing antennae.

Bare Bones

- Dowsing is the ability to find hidden things using psychic means. It has been used to find water, lost objects, and even missing people.

- Most dowsers use a tool such as dowsing rods or a pendulum, but some claim they can dowse using only their hands.

- Experiments have failed to prove scientifically that dowsing works, but dowsers maintain that their abilities work if there is a genuine need.

In Europe dowsing for water became commonplace during the Middle Ages, when its association with the supernatural gave rise to names such as water witching. Dowsing is a form of divination, in which the dowser uses a stick, rod, or another device, such as a handheld and suspended pendulum, to locate whatever the dowser wants to find. Underground water, oil, coal, or mineral deposits are favorite targets, while dowsing has also been used to locate missing persons, murderers, their victims, lost objects, and animals, and to aid in the mapping of archaeological sites before excavation begins.

RODS AND PENDULUMS

Water dowsing is almost certainly the oldest form of the procedure. The traditional method involves the dowser walking around a predetermined area, holding out a forked rod or stick horizontally in front of him or her. The rod is usually made of hazel, ash, rowan, or willow, though occasionally metal, whalebone, and even plastic ones are employed. When water is located, the rod starts to twitch and jerk up and down, sometimes violently. Some dowsers use two rods, in which case the rods cross when water is detected.

In Europe many dowsers today prefer the use of a pendulum as their dowsing instrument. The pendulum, customarily made of

A traditional dowser demonstrates his powers using forked wooden dowsing rods. A form of divination, dowsing has been practiced for centuries. It is employed mainly for detecting water, mineral ores, and buried treasure.

either crystal or wood, is suspended on a string. It swings, practitioners claim, in response to so-called closed questions or if held over a map. This is known as map dowsing and can be practiced even at a distance. In 1949 Henry Gross, a well-known dowser, was attending a reception in Maine, his home state, when a dinner conversation about the extreme drought then prevailing on the island of Bermuda led him to use a map to try to locate new, hidden water reserves. Water was located in three out of the four sites he selected when wells were dug there.

Pendulum dowsing is not limited to the areas in which dowsers have traditionally operated. According to some of its practitioners, it can be used to diagnose illness. The belief is that the pendulum can pinpoint an energy blockage, an area of discomfort, or a malfunctioning body organ by circling as it would to indicate the answer no to a question, generally counterclockwise. Alternatively, it may simply stop moving altogether.

Map dowsing, also known as remote dowsing, or over-the-horizon dowsing, is regarded by many practitioners of the art as the most sophisticated form of dowsing. Dowsers claim that it is possible to search for virtually anything irrespective of the distance from the site they dowse.

HOW DOWSERS WORK

Regardless of the tools they employ, all dowsers claim to possess psychic abilities—that is, the ability to tune mentally into whatever is being sought. In a few exceptional cases these abilities are so strong that dowsers can dowse unaided, without any form of instrument. The celebrated Israeli-born psychic Uri Geller, for instance, dowses with nothing but his hands.

Dowsers start by tuning their chosen instrument and concentrating mentally on the item for which they are looking. Procedures vary according to each case. If, for instance, a dowser is trying to locate a missing person, he or she may first hold their dowsing tool over a personal item to help them focus.

Before a pendulum is used for the first time, it is cleansed and the dowser charges it with personal energy. The dowser then mentally asks the pendulum to indicate yes. In response, the tool should start swinging gently from side to side and then circle clockwise. To confirm, the dowser stops it swinging, then asks it to indicate no. The pendulum should start to circle in the opposite direction.

TESTING THE DOWSERS

Though thousands of instances of successful dowsing have been recorded over the centuries, scientific testing has been sparse. The main evidence comes from testimonials provided by the dowsers and those who have observed them. Indeed, some dowsers have actively resisted attempts by scientists to test their powers. Sir Charles Jessel, President of the British Society of Dowsers, said that he was not willing to participate in anything that would "put dowsing to the test." His argument was that "the dowsing faculty does not always behave to order, when real need is not being expressed or fulfilled."

"...even after we've demonstrated that they can't produce results...they'll still go away believing in their abilities." —JAMES RANDI, MAGICIAN

The proposition is simple. Dowsers find the items for which they dowse, believers argue. Therefore, what more proof is needed? Skeptics, however, say that this kind of reasoning is unscientific and fallacious. They contend that every reputable scientific dowsing experiment that has been conducted, such as the exhaustive tests on 30 dowsers in Kassel, in Germany, in 1992, indicates that, statistically, dowsers do little or no better than chance.

It is unlikely that many dowsers are out-and-out fraudsters. Most genuinely believe they possess paranormal powers. More likely, according to the skeptics, is they have fallen victim to what is known as the ideomotor effect: unconscious muscular movements initiated in the dowser's mind. Thus, in dowsing, the rods move or the pendulum swings as a result of involuntary motor behavior, not because of supernatural force.

Dermo-optical Perception: Eyeless Sight

Otherwise termed bio-introscopy, dermo-optical perception (DOP) is the alleged ability to see without the use of the eyes. People claiming to possess DOP often say that they can see through the skin of their fingers or hands, frequently demonstrating their ability by reading while blindfolded. For this reason it is often referred to as eyeless sight or fingertip vision.

Bare Bones

- Dermo-optical perception is the ability to see without the use of the eyes, usually using a part of the skin, such as the fingertips, as a substitute.

- Some say that this ability is innate in a gifted few, while others claim it can be taught to anyone.

- A reputable team of French scientists conducted tests in 1996 that appeared to confirm the existence of DOP, but independent confirmatory tests failed to replicate the results and fraud was suspected.

In 1990 it was claimed that a group of Chinese children could read bits of paper that had been crumpled up and placed in their ears or armpits. Back in the days of the U.S.S.R., the Russian psychic Rosa A. Kuleshova was said to be a noted practitioner of the art. It was claimed that she had started blindfold reading at the age of five, and she was declared genuine by the Soviet Academy of Sciences in 1978—the year in which the 23-year-old Kuleshova died of a brain tumor.

THE SKEPTICS' VIEW

If such claims were provable, DOP would be a classic example of what psychologists term Extraordinary Human Function. Instead, it has been roundly condemned as a confidence trick. James Randi, the well-known skeptic and debunker of psychics, accused Nina Kulagina, another celebrated Russian practitioner, of fraud. Kulagina was filmed reading letter cards on a wall behind her. Having studied the film carefully, Randi concluded that Kulagina was nothing more than a clever trickster. Prior to reading the cards, she raised her hand up to her eyes, slipped it into her pocket, took it out again, and displayed it to the camera to show that it was empty. Randi thought the actions suggested that Kulagina was peeping at the cards with a small handheld mirror, which she pocketed once she had taken a glance. To support his supposition, Randi noted that Kulagina read all of the cards, including a two-digit number, in reverse order, which strongly suggested to him that a mirror was involved.

TEACHING DOP

Dermo-optical perception was historically claimed to be innate. Then, in the mid-1990s, BUKVA-A, a Russian company, announced that it could teach DOP to anyone prepared to pay its fees. In Paris in 1996, a reputable French team of an ophthalmologist, neurologist, and radiologist tested two volunteers put forward by the company and were amazed by the results. Both volunteers seemed to possess the ability to see images without using their eyes. At last it seemed that proof of DOP had been found.

Obviously, independent confirmatory tests were needed. These were conducted by scientists from the Medical Research Center of the French Ministry of Defense. From the Russian standpoint, the first experiment was a total failure. Not only was its blindfolded subject unable to identify accurately any of the images presented to her on a computer screen, but she also declared she could see something on the screen even when it was blank. The same thing happened when the second experiment was conducted with the other volunteer. Out of a total of 24 images, the participants had identified none accurately.

"Just because a man lacks the use of his eyes doesn't mean he lacks vision."

—STEVIE WONDER, MUSICIAN

In response, the Russians claimed that this was the first time in four years that the volunteers had failed such a test, that perhaps their failure was due to the use of aluminum-foil blindfolds, or the fact that a computer screen had been used to display the images. The French replied that the way in which the experiments would be conducted had been agreed in advance. They refused a Russian request to repeat the tests using a type of blindfold that they knew to be unreliable and concluded that no evidence of DOP had been found. Once suitably blindfolded, the Russians lost all the amazing abilities that had impressed the experts in Paris.

Psychic Surgery: Faith or Fraud?

Psychic surgery is about as far removed from conventional surgery as a medical procedure could be. Originating in the Philippines, it is practiced widely there and in Brazil. Approximately 400 psychic surgeons practice in the islands, and these surgeons have performed more than 3 million operations over the last 40 years.

Bare Bones

- Psychic surgery is performed by psychic surgeons, who claim to make incisions in the body and remove diseased tissues without the use of any anesthetics or surgical instruments.

- Although it takes place throughout the world, the practice is particularly prevalent in the Philippines.

- Some recipients of psychic surgery claim to have benefited, but experts agree that most practitioners use conjuring tricks to deceive onlookers and perform no genuine medical procedure.

The procedure is performed by self-styled psychic healers, who claim to extract tumors and other potentially harmful objects from the human body through a bloody, but painless and invisible, incision, often made with the bare hands. The incision heals spontaneously after the procedure has been completed. No antiseptics or anesthetics are employed.

The practice has come under sustained and continuing attack from public and private bodies and individuals. In 1975 the U.S. Federal Trade Commission won an injunction against travel agents promoting psychic surgery tours. For its part, the American Cancer Society maintains its 1990 position that there is "no evidence that psychic surgery results in objective benefit in the treatment of any medical condition," while the British Columbia Cancer Association is just as blunt. It "strongly urges individuals who are ill not to seek treatment by psychic surgeons." This is in line with the verdict of the National Council Against Health Fraud in the United States, which cautioned that psychic surgery "wastes money, causes psychological harm, may cause needless deaths, and may result in needless suffering and discomfort."

WHAT PSYCHIC SURGERY INVOLVES

Most medical professionals and skeptics condemn psychic surgery outright as sleight of hand. Any positive results it may produce, they say, are classic examples of a placebo effect. Some lay people, however, claim to have physically benefitted and found solace in it. They believe that the healers are divine agents or divinely inspired. Many people believe that Stephen Turoff, Britain's best-

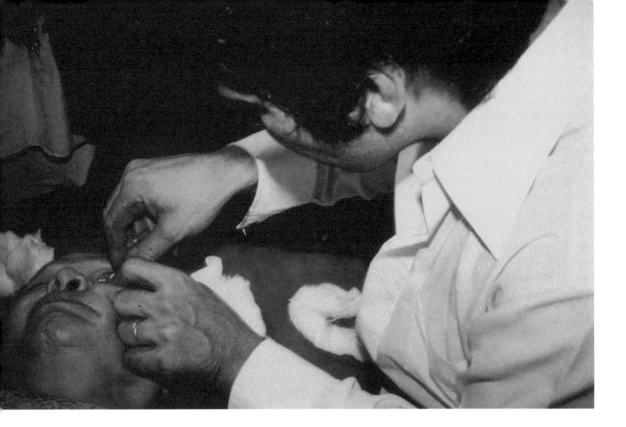

Ivan Trilha, a psychic surgeon from Paraguay, is caught in action performing an operation in 1978. Skeptics say that the whole thing is a fraud, in which sleight of hand is employed. Practitioners, however, claim to cure a range of diseases, including diabetes and cancers.

known psychic surgeon, may be an instrument of God, though others dismiss him as nothing more than a pious fraud.

The most commonly used props for performing psychic surgery are a table, a bowl of water, and cotton balls. The procedures differ between its practitioners, since all individual healers develop their own trademark gimmicks. One psychic healer, for instance, appears to extract palm leaves, grass, plastic bags, corncobs, and other nonanimal objects from his patients' bodies. Another administers so-called spirit injections from several feet away. These are felt, so it is claimed, as needlelike jabs. Another appears to make an incision with hands held high 6 inches (15 cm) or more above the skin. Some claim to diagnose with x-ray vision, while several perform a ritual in which it appears that the patient's eyes are removed, cleaned, and then reinserted into the eye sockets.

Alex Orbito, a leading Filipino psychic surgeon, describes the way he treats his patients as magnetic. According to him, his hands are "like a magnet, so that even if the sickness is at a distance from my hand, it is drawn to me, and I feel the current. When I feel the current, I know the sickness is now in my hand, and I remove it

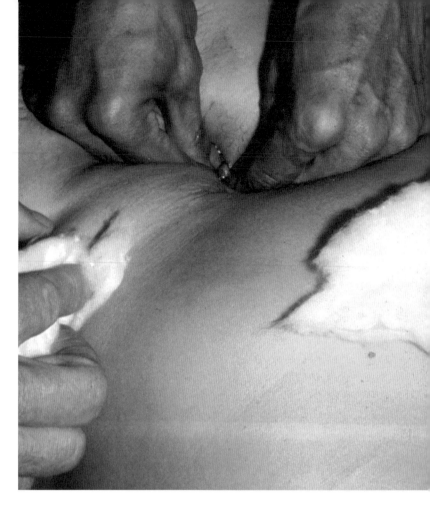

In the Philippines, where this photograph was taken, psychic surgery started in the 1940s. The healer uses his or her mind to project spiritual healing powers into the body via the hands. Among the hundreds of people who have turned to psychic surgeons over the years are Hollywood actress Shirley Maclaine, British comedian Peter Sellers, and Saudi royalty.

immediately." In Australia, psychic surgeon Chris Cole has been practicing in Sydney since 1991. She employs what she describes as a more energy-based form of the procedure, acting as an energy channel to direct recuperative divine energy into her patients. It is that energy, she claims, that helps to initiate the healing response. The patient's innate healing wisdom does the healing.

Healing rituals often include prayers and meditation. Healers often recommend repeat treatments, telling patients that the healing will take place a month or two after the procedure has been completed. Most healers also claim to detect and remove previously undiagnosed illnesses, in addition to any that the patient may have disclosed prior to treatment.

Psychic dentists are available for those people who prefer dentistry without anesthesia or dental probes and drills. Willard Fuller, one such dentist, has supposedly healed more than 40,000 people since he began practicing in 1960. Those who flock to his clinics claim that his magic touch can fill cavities, make bad teeth whole again, and even produce a new set of teeth.

EXPOSING FRAUD

The experts say that some 80 percent of psychic surgeons are simply fakes. Quite a few have been exposed over the years. Gary G. Magno was arrested in Phoenix, Arizona, in 1986. When he was searched, the police found vials of red fluid and packets of meat tucked under his waistband. Three years later Placido Palatayan was arrested in Colville, Washington, where he was charged with theft and practicing medicine without a license. A bucket containing blood and tissue that purportedly had been removed from his patients was found to contain nonhuman animal tissue.

Perhaps the most significant test of the claims made for psychic surgery was the demonstration conducted by the Reverend Philip Malicdan in a Michigan University laboratory in 1987. After it, three observers—a magician, an audiovisual expert, and a pathologist—reported their findings. The magician claimed to have detected the use of conjuring methodology and concluded that Malicdan was "a willful fraud." The audiovisual expert found that the videotape of the proceedings "indicated beyond any doubt that sleight of hand was used..." According to the pathologist, the blood and tissue Malicdan claimed to have removed from the patients was actually weeks or months old.

"Psychic surgery is nothing more than a total hoax." —U.S. FEDERAL TRADE COMMISSION

James Randi, the renowned magician who has been debunking paranormal claims for decades, has no doubts. He is certain that psychic surgery is nothing more than a hoax. "I've witnessed psychic surgery in the Philippines and in the West, and I've got many hours of videotape of it—in the unedited versions—that show very plainly what the gimmicks are," he says. "But you will see them only if you know what to look for." Perhaps this explains why so many people continue to have psychic surgery performed.

Psychometry: Seeing History

Psychometry is the ability to access information from an object or place using psychic means. If giving a personal reading, a psychometrist will hold an individual's personal possession and attempt to gain information about the owner's past and present circumstances. In place psychometry, the psychometrist either holds an object from a given spot or, more usually, simply visits the given location and enters a quiet, almost meditative, mental state to receive impressions or visions of what has happened there.

Bare Bones

- Psychometry is the term used to describe gaining information about a place or object psychically, simply by visiting the place or holding the object.

- Experiments in psychometry have taken place since the 1840s with some successful results reported. This research continues to this day.

- One application of psychometry is in archaeology. While this technique has yielded important information that has later been verified, it is not always reliable.

The term psychometry (*psyche*, spirit, and *metron*, measure) was coined in 1842 by Joseph R. Buchanan, a professor of physiology and early investigator of this apparent ability. He put different drugs in glass vials and asked his students to identify the substances simply by holding the vials. The positive results proved better than chance, and he published his findings. His work has been followed over the decades by sporadic attempts at experimentation by various other people.

THE EARLY DAYS

In 1854 geologist William Denton tested the idea of psychometry by wrapping geological samples in cloth and asking his sister, Ann Denton Cridge, to hold them to her forehead to see if she could identify them by extrasensory means. She obtained vivid mental impressions that enabled her to do so. In the early 1920s Gustav Pagenstecher, a German physician, found that one of his patients, Maria Reyes de Zierold, could enter a trancelike state while holding an object and experience multisensory impressions of what had happened to it.

In 1935 the Russian-born medium Stefan Ossowiecki underwent a test devised by a wealthy Hungarian called Dionizy Jonky. The Hungarian had a sealed package he wanted Ossowiecki to open after his death. When that time came, Ossowiecki was presented with 14 photographs of different men and asked to identify the one that showed Jonky. Ossowiecki did not know Jonky, but he successfully identified the Hungarian's picture and was handed the package. On touching it, the medium stated that it contained volcanic materials and that he had the impression of "another planet." The package contained a meteoric fragment. Fifty scientists and other observers witnessed the experiment firsthand.

PSYCHIC DETECTIVE

During the 1940s Dutchman Gerard Croiset gained a reputation as a psychic detective because of his seeming ability to use psychometry to help police departments from various countries solve crimes. In one of his more celebrated cases—that of a missing little girl from Brooklyn, New York—Croiset correctly determined that she was dead, gave the location of her body, and supplied information regarding the man who murdered her. The information led to the recovery of the body and the arrest of the man. Croiset did all this simply by being given a photograph of the girl, an item of her clothing, and a map of New York City.

Experiments with psychometry continue to the present day. One mass experiment conducted over the summer of 2007 in Ontario compared people's impressions of specially selected objects with their actual history. Organized by historian Chris Laursen, the experiment was conducted at specified times and places in the southern Ontario region. People ranging from those who had never had a psychic experience before to people who had had inexplicable events occur in their lives, to people who asserted that they had psychic abilities were invited to participate. Results are to be disseminated in due course.

PSYCHIC ARCHAEOLOGY

Visitors to ancient monument sites typically try to visualize what originally took place there, so it is not surprising that the apparent ability of gifted psychometrists to see past events at places has attracted unorthodox, alternative archaeologists. One of the earliest such collaborations on record was by the architect Frederick Bligh Bond, who in the early twentieth century was appointed

No Success Like Failure

Following the apparent success of the earlier Jonky experiment (*see* "The Early Days"), the Russian psychometrist Stefan Ossowiecki was subjected to 33 sessions by academic Stanislaw Poniatowski to test the extent and reliability of his powers.

In each session, Ossowiecki was handed objects from the remote past to see what impressions he might gain from them. He often gave details concerning items like Stone Age tools and a 300,000-year-old skull that corresponded with known facts, but sometimes he seemed to fail, giving information that was thought at the time to be in error.

In one case, for instance, he said that the Sahara had been a fertile and well-irrigated land thousands of years ago. Although assumed to be false at the time, current-day satellite imagery has revealed the dried-up courses of rivers crossing the vast expanse of what is now the great desert, and archaeological findings have also confirmed the former existence of civilizations that thrived in the lush environment of the earlier Sahara region.

Ancient Magicians

Geoffrey Hodson, a well-known visionary painter in his day, psychometrized a number of ancient sites. In 1922 he visited the Castlerigg Stone Circle in England's Lake District, where he claimed that with his inner vision, he could see a tall man with long dark hair and a beard, dressed in a flowing white garment, standing within the ring of stones in the company of other priests.

He and they were engaged in a ritual in which energy, visible to Hodson as a column of rosy-tinged opalescent light, was brought down from the sky and fused with the ground inside the ring of stones. Hodson's visionary snapshot also included glimpses of banners emblazoned with symbols draped over some of the stones.

On another occasion, in Mexico, Hodson psychometrically perceived rituals taking place on the summit of the Pyramid of the Sun in the 2,000-year-old ruined city of Teotihuacan (Birthplace of the Gods), a name given to the vast complex by the later Aztecs. Hodson interpreted the scene as being descendants of Atlantis manipulating "cosmic energies."

director of excavations at the ruined site of Glastonbury Abbey in England. Between 1907 and 1912 Bond worked with John Bartlett, a medium who conducted automatic writing, supposedly dictated by discarnate people, to glean information about the best locations at the site to excavate. Bond amassed screeds of automatic writing through Bartlett in Low Latin, Middle English, and modern English purporting to come from long-dead Glastonbury monks. Architectural information regarding the site was included, and Bond confirmed some of it by his excavations. In his *The Gate of Remembrance*, Bond revealed the unconventional source of his excavational guidance, resulting in unfortunate consequences for his career.

By the 1920s and 1930s it had become quite fashionable within a certain circle of antiquarians to invite psychometrists along to ancient sites. Two psychometrists in particular were in great demand—Geraldine Cummins and Iris Campbell. Working in Ireland with the archaeoastronomer, Admiral Boyle-Somerville, Cummins visited the standing stones known as the Three Fingers. She claimed she could see robed priests in antiquity "drawing power" from the stones, while at the stone circle of Drombeg, County Cork, she psychometrized ancient rituals in which "earth power" was drawn up from the ground and used in a low form of elemental magic.

In 1971, carpenter George McMullen, who discovered his psychic abilities during childhood, undertook a series of psychometric tests organized by educator J. N. Emerson. McMullen provided detailed and accurate information concerning archaeological objects handed to him, and when taken to Iroquois sites in Canada, he provided exceptionally detailed information about the people who lived at them—he even claimed to hear them talking.

THE STONES SPEAK

American explorer David Zink used the on-site impressions of psychometrists to extend his understanding of the ancient sites he visited around the world. In his book *The Ancient Stones Speak*, one of his psychometric informants claimed that the Scottish stone

circle complex of Callanish was linked to the Pleiades constellation in some mysterious way, creating energy vortices at the stones. Another stated that the Stone Age temple of Hagar Qim on Malta had helped humans to communicate with extraterrestrial beings. As might be expected, Egypt's Great Pyramid elicited many psychometric responses, such as it being "an energy collector and beacon," that its stones could trigger out-of-body experiences, and that that it had been built by Atlanteans. At the ancient ruined Andean city of Tiahuanaco on Bolivia's altiplano, a psychometrist told Zink that the Gateway of the Sun had been moved to its present location from elsewhere—a fact now confirmed by archaeology. But she also said that there was no cultivation conducted in the area by the ancient Tiahuanacos; this is now known to be untrue. Another psychometrist informed Zink that the founders of Tiahuanaco had come from Mars.

It seems that psychometry can produce flashes of reliable information, though blended with a number of fanciful impressions.

The Pyramid of the Sun, Teotihuacan, Mexico. This 200-foot (60-m) tall edifice was built around A.D. 150 above a ritual cave that had its opening facing the setting point of the Pleiades star cluster. The pyramid was similarly aligned, and this provided the angle for the whole axial layout of the city.

Divination: Uncovering the Truth

Divination is the art of discovering future events or unknown things. In his *Mysmantia* of 1652, clergyman and author John Gaule listed some 53 different categories of divination, and that was far from being exhaustive. Some people may be familiar with the reading of tea leaves, water divining, crystal gazing, and palmistry, but there are more bizarre methods, such as monitoring the coagulation of cheese (tyromancy), interpreting the creaking of doors, or even stomach rumbles (gastromancy). Certain prehistoric standing stones had divinatory lore attached to them, as did holy wells and springs—the origin of the wishing well.

Bare Bones

- Divination is the art of revealing hidden information, primarily foretelling the future. Throughout history many different practices have been used for divination.

- Ancient systems of divination included geomancy, the casting of handfuls of soil, and divination by reading bodily signs. Some systems involved the sacrifice of animals and even humans.

- Astrology is a form of divination that interprets the movements of planets and stars and is still popular today.

TWISTS OF FATE

Most forms of divination used randomization of one kind or another, some more obviously so than others—scatoscopy, for example, involved the inspection of excrement—but the most pervasive category of chance divination was, and remains, sortilege, the casting or drawing of lots.

Today's lottery systems are, of course, merely modern electronic forms of sortilege, but a widespread ancient form, which also survives to this day, was geomancy, the casting of handfuls of soil or, sometimes, pebbles, twigs, seeds, beans, bones, or other small objects. The geomancer marked a grid on the ground onto which he then cast the soil or other particles, interpreting the resulting pattern using learned formulas.

EMBODIED DIVINATION

The human body itself has been not exempt from divinatory attention, especially the hand. In old European tradition the thumb was sensitive to supernatural influences, and it is noteworthy that one of the witches in Shakespeare's *Macbeth* foretells the arrival of evil by "the pricking of my thumbs." In the continued popular practice of palmistry, the lines running across the palm of the hand, the forms of specific parts of the palm, and the shape of the fingers and hand as a whole are considered fraught with meaning.

ANIMAL MAGIC

Divination has also involved the animal world in various ways. One example is scapulomancy—the use of the shoulder blades of animals as divinatory tools. In the Highlands of Scotland it was known as *slinneineachd*, and the right scapula of a black pig or sheep was considered most suitable. The bone would be thoroughly boiled so all the flesh was removed, then carefully inspected for holes or markings, each having its own meaning.

A widely used system was haruspicy, the study of the entrails of a sacrificed animal, as was hepatoscopy, extracting meaning from the liver of an animal. The shape, condition, and color of the liver was studied. Archaeologists have found clay models of animal livers

A Dogon geomantic diviner at work in Africa. The geomancer draws a grid on the ground with a stick. He leaves it overnight and comes back the next morning to see what animal tracks have been left on it. Relating them to their positions in the grid, he is able to give his client a reading.

marked with cuneiform writing, indicating that hepatoscopy dates back at least 4,000 years to Babylonian times.

Birds were seen as messengers of the gods. The classic examples of divination by studying the behavior of birds were Etruscan and Roman augury, but the Iron Age priesthood called the Druids also divined things by the flight patterns or songs of birds.

DIVINATION AND DEATH

Ritual killing, of humans or animals, was often used for divination. The Druids practiced hieromancy—the study of the sacrificial victim's death throes, the angle the eyes took at death, or the patterns created by blood from the body. The Aztecs employed similar methods. Divination by means of communication with the spirits of the dead is called necromancy. The classic example of this black art is the Bible story of the witch of Endor, who raised the soul of the dead Samuel to seek knowledge of the future from it.

Men-an-Tol, Cornwall, England. According to tradition, the local seer could divine the future or answers to questions by placing two brass pins, one across the other, on top of the stone. It is said the pins would acquire "a peculiar motion" and the seer would give his reading by interpreting these movements.

MAJOR DIVINATORY SYSTEMS

Some divinatory methods became especially sophisticated, like the *I Ching* (The Book of Changes). This requires the casting of yarrow stalks or coins to obtain negative-positive (*yin-yang*) combinations, which enable a set of hexagrams from a total of 64 to be identified, allowing for a broad range of formulaic interpretations.

The best-known and most widely used type of formalized divination today is undoubtedly astrology. The term covers a range of similar divinatory systems designed to plot the influence of heavenly bodies on earthly events. Its origins reach back to when human beings first gazed at the night sky, and the astronomical orientations of the great prehistoric megalithic monuments like Stonehenge were more than likely part of an astrological science now lost to humankind.

TRANCE DIVINATION

Diviners have used a variety of methods based on hypnotic gazing at lustrous surfaces to access prophetic trance. The use of crystals (scrying), mirrors (catoptromancy), and bowls or pools of water (hydromancy) was common in many ancient cultures. In Hungary seers would apparently use a fingernail smeared with poppy-seed oil, or even spittle, to provide a reflective gazing surface. Mayan diviners used obsidian (black volcanic glass). Seers in some cultures obtained shiny dark surfaces, similar to obsidian, by moistening the surface of a piece of slate.

Trance divination was also often associated with the phenomenon of oracles. Probably the most famous oracle temple of antiquity was Delphi, Greece. People came from far and wide to consult the prophetess, the *Pythia*, there. She seated herself on a special three-legged stool that was said to span a fissure in the ground. Long discounted by scholars, it has now been scientifically confirmed that a geological fault does indeed pass beneath the site of the divination chamber and that hydrocarbon fumes once issued from it. These fumes would have caused the *Pythia* to fall into a trance—she was, in effect, the more controlled equivalent of a modern glue sniffer.

Fortune-Telling: The Future Foretold

When people think of fortune-telling, what comes to mind is a Gypsy woman practicing palmistry, gazing into a crystal ball, or dealing and reading cards. Most Gypsies say that palmistry is the most popular method they use to predict the future. This is followed by crystallomancy, the art of scrying, and cartomancy, reading the cards.

Bare Bones

- Fortune-telling is an informal term for divination, most often applied to the forms of the art traditionally popular with the Romany people.

- These forms of divination include palmistry, crystallomancy, cartomancy, and rune casting.

- Palmistry, or chiromancy, involves interpreting the lines on a subject's hands.

- Crystallomancy, or scrying, involves staring at a highly reflective surface, most often a crystal ball, until an image appears, and cartomancy is the art of reading the cards.

Records show that Gypsy fortune-tellers practiced in both France and Germany as early as 1414, the year when the presence of Gypsies was first noted in Europe. Because they arrived there from the East, Europeans of the time thought that they originated in Turkey, Nubia, or possibly came from as far away as Egypt. Among other things, they were christened Gyptians, which is how the word Gypsy originated.

CHOVIHANI, DRABARDI, AND DUKKERING

Many people believed that Gypsies, or Roma, possess remarkable psychic abilities. These are said to be innate, springing from a close relationship with nature and a consequent bond with the spirits of the outdoors. This combination apparently allows psychic powers to evolve over time, and the ability to perform various types of magic naturally follows.

Gypsies who possess this ability are called *chovihani*. They are the witches, warlocks, and wizards of the Romani world. The majority of them are women. The fortune-tellers are *drabardi*, and what they do is termed *bocht* and *dukkering*. *Dukkering* appeals to the Roma for several reasons. First, there is the obvious attraction of the mystery and magic it provides. Second, it is a relatively simple way of making money. A skilled practitioner can probe the character of the client and manipulate his or her desires accordingly.

UNDERSTANDING PALMISTRY

Palmistry is said to have originated in India more than 3,000 years ago. What it cannot do is make specific predictions, but according to palmists, it is a useful tool in helping people shape their destinies. The argument is that the hand is like a graph that reflects emotional and physical changes over time.

According to palmists, if you are right-handed, the left hand indicates inherited personality traits, while the right hand shows potential. If you are left-handed, this is reversed. A reading involves having both palms read. The lines on them all have specific names, relating to the aspects of the personality that they govern. The life line indicates physical vitality, the head line intellectual capacity, the heart line emotional nature, and so on. Some palmists also claim they can tell what a person is like by the overall

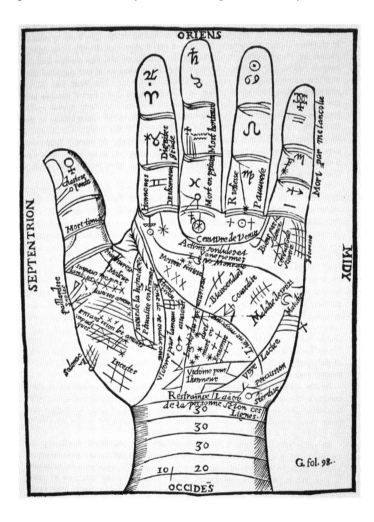

Palmistry is an ancient form of fortune-telling that remains popular today. As well as the major lines on a hand, palmists study its overall shape and features, such as the mounts of Jupiter, Saturn, Venus, Mercury, Mars, and the moon to give a personalized reading.

At the Bottom of a Teacup

Reading tea leaves to predict the future became extremely popular in Victorian times and is still practiced widely today, as is the reading of coffee grounds. It is technically known as tasseomancy.

The idea is that the fortune-teller drinks from a cup of tea until only a teaspoonful is left in the cup. Alternatively, the questioner, or querant, is asked to drink the tea. Either way, the dregs are swirled around three times before any remaining liquid is drained into the saucer and the tea leaves then read.

The patterns formed by the leaves in the cup are the basis for the fortune-teller's predictions, which usually focus on the immediate and near future. Straight lines, for instance, indicate careful planning and peace of mind, while a cup shape signifies love and harmony. Bubbles are said to represent money, while drops signify tears or some sort of sadness.

shape of their hands. Creative people, for instance, often possess fan-shaped hands, while sensitive ones have narrow pointy fingers and fleshy palms.

SCRYING IN ACTION

Though crystallomancy, or scrying, is commonly thought to depend on the use of the traditional crystal ball, any reflective surface, which may be flat or spherical, can be employed. In the sixteenth century the renowned French seer Nostradamus, for instance, chose to scry into a bowl of water. Dr. John Dee, the equally celebrated astrological adviser to Queen Elizabeth I of England, scryed into a polished obsidian disk—a "black mirror" that had been brought back from Mexico.

According to its practitioners, the art is a fairly easy one to master. It should be done in a darkened room, with a candle or table lamp positioned so the light does not distract from the task. This involves focusing intently on the crystal ball or whichever tool is being employed. The ball will eventually start to cloud over. The clouds then clear and a void appears, from which images should start to arise. Ideally, they should appear midway between the practitioner and whatever instrument he or she is using. This is a clear indication that the practitioner is seeing with the "inner eye."

The images can be literal or symbolic. Generally, whatever images appear to the left are concerned with the present. Any images to the right are symbolic—clouds, for instance, are said to be a sign of trouble ahead—and the practitioner needs to interpret them in detail. Those to the front and the back reveal events in the future and the past respectively.

RUNES AND RUNE CASTING

Rune casting is another widely practiced form of divination, though its origins do not go as far back as some other fortune-telling techniques. Runes may have gained their reputation for being tools of divination, thanks to the medieval church, whose leaders claimed that they were being used to cast magic spells and to communicate with the devil.

The runes themselves are characters in three ancient alphabets (or *futharks,* as they are more properly known), which are generally carved on wood or stone. The belief is that by casting them, it is possible to see into the future by analyzing the way in which the symbols fall. The runes are placed in a special bag, sight unseen. The rune caster than swirls them around gently with his or her writing hand until finally one falls naturally into the fingers. The process is repeated one at a time until all the runes required for the particular cast are drawn.

As each rune is drawn, it is placed on a cloth. This is known as the field, and it stands for the world in which people live. The right of the field represents the past, the left represents the future, and the central area represents the present. The vertical area closest to the rune caster—near—represents the issue and the one furthest away—far—the outcome. The runes are positioned working from right to left and then vertically from near to far. They should always be placed exactly as they come to hand.

"We still do not know one-ten thousandth of one percent of what nature has revealed to us." —ALBERT EINSTEIN, PHYSICIST

BELIEVERS AND SKEPTICS

Whether or not paranormal powers are involved in fortune-telling is open to dispute. Most psychics say that the instruments that may be employed in it—crystal balls, tarot cards, runic symbols, and the like—do not possess any powers of their own. Rather, they act as a focus for the practitioner's own psychic sensitivity, stimulating what psychics call the Third Eye.

Skeptics argue that, as there is no scientific proof to support the existence of such a phenomenon, it is wishful thinking at best and deliberate fraud at worst. Claims of success, they say, are the result of cold reading and the exercise of selective memory. It is also true, they opine, that humans are very clever at finding meaning where there is none and giving significance to what is actually meaningless.

Tarot Reading: All in the Cards

Tarot traces its origins back to the first half of the fifteenth century, when someone in northern Italy devised the first set of tarot cards. This consisted of 78 cards, which were used to play a newly devised and soon popular trick-taking card game called Triumphs. In North America today, the most common tarot deck is the Rider-Waite deck. A. E. Waite, a prominent member of the occult group Hermetic Order of the Golden Dawn, devised it in 1909 in conjunction with publisher Rider & Company.

Bare Bones

- Tarot reading is a popular form of divination in which cards from a tarot pack are laid in a pattern and interpreted by the reader.

- The origins of the tarot pack are obscure, dating back as far as the early 1400s, when it was used to play a card game.

- There are many tarot decks available, each with different designs. The most popular is the Rider–Waite deck.

The link between tarot and the occult was forged in the late eighteenth and early nineteenth centuries, when devotees of the occult arts in France and England first began to claim that they could see mystical, magical meanings in the symbolism of the cards. Eventually, this led to tarot's worldwide recognition as a major fortune-telling tool.

HOW TAROT WORKS

Traditionally, the tarot deck consists of two sets of cards. One contains 22 picture cards, including the Fool, the Devil, Temperance, the Hermit, the Sun, the Lovers, the Wheel of Fortune, the Hanged Man, and Death. These are the so-called major arcana. The other set—the minor arcana—contains 56 cards and mirrors a traditional set of playing cards with kings, queens, knights, and pages as the court cards. The four tarot suits are wands, swords, pentacles, and cups. These correspond to the four traditional elements—fire, air, earth, and water. Symbolically, they are associated with spirit, intellect, matter, and emotion.

Before a reading, the cards are gathered together, shuffled, and cut, the shuffle being performed by the person receiving the reading. Following this, the reader arranges the cards one by one in a pattern known as the spread. Sometimes the first card dealt is selected as representing either the question raised or the questioner. If so, this card is termed the significator. Generally, each

card in the spread is assigned a number and the cards are flipped accordingly. Each card is interpreted individually before moving to the next. The placing of each card is important since each position indicates to what aspect of the question the card in that position refers.

READING THE TAROT

There are many varieties of spreads, ranging from one incorporating just a single card to others that use all 78 cards in the deck. The reader decides which spread to use, though the choice is often influenced by the nature of the question being asked or the type of reading required. The Celtic Cross is probably the spread most often employed. It consists of 10 cards, five arranged in a cross and four placed vertically beside it: these four are known collectively as the staff. The remaining card is positioned horizontally across the central card of the cross.

There are several ways to determine what the cards are saying, and each reader will have their own favorite interpretation. The

The Celtic Cross, the most frequently used tarot spread, revolves around the dealing of 10 cards. Normally, the first six are dealt faceup and the remaining ones facedown. The first six cards are interpreted before the remainder are exposed and interpreted in turn in the context of what has been revealed before.

The Death card. In tarot the Death card rarely, if ever, symbolizes death. Rather, it is an indication that life is about to change. It signals that although it is time for something to come to an end, it is also the moment for something new to begin.

reader starts by examining the cards in the cross. These represent what is currently going on in the questioner's life. He or she starts by looking at the cards in pairs. The bottom card of the center pair concerns the present and the top one the challenge facing the questioner. The third card to the right of this deals with what tarot experts define as the distant past and the fourth card below it the immediate past. The fifth card—the one at the top of the cross—indicates the most that can be achieved, while the sixth—to the left of center—is concerned with the immediate future.

The cards in the staff are then examined, starting at the bottom. Card 7 reveals any personal factors affecting the situation, card 8 external influences, and card 9 hopes and fears. Card 10 is concerned with the final outcome. If this is ambiguous, tarot experts advise drawing three more cards to clarify the reading.

Other commonly used spreads include the Horseshoe, the Three-Card spread, and the Astrological spread. The Horseshoe is second only to the Celtic Cross in popularity as a question-asking spread. It consists of seven cards, arranged in a semicircle or in a V shape. From left to right, they represent past, present, influences, obstacles, expectations, best course of action, and likely outcomes. The three cards in the Three-Card spread represent past, present, and future, while in the Astrological spread 12 cards are spread in a circle, so as to represent the signs of the Zodiac. A final card, which is placed in the center of the circle, is the significator, representing the questioner.

FOR AND AGAINST

Tarot certainly does not lack advocates. Emile Grillot de Givry, a noted French writer on the occult, was one who did not stint his praise. In his book *Witchcraft, Magic & Alchemy* he noted that tarot "is one of the most wonderful human inventions…in which destiny is reflected as in a mirror with multiple facets."

The pioneer Swiss psychologist Carl Jung was another tarot enthusiast. He attached special importance to its symbolic elements. He saw the cards as representations of what he called archetypes—that is, the fundamental patterns or forms of thought and experience that lie embedded deep in the subconscious. He believed that all the tarot images, "descended from the archetypes of transformation." This followed from Jung's belief in a connecting principle governing human life that was totally independent of cause and effect. He called this synchronicity. According to this principle, things that on the surface seem like a coincidence can actually help people make decisions and regulate their lives. Tarot cards provided a way of locating the necessary pathways.

The skeptics, however, are dismissive, arguing that it is irrational to expect anyone's fate to be contained in a pack of cards. They say that, in common with other types of fortune-telling, a belief in tarot and its powers is simply misguided mysticism.

Questions and Answers

Broadly, there are two different types of tarot reading—question readings and open readings. In the former a specific question is addressed. The latter examines the larger issues of life, rather than the specifics. Tarot experts believe the way in which a question is stated is extremely important.

The vital points to remember are to keep options open, make sure that the question, though focused, is not overly detailed and, if making a reading for yourself, the focus is on you, rather than anyone else. When it comes to detail, rather than concentrating on one particular aspect of a problem, try to find a way of looking at the issue broadly.

Questions should also be neutral and stated positively, not negatively. Instead of asking why something has failed to happen, for instance, the questioner should always ask what he or she can do to make it happen.

Witchcraft

People have believed in the power of witchcraft since the dawn of recorded time. Witches—most of whom were women—were originally seen as wise healers, with the power to nurture as well as to destroy. Eventually, though, respect turned to fear. As a result, witches were often forced to live their lives as outcasts; some of them even lost their lives.

Witch Hunts and Witch Trials

Witch hunts in Europe began in earnest in the late fifteenth century, shortly after Pope Innocent VIII ordered the treatise *Malleus Maleficarum* (Hammer of Witches) to be published. Its message was clear and simple. It was the duty of all Christians to hunt down witches and kill them. Witchcraft was feared and misunderstood, and anyone who used potions for healing or exhibited psychic powers was blamed for outbreaks of plague, famine, and other disasters.

Hysteria grew apace from the early 1500s onward. In the period between 1500 and 1650, the European continent saw the execution of between 50,000 and 80,000 suspected witches. By the late seventeenth century the mania was abating. The coming of the Enlightenment contributed greatly to this; its rational ideas helping to defeat the superstitions that had plagued past ages. The last judicial execution for witchcraft in Europe took place in Poland in 1793.

Witchcraft in the Spotlight

Witchcraft has been the theme of many successful movies, including the classic romantic comedy I Married a Witch *(1942) which starred Veronica Lake and Frederick March, and Disney's lighthearted* Hocus Pocus *(1993), which cast Bette Middler and Sarah Jessica Parker as seventeenth century Salem witches who return to wreak havoc in the twentieth century. The darker side of the art is portrayed in* The Craft *(1996), which examines the consequences when four teenage girls dabble in powerful magic. On television one of the best-loved and longest-running supernatural-themed shows was* Bewitched, *which ran from 1964 to 1972.*

The Salem Witches

In the United States there was one great outbreak of witchcraft hysteria. It took place between June and September 1692 in Salem, Massachusetts, in the heart of Puritan New England. Several hundred people were accused. Many were held in prison for months without trial, while 19 were sentenced to be hanged.

Modern Witchcraft

Today belief in witchcraft survives in places as far removed as Central Africa and the Appalachian Mountains of North America. As well as traditional witches, there are green witches, hedge witches, hereditary witches, and kitchen or cottage witches. In Pennsylvania, the so-called Pow-Wows consider themselves Christians endowed with

Wicca is now one of the largest minority religions in the world, with an estimated 750,000 active adherents in the United States alone. These Texan Wiccans are taking part in one of the religion's major festivals, known as sabbats.

supernatural powers. Their rituals feature charms and incantations dating back to the Middle Ages, as well as elements borrowed from the Jewish kabbalah and the Bible.

The majority of modern witches, though, are followers of Wicca. This is a pagan religion established in the late 1940s and 1950s largely because of the efforts of Gerald Gardner, an English mystic, who redefined witchcraft as a life-affirming, positive force, which harnesses natural powers for the good of the individual and the community. His main tenet was, "If it does no harm, do your own will."

Wiccans believe in neither the devil nor the Christian notion of hell. They believe that they can become one with what they term the life force, or cosmic energy, by performing various rituals, and that they can control and direct it to bring about personal change through the application of magic. Wicca, however, must never be used to harm another person. If it is abused, the magic will rebound on the abuser threefold. A 2001 study by the Graduate Center of the City University of New York reported that Wicca is, in percentage terms, the fastest-growing religion in the United States.

Voodoo: A Multitude of Spirits

Despite its popular associations with black magic, zombies, and hexing enemies by sticking pins into wax dolls, voodoo is more like a religion than anything else. This oral tradition originated in West Africa some 6,000 years ago and varies from person to person and place to place. It has no sacred text or prayer book, and no fixed rituals or beliefs.

Bare Bones

- Voodoo is an oral spiritual tradition that originated in West Africa 6,000 years ago. Its practices vary widely between different regions and from person to person.

- It is a monotheistic tradition that acknowledges a single, supreme deity. Followers may only communicate with this deity through the agency of spirits.

- During voodoo ceremonies the participants ask the spirits for help, advice, or protection. In return they must perform certain rituals, the most notable of which is animal sacrifice.

BONDYE AND IOA

The Voodoo tradition affirms one supreme god. In Haiti he is called Bondye, which is derived from the French *bon dieu* (good god). In other places Bondye goes by different names, but no matter what name people use, he is immensely powerful. He is also unapproachable, which is why practitioners of voodoo rely on thousands of other spirits to communicate with their god.

In Haiti these spirits are known as Ioa or Iwa, and there is a strict hierarchy. There are major spirits and minor ones, all of whom receive their power from Bondye and communicate with him on behalf of their followers. In addition, most communities and even individual families have their own special Ioa. These are more often than not the spirits of loved or influential deceased community or family members.

During voodoo ceremonies the participants ask the spirits for help, advice, or protection. In return they must perform certain rituals, the most notable of which is animal sacrifice. The Ioa communicate with their followers through what is termed possession. This means temporarily displacing the soul of its host—the medium—and taking control of his or her body.

VOODOO TRADITIONS

The notion of possession unites the two distinct voodoo traditions—that of the northern and central parts of the West African coast and the form of voodoo practiced in Haiti and parts of North and South America. African voodoo today is centered in Benin, Togo, and Ghana, where it has around 30 million adherents.

A Haitian man balances a human skull on his head in honor of Fet Gede, a voodoo holiday commemorating one's dead ancestors. Fet Gede is a national holiday in Haiti, where voodoo has been actively practiced since French colonial rule.

In the Caribbean a somewhat different tradition evolved, primarily as the result of the official requirement for all African slaves to be baptized as Christians. As a result, the forcibly converted slaves borrowed many elements of Catholicism and incorporated them into traditional ritual.

VOODOO AND HOODOO

Voodoo is widely practiced in Haiti, and in 2003 it was made the official state religion. However, in other parts of the Western world, it is regarded with intense suspicion. One of the reasons for this is the way voodoo has been portrayed in books and movies. Another is the growth of a bastardized variant of voodoo, known as hoodoo. Hoodoo's stronghold is New Orleans and other parts of the American South. Its practitioners are said to use evil magic—bad juju—to inflict harm. Hence, casting love spells and making curses should be classified as hoodoo rather than voodoo. These are not voodoo practices at all.

Ghosts & Hauntings

The strangely pleasant thrill of terror when confronted with the unknown forms the basis of many horror movies and books. Nothing has provided more inspiration to the masters of film or written horror than those spirits of the dead that return to stalk the Earth on macabre, terrifying business. Leaping through solid walls and floating on wispy tails, these ghosts are, almost without exception, hostile to the living and come armed with all manner of gruesome surprises. As with so much of the unseen world, "real" ghosts are quite unlike their fictional counterparts. But they are no less unnerving.

Defining Ghosts

In the popular imagination a ghost is the spirit of a dead person—or occasionally animal—that is seen moving around as if it were still alive. Such spirits are generally thought to come equipped with clothes, tools, or other objects that they used in life. Ghosts like these may indeed exist, but there is also far more to the world of specters.

Bare Bones

- Ghosts are believed to be the spirits of dead people that have survived their bodily deaths, though apparitions of the living have also been reported.

- Because ghosts are often reported to repeat the same actions, some have suggested they are not returning spirits, but a recording of past events that somehow gets replayed.

- Poltergeists are different from other ghosts. They remain invisible, fling objects around, and even attack people.

BACK FROM THE GRAVE

Apparitions of living people are occasionally reported, but the vast majority of recorded ghosts are of deceased individuals. The actress Vivien Leigh (1913–1967) has been seen haunting Culver Studios in Hollywood for the past 10 years, and Abraham Lincoln has been spotted several times strolling around the White House in Washington, D.C. Most ghosts cannot, however, be so easily identified. The warship USS *Alabama* is preserved in Mobile Harbor. Several visitors have reported seeing the figure of a tall thin-faced blond man walking the ship in naval uniform. Presumably the ghost is that of a former officer on the ship, but which one is unknown.

One thing most ghosts have in common is that, when seen, they appear quite solid. They are not semitransparent, nor do they walk through walls. Were it not for their old-fashioned clothes, they might be mistaken for living humans. But often witnesses who see ghosts state that there was something odd about them that first attracted attention. This oddness can be difficult to pin down. A witness who reported seeing a ghost at McLoughlin House in Oregon City reported that the phantom seemed to "shimmer somewhat like I was seeing it through one of those weird filter things they use on sci-fi shows on TV."

REPEATING PATTERNS

Such apparitions might be described as being classic ghosts. The vast majority of phantoms fit this pattern. They haunt specific places and do not move objects around or interact with the humans who see them. Often they do the same things time after time. Ball Cemetery, on Highway 50 outside Omaha, Nebraska, is haunted by a man in a small two-wheeled carriage pulled by a horse. The carriage pulls up outside the cemetery entrance, and the man climbs down. Then the whole apparition vanishes.

Some say that these ghosts are *not* the returning spirits of the dead. If they were, surely they would soon tire of repeating the same routine. Instead, it has been proposed that they represent some kind of recording of past events that is replayed from time to time. This is supported by the fact that many hauntings seem to be affected by their surroundings. A former hotel in Chicago, Illinois, had been converted in the 1980s into a fashionable apartment development. There was no report of supernatural activity until the construction. Then a man in a long gray 1940s-style overcoat, with a fedora hat pulled down over his face, started showing up with some regularity.

The fact that many of these ghosts seem to be subject to strong emotions has led some to suggest that these apparitions are caused by the power of strong feelings that have become imprinted on the places where they occurred. Many ghosts are unidentified, but when their background *is* known, they are often linked to murder, unrequited love, or family tragedy of one kind or another.

OTHER SPIRITS

Any explanation for these classic ghosts cannot extend to cover all ghostly manifestations. Poltergeists show a different range of characteristics. Objects are not only moved, but are flung about with great strength. The supernatural agent that causes this mayhem is never seen and rarely identified. Less easy to explain are the spirits that seem to be at work in the cases of possession or demonic work reported from time to time. If classic ghosts are indifferent to humanity and poltergeists apparently mischievous in intent, these entities seem positively hostile.

Clearly there is no single explanation that can cover the range of ghosts and specters that are reported around the world. Whatever is happening is more bizarre and inexplicable than that.

Ghosts in the Spotlight

Film and television producers have always been quick to cash in on our fascination for all things ghostly. Tsui Hark's Cantonese-language movie *A Chinese Ghost Story* proved a roaring success when it was released in 1987.

The story follows the adventures of Ning, a timid tax collector, as he attempts to save the spirit of the beautiful Nie, whose soul was enslaved by a powerful tree demon when her ashes were inadvertently buried beneath it. The movie provided a catalyst for a whole new wave of folklore ghost films in the Hong Kong film industry.

One of Hollywood's more famous depictions of life after death was the 1990 romantic thriller *Ghost*. Its famous potter's wheel scene inspired a host of parodies. Tim Burton's *Sleepy Hollow* (1999) was a memorable modern interpretation of the enduring legend of the headless horseman and was loosely based on Washington Irving's chilling story *The Legend of Sleepy Hollow* (1820). Irving's story was first brought to the big screen in the 1922 silent movie *The Headless Horseman*, directed by Edward Venturini and starring Will Rogers as Ichabod Crane.

Ghost Hunters and Their Methods

There is no recognized body that controls the activities of ghost hunters, nor is there any exam or test that would-be ghost hunters need to pass to qualify for the title. Ghost hunters come in all shades of seriousness, dedication, and skill. Some merely delight in collecting tales of haunted houses, while others investigate further, determined to learn what facts lie behind each ghost story.

Bare Bones

- Ghost hunting is a relatively modern occupation, with one of the earliest accounts coming from 1901.

- Most ghost hunters are amateurs, although they often organize themselves into groups.

- One of the most prolific recent ghost-hunting partnerships was that of Ed and Lorraine Warren, who founded the New England Society for Psychical Research.

- Ghosthunters employ a variety of tools, from the Ouija board and trigger object to the high-tech EMF detector and motion-sensitive camera.

The vast majority of ghost hunters are amateurs, simply because there are no paid jobs for ghost hunters. Even those universities and other institutions willing to fund investigations into the paranormal stay away from the subject of ghosts. They prefer to put money into phenomena that can be replicated and tested in laboratory conditions. A wraith seen in a shop or house once every few weeks does not match the criteria for funding. The study of such phantoms is left to those who choose to spend their leisure time on such investigations. The amateur status of ghost hunters does not mean that their work is not serious and carefully conducted. Many investigations have become minor classics of investigative scientific work.

EARLY INVESTIGATIONS

Although ghosts have been reported for centuries, the activity of ghost hunting is a twentieth-century innovation. One of the earliest accounts dates from May 1901. Earlier that year, a writer for the *Daily Mail* newspaper in London had abruptly changed his address. When Ralph Blumenfeld, the paper's editor, asked why, he was told that the man was leaving because the rooms in Lincoln's Inn were haunted. Intrigued, Blumenfeld contacted the landlord and rented the rooms for a week to investigate the haunting, planning to write up the experience for his newspaper.

Blumenfeld arranged for the rooms to be stripped of all furniture and window treatments so that there would be nowhere for a hoaxer to hide. He then sealed the windows, checked for hidden

This famous picture appears to be the holy grail of ghost hunters; it is a clear image of a ghost. It purports to show the Brown Lady of Raynham Hall in England, but skeptics have largely dismissed it as the result of either deliberate double exposure or failure of the camera equipment, resulting in a light anomaly.

access, and filled any holes in floorboards and walls. On the evening of May 11, Blumenfeld and a friend, Sir Max Pemberton, went to stay the night in the supposedly haunted rooms. On arrival they locked the front door and sprinkled chalk powder liberally around the rooms. During the course of the night, the doors opened and closed by themselves several times. The performance ceased at 2:07 A.M., and it was then that the two men noticed the footprints of a large bird in the chalk.

The events were odd, but they fell short of the hoped-for ghost sighting. Blumenfeld wrote a short article for his newspaper. A week after it was published, he received a letter from a Spiritualist medium named Margaret Verrall. At the time that Blumenfeld and Pemberton were watching the doors open and close, she had been receiving a spirit message in the form of automatic writing. The message read, "Chalk sticking to the feet has got over the difficulty. You help greatly by always persevering." The message ended with a drawing of a turkeylike bird with a smiling human face.

Ghost hunters claim that orbs such as this one are the first stages of the manifestation of a ghost, but others believe that they are nothing more than out-of-focus images of flecks of dust or insects.

MODERN GHOSTBUSTING

These days things have progressed considerably. Ghost hunters go to work armed with all sorts of high-tech equipment. Numerous witnesses have reported that the temperature of a room drops when a ghost is around. Meteorological equipment designed to record air temperature is standard for a ghost-hunting expedition. This can be left in a room for hours to record the temperature. Sound recorders may also be left in sealed rooms to record any supernatural sounds that occur, and ghost hunters may also employ motion-sensitive cameras.

In October 2003 a motion-sensitive camera produced a startling image at Hampton Court Palace in the UK. A security camera was triggered when a door flew open, and the subsequent photo showed a female figure dressed in Tudor-style costume. Nobody had been near the door at the time, and nobody had such a costume.

One of the better-known modern ghost-hunting organizations is The Atlantic Paranormal Society (TAPS), which has been in Warwick, Rhode Island, since 1990. Its fame is partly due to the fact that in 2004 it became the subject of a weekly reality television series for the Sci-Fi Channel entitled *Ghost Hunters*. The Society typically puts together a team of up to six members to undertake a 12-hour investigation into hauntings reported to them. They go equipped with all the most modern equipment available to ghost hunters. The Atlantic Paranormal Society does not charge for their services and, unlike some groups, are as content to disprove a haunting as to find evidence of genuine paranormal activity.

Another hugely successful ghost-hunting team were Ed Warren and his wife, Lorraine. They began work in the 1950s and continued until Ed's death in 2006. The couple founded the New England Society for Psychical Research (NESPR), which undertakes investigations and shares information with other organizations and individuals. The NESPR has investigated over 4,000 cases of alleged hauntings, with most of the work done by the Warrens themselves. It has amassed an impressive amount of data and personal testimony about all aspects of the paranormal.

TOOLS OF THE TRADE

Ghost-hunting tools of long standing are the Ouija board and the planchette, used to channel messages from spirits of the deceased, but a recent addition to the ghost hunter's toolkit is the electromagnetic field (EMF) detector. This piece of the kit has become so well regarded that some refer to it as a ghost detector. Leaving aside the fact that no serious theory has been put forward to explain how EMFs are linked to ghosts, relatively minor factors can affect an EMF. A room on top of a major electricity cable will have a much different EMF from an identical room without such a cable. The use of an EMF detector is most problematic when it is handheld and moved around a building. Passing close to hidden cables and pipes can cause dramatic changes. That said, many haunted sites do seem to have an EMF considerably stronger than the normal background field, and when an EMF meter is left static and monitored carefully, it will sometimes give a dramatic leap or spike in a reportedly haunted location.

IN THE MIDDLE OF THE NIGHT

Many aspects of ghost hunting are subject to debate among dedicated ghost hunters. Some believe that ghost hunts are best held at night. This is not just because that is when ghosts appear—they may actually be seen at any hour—but because in the modern world, motor traffic, machinery, and humans add noise and distractions to the experiment. The night is quieter and calmer, so any anomalous sounds or sights are easier to spot.

Another dispute involves the optimum duration of a ghost hunt. Time is usually limited for those taking part, so in recent years it has become the norm for a ghost-hunting team to stay in a haunted building all night to maximize the chances of a ghostly experience. Some claim that by around 4:00 A.M. tired ghost hunters are more likely to imagine sounds or sights.

Such disputes reflect the uncertain nature of ghosts and ghostly phenomena. They also demonstrate that most ghost hunters take their task seriously and genuinely try to find reliable evidence of elusive phenomena.

Orbs

Since the 1970s increasing numbers of ghost hunters have reported the phenomenon of orbs in the course of their work. These orbs are luminous balls of light that seem to have no solid reality, but flick in and out of existence. They have been seen occasionally with the naked eye but turn up more often in photographs.

Photos including orbs have been submitted to photographic experts for analysis, and the results proved that the photos had not been tampered with in any way and that they did, indeed, show spherical luminous objects floating about. During the 1990s the number of orbs appearing in photos increased dramatically with the wider ownership of digital cameras.

Some investigators have noticed that orbs tend to appear in photos taken with a flash in dark or gloomy rooms. It has been suggested that orbs are, in fact, specks of dust close to the camera that are reflecting light from the flash but are so out of focus that the tiny specks are distorted and thus appear as round balls of semitransparent light.

Famous Hauntings

Some ghosts become internationally famous, becoming bywords for horror and terror. No one knows why some become so well known, while other, equally horrific stories are known only to those who live close to their origins. Sometimes the ghost may take its fame from the building it haunts—such as the phantoms that stalk the Tower of London—others from the fame of the person whose shade they are. A few, however, hit the headlines simply because they are newsworthy in themselves.

Bare Bones

- One of the first hauntings to achieve notoriety was the case of the Bell Witch of Tennessee, which began tormenting the Bell family in 1817.

- The haunting of 112 Ocean Avenue, Amityville, New York, is perhaps the most famous haunting of all, but to what extent the phenomena reported were genuine is fiercely debated. Some have suggested that the case owes its fame more to media coverage than to facts.

THE BELL WITCH

One of the first such hauntings to achieve international notoriety was the Bell Witch of Tennessee. In 1817 the Bell family of Robertson County were subjected to a violent paranormal assault that became famous in its day and was subsequently recorded by one of the family members. The Bells were a respectable Christian family that owned a cotton plantation and treated their slaves well by contemporary standards. A close family friend was Andrew Jackson, later to be President of the United States, and he witnessed some of the events.

The trouble began with loud knocks on the door and windows of the house. Thinking they were the victims of mischievous children or somebody with a grudge, John Bell, the father of the family, set watchmen outside his house. They never saw anybody approaching the building, but the knockings continued. The Bells became alarmed when they heard sounds of a human coughing and choking, followed by lip smacking and gulping. After a few months of these noises, the mysterious intruder turned nasty. Three of the Bell's children, Richard, Joel, and Elizabeth, had their hair pulled so violently that they each fell out of bed, screaming in terror and pain. Eventually John Bell called in a neighbor named James Johnson who conducted an impromptu exorcism. The disturbances ceased.

A month later they were back with redoubled fury. The disturbances now centered around the 12-year-old Elizabeth and her father. Invisible hands pulled Elizabeth's hair and slapped her face, while John's bed was shaken as he slept. The knocks sounded loudest when he was present.

By 1818 the supernatural visitor had begun to acquire a voice. At first the family only heard muttered whispers, but within a couple of months, the voice could be heard clearly. It seemed to be the voice of an elderly woman. At first it repeated phrases from the Bible or from the sermons of local preachers but soon turned to obscenities and lewd remarks.

One neighbor, perhaps bolder than the others, asked the spirit who it was. After muttered obscenities, the voice declared, "I am old Kate Batt's Witch." The Kate Batt referred to was a local woman who prepared herbal medicines for the slaves and poorer white folk and occasionally told fortunes. Batt denied all knowledge of the troublesome spirit or of witchcraft, but the idea that it was a witch causing the trouble stuck, and the spirit became known as the Bell Witch.

For months the Bell Witch continued to torment the unfortunate family. Noises and disgusting smells became commonplace around the house, and objects were thrown about by invisible hands. On December 19, 1820, John Bell was found in bed in a stupor. Nearby was a bottle of smoky brown liquid instead of his usual tonic. "It's useless for you to try to relieve Old Jack," called out the Witch. "I have got him this time. He will never get up." When John junior demanded to know what she meant, the witch replied, "I put it there and gave old Jack a big dose out of it last night while he was asleep. That fixed him." It did, indeed, for John Bell was dead within hours.

Some believed that the Bell Witch had, indeed, killed John Bell. Others thought that the poor man had committed suicide because he had been suffering from depression. Whatever the cause, his death was the beginning of the end. Within weeks the Bell Witch's antics had virtually ceased. Early in 1821 the voice called from behind a chimney, "I'm going and will be gone seven years." Seven years later some scratching sounds were heard in the house, but the Bell Witch did not return.

The Wicked Major

The haunting of West Bow in Edinburgh, Scotland, shows how even a famous haunting can sometimes be based more on rumor and scandal than fact.

Major Thomas Weir lived for many years in the seventeenth century in West Bow, off Grassmarket, in Edinburgh. He was a famously devout Protestant with a distinguished career as an army officer. Then, in February 1670, Weir confessed to being a powerful magician who was in league with the devil, who had led him into sexual perversity, violence, and murder. His friends were shocked and astonished, and he was duly hanged in the Grassmarket.

Within weeks the major's house was said to be haunted. It could not be rented out, so it was demolished and replaced. The tales of hauntings then moved to the Grassmarket, where the major was said to gallop by on a phantom, fiery steed. These stories are repeated regularly to this day. But although most citizens of Edinburgh know of the ghostly major, nobody has ever recorded actually seeing the phantom. It seems the notorious events prompted stories of a haunting that never happened.

The Ghost of Griffintown

Every seven years on the anniversary of her death, the ghost of murdered prostitute Mary Gallagher is said to return to the very spot in Montreal where fellow prostitute Susan Kennedy killed her in a jealous, drunken rage.

Gallagher's murder, in the largely Irish neighborhood of Griffintown, occurred on June 26, 1879, as the two women were fighting over the favors of the same customer.

Kennedy, who was eventually convicted and jailed for her crime, hacked off Gallagher's head and put it in a bucket. Ever since that day, witnesses have reported occasional sightings of a headless figure wearing a black cloak passing them on the street.

To this da, dozens of curious onlookers gather at the corner of Murray and William streets every seven years in hopes of glimpsing the phantom apparition. The next spirit vigil will take place on June 26, 2012.

THE AMITYVILLE HORROR

Surpassing the Bell Witch with its fame is the nameless, shapeless terror usually referred to as the Amityville Horror, though many suspect that events surrounding this haunting may have been exaggerated in an attempt to cash in.

The story began in the early hours of November 15, 1974, at the large house at 112 Ocean Avenue in Amityville, New York. For no apparent reason Ronald DeFeo got out of bed, took his father's gun, and shot his parents, two brothers, and two sisters dead. He later claimed that a voice had told him that his family members were plotting to kill him, so he had shot them all in self-defense.

In December 1975 George and Kathy Lutz bought the home and moved in together with Kathy's three children from a previous marriage. According to the Lutz's later account, strange things began happening almost at once. George heard the sounds of a brass band playing. Doors and windows that had been shut were found open, and those left open were found closed. The Lutzes called in a local priest, who blessed the house and expressed concern about a possible presence.

The blessing did little good. The Lutzes reported that a face like that of a devil was seen peering in through the windows, and cloven-hoofed prints were seen in snow in the garden. George Lutz said that he thought that he was intermittently possessed by an evil spirit. Hundreds of flies appeared from nowhere in one of the rooms on a regular basis, while disgusting smells permeated the house. When the family began to see ghosts and one child reported that it was being visited at night by a ghostly pig, the Lutzes had had enough. They moved out.

A month later a TV network moved in with a team of mediums to conduct a televised séance. This and subsequent attempts to contact the spirits revealed that the house was haunted by demonic spirits. The area had allegedly been used by the local Shinnecock Indians as a place where the sick and insane were left to die. Later that year a book entitled *The Amityville Horror*, authored by the Lutz couple and writer Jay Anson, came out. This gave a lurid account of the events that had plagued the Lutz

The house in Amityville that was to become famous as the scene of the Amityville Horror hauntings. The house is currently in private hands, and no supernatural events have been reported there for many years.

family. A movie followed that was even more spectacular in its effects. The story spread around the world and became perhaps the most famous haunting of the later twentieth century.

It was not long, however, before doubts surfaced. Paranormal investigator Dr. Stephen Kaplan came forward to claim that he had been contacted by Lutz to investigate the haunting but had been dropped when the TV company took an interest. Kaplan investigated anyway and turned up inconsistencies in the Lutz account—such as the fact that there was no snow on the day they claimed to have seen footprints. Lutz was later to admit that he had exaggerated some events to make the book and film more sensational, but to his dying day he maintained that there had been a real outbreak of demonic activity.

Whatever the truth, the house is now quiet. The family that lives there seem unperturbed by the property's controversial history and do not welcome sightseers.

Haunted Highways

From ancient times people of all cultures have often believed their landscape to be haunted by ghosts of the dead, wraiths of the living, and various kinds of nature spirits. Bronze-Age rock carvings in southern Sweden depict footprints descending from hilltop cemeteries. On Pony Hills, a modest ridge in the New Mexico desert, tiny spirit footprints carved on rocks by Native Americans 1,000years ago mark what they thought were the tracks of nature spirits. The land still seems to be haunted today, but now people register this in terms of highway apparitions of various kinds.

Road Ghosts

The B4068 country road close to the remote village of Naunton near Gloucester in central England seems to be particularly haunted. Around 10:00 P.M. on August 26, 1998, hospital anesthetist Guy Routh was driving along that road when he saw a woman in a cream-colored dress standing on the roadside. She smiled and waved at him. Routh stopped to make sure she was all right. He looked for the woman in the pale dress, but she was nowhere in sight. On another late evening, this time in April 2000, a night security guard was driving to work on the same stretch of road. "A figure all in white appeared in front of the car out of nowhere," he reported. "It looked like a monk and was six feet tall." He saw him before he had a chance to hit the brakes and drove right through the figure. When he stopped to look, there was nothing to be seen.

Phantom Hitchhikers

A celebrated subcategory of the road ghost is the phantom hitchhiker. The accounts that come from Greensboro in North Carolina are surprisingly consistent. In 1923 drivers began to report seeing a beautiful girl in an evening gown standing next to the U.S. Highway 70 underpass and waving for someone to stop. Those drivers who take pity on her discover her name is Lydia and she wants to be taken to an address in High Point. Her story is always the same: She is returning from a dance in Raleigh but has run into problems with her car. The

Eyewitness

PAUL DEVEREUX, AUTHOR OF *HAUNTED LAND* (2001), HAS HIMSELF WITNESSED A PHANTOM VEHICLE.

"I was traveling along the M6 motorway in central England in the early morning. As I passed a shabby-looking pickup truck that had just joined the highway, I glanced sideways at the driver's cab. It looked empty. Puzzled, I sped on. After a short distance I glanced in my rearview mirror, only to see a deserted motorway behind me. With a kind of primal chill it dawned on me that I had just seen a phantom vehicle. It was no trick of the light. The incident occurred over 20 years ago, but it has never left me. If ghosts are supposedly spirits of people, I want to know how there can be spectral vehicles, things that have no souls."

One of the ancient, carved spirit footprints at Pony Hills, New Mexico, compared to an adult foot.

lady vanishes just as the car arrives at the address she has given, and upon inquiring at the house, the drivers are told that Lydia died many years ago in a car wreck on her way home from a dance in Raleigh.

The popular American actor Telly Savalas once picked up a young female hitchhiker and found that he had to borrow a few dollars from her for gas. Anxious to return the money, Savalas got the girl to write down her address before she entered the house. When he returned shortly afterward to repay his debt, the girl's mother answered the door and informed the actor that her daughter had died several years previously. Savalas recognized the girl he had picked up from photos that her mother showed him, and the mother also verified that the address Savalas had was indeed written in her dead daughter's handwriting.

Phantom Vehicles

Not all highway apparitions take human form. There are numerous accounts of ghostly vehicles—typically trucks—bearing down on alarmed drivers with such swiftness that an impact seems inevitable, but they always fade away at the critical moment. The predecessors of ghostly motor vehicles were phantom stagecoaches, a celebrated supernatural motif that has been reported for centuries. A typical sighting occurred in the 1970s, when a young couple saw the outline of a stagecoach on the lane between the Bear of Rodborough Hotel and Woodchester on Rodborough Common just south of Stroud in Gloucestershire, England. Although the form of the apparition may change with the times, it seems the phenomenon of the haunted highway is timeless.

The World's Most Haunted Places

The majority of haunted places play host to just a single specter; a few may have a pair. But some places appear awash with phantoms and specters. What causes these places to apparently attract supernatural activity is not altogether clear.

Bare Bones

- Some places seem to act like a magnet for supernatural activity. The village of Pluckley in Kent, UK, claims to be the most haunted place in the world.

- The reason for the number of ghosts associated with Gettysburg, Pennsylvania, is clear: Many men suffered trauma and lost their lives here during the climactic battle of the American Civil War.

- Burlington in Ontario claims to be the most haunted place in Canada, with ghosts in the museum, several restaurants, and a pub, as well as a haunted war memorial.

ENGLAND'S FINEST

The village of Pluckley, Kent, in England claims to be the most haunted place on Earth. There are plenty of ghosts attached to the place, though some have not been seen in recent years. The village is clustered around a large green, a church, and a small high street, and the area is fairly unremarkable—at least to human eyes.

The oldest of the various phantoms to lurk here is that of Lady Dering, who died some four centuries ago. The Derings were the local land-owning family and were well connected at Court. This particular Lady Dering was beautiful and greatly loved by her husband, but by few others. She was a ruthless and inveterate schemer who would happily ruin the lives of others to gain advantage. Like all her family, she was laid to rest in the Dering Chapel inside the parish church, but unlike them she did not rest. Within a few weeks her wraith was seen pacing around the churchyard. This Lady Dering is also blamed for knocking noises that come from the Dering Chapel and lights seen through the stained-glass windows. Lady Dering is not alone in the churchyard. A middle-aged lady in tweed has been seen flitting about the gravestones, though who she might be nobody seems to know.

Also unrecognized is the handsome young man who haunts the barn of Elvey Farm just outside the village. This ghost appears to be around 20 years old, with a neatly trimmed beard and dressed in the fashion of the later Victorian era. He has a pale face and is sometimes accompanied by the scent of singed wool.

The man who haunts the old brickworks near the railway station is a Victorian specter. This unfortunate man fell into a pit one dark night and was killed. He is not *seen* often, but the heart-rending

scream of terror from his fall echoes out frequently. Not far away is the site of the old mill, demolished around World War I. The miller who worked here in the 1860s was jilted by his fiancée. His body was found the next day swinging from a beam in the mill. His ghost lurks around the site but can only be seen by women.

Perhaps the most active of Pluckley's ghosts is the man who haunts the Black Horse Inn. The ghost of a former landlord is seen often, and he seems to take a great delight in hiding things. Keys, papers, and books have all gone missing, only to turn up again a few days or weeks later.

Among the assorted Pluckley ghosts fading from view, not having been seen for a number of years, is the army officer dressed in the bright red coat and white breeches of the eighteenth century. He is supposed to haunt the Dering Woods, striding along one of the footpaths that run out of the village. He is thought to have been one of several younger Derings who joined the army as a career. The spectral coach and four horses that is said to drive out of Pluckley along the lane toward Smarden has likewise not been seen for decades. This is a shame, for it was a most spectacular phantom, complete with a headless coachman.

The English village of Pluckley claims to be the most haunted village in the world, with several of its quaint cottages harboring a phantom or spirit of some description.

THE GHOSTS OF GETTYSBURG

Just as Pluckley is said to be the most haunted place in England, the same claim has been made in the United States for Gettysburg, Pennsylvania. Like Pluckley, Gettysburg is a pleasant if unremarkable place. But unlike Pluckley, there is no mystery as to why Gettysburg has become so haunted. Between July 1 and 3, 1863, this little town and the hills around it were the site of the turning point to the American Civil War.

The southern Confederates under General Robert E. Lee were invading the North when they stumbled on to an outpost of the

The grim aftermath of the Battle of Gettysburg, photographed the day after the battle. The battlefield and the surrounding area are said to be haunted by several of the men who died here during the U.S. Civil War.

northern Union army under General George Meade. The Unionists were driven back in the first two days to take up a last defensive position on the ridge south of the town. On the third day they drove off a determined charge led by Confederate general Pickett amid frightful slaughter. Over three days the Confederates lost 20,000 men, the Unionists 23,000.

The first sightings of ghosts began just weeks after the battle. Soldiers were seen marching over the hills, sparking fears that war was returning to the area, but it was soon clear they were ghosts. To the present day, phantoms continue to be reported by visitors to the battlefield. Some take the ghosts to be modern re-enactors in period costume, but their sudden disappearance makes it clear that this cannot be so.

Among the ghosts to be seen most often are those on Seminary Ridge, where the most intense fighting took place. One ghost is that of a Unionist cavalry officer who haunts a particular spot, presumed to be where he died. The open fields across which Pickett's men charged are haunted by several Confederates, and the sound of the famed rebel yell has been heard. Seen almost as often is the Confederate officer, nicknamed the General, who stalks down Carlisle Street. Which officer he is and whether or not he survived the battle is unclear. South of the town on Oak Ridge, a Confederate cavalryman has been seen galloping past in a great rush. Some witnesses report that he has in his hand a scrap of paper. He is thought to be the messenger sent by Lee to find General Stuart and urge him to bring his men to join the battle. Stuart arrived too late.

One non-military ghost linked to the battle is the undertaker seen near the church. During and after the battle, the church was used as an impromptu hospital. So many amputations were performed here that holes had to be drilled in the floor to drain away the blood. The ghostly undertaker walks from the church to the graveyard, located a couple of blocks away. Another building, now a hotel, which was used as a hospital after the battle, has a phantom that is both disturbing and possibly unique. It is of a severed, bloody arm that appears on a windowsill from time to time.

Most Haunted

The reason some places are haunted and others are not is as obscure as why some people seem to be more prone to seeing ghosts than others. There can be no doubt that some places that have a reputation for being haunted have acquired their notoriety simply because of their appearance or their history.

The Tower of London, for instance, has been a fortress, palace, and prison as well as a venue for murders and executions. Londoners firmly believe it to be the most haunted place in their city and tell hair-raising tales of phantom executions, ghostly bears, and headless soldiers. Investigations have shown that actual eyewitness accounts of ghosts from the Tower are rare. By way of contrast, the pleasant, welcoming, and decidedly nonspooky Tontine Hotel in Shropshire, England, produces regular reports of ghostly activity.

Non-supernatural Ghosts

Some ghost sightings have, on investigation by a ghosthunter, turned out to have non-supernatural explanations. Even the most haunted of sites may not display any spooky activity at all upon examination. A white lady ghost in a street in northern England, which locals reported seeing regularly on winter evenings in the 1980s, stemmed from the steam that escaped from a drain and caught a streetlight beam when seen from a particular angle. Another active ghost that was proved untrue came from Wiltshire, England, in the 1930s. The rural phantom was actually a white goose protecting its nest.

Other hauntings have resulted from low-frequency sounds. The shape of some rooms traps and enhances such sounds, produced by nearby traffic, for instance. These vibrations are known to affect sight, creating the illusion of fog or mist. Several apparently haunted places have turned out to have strong low-frequency sounds.

BURLINGTON BOO

Some claim that Burlington in Ontario is the most haunted place in Canada. The Joseph Brant Museum, nineteenth-century home of the Indian leader of that name, is haunted by a rather plump lady in white with the name Elisa. Reports of the ghost have been traced back to the 1870s, but she seems to have become more active since the 1970s. Elisa is seen most often on the upper floors of the building and has been glimpsed peering out of an attic window by visitors in the grounds.

The nearby Pearl Diner is located in a house built in the 1880s. The staff members have reported that doors open and close by themselves and footsteps have been heard walking up to the second floor when nobody is there. A murder was committed here in the early 1900s, and that is blamed for the supernatural activity, though whether it is the killer or the victim who returns is unclear. Another restaurant in the town, the My Thai, is haunted by a thin man in dark clothes whom the staff members nicknamed Luther. He has a habit of moving glasses and other small objects around.

The Poacher Pub, which dates back to 1826, has no less than three ghosts. One is a chimney sweep who stands quietly in a corner watching the bar as if waiting for someone. Rather more enigmatic is the ghostly Abigail, who seems to be attached to the large mirror in the bar rather than to the building. She came with the mirror and is seen most often next to it. She is a middle-aged lady dressed in late-nineteenth-century clothing. Seen more often than either of these two is the dark-haired waitress who appears rushing around the kitchen, the lounge, and an upstairs room.

Just as active is the ghost that lurks around the war memorial, which in Burlington takes the form of a statue of a World War I soldier. The ghost is generally identified as that of Alfred Edward Johnson, who was killed on August 18, 1942, during a raid on the German-occupied French town of Dieppe that went badly wrong. Johnson died a hero, holding off a determined German counterattack so that his comrades could escape back to their boats.

The ghost is often heard muttering to itself and was once heard saying, "My name is Alfred." Most astonishing are the reports that

The Princess Theater in Melbourne has the most active ghost in Australia. A phantom singer returns with regularity to haunt the stage, where he died of a stroke in 1888.

the statue moves. Its lips are seen to open and close as if the statue were talking, its eyes open and close, and the fingers move on the rifle it holds. On October 29, 2003, blood seemed to flow from the statue and was seen by more than 20 people.

TAKING A BOW

Melbourne's Princess Theater has been cited as the most haunted building in Australia. There is only one ghost here, but he is seen with astonishing regularity. On the night of March 3, 1888, the popular baritone singer Frederick Baker, who used the stage name Frederici, was playing Mephistopheles in the opera *Faust*. At the end of the performance, Frederici left the stage and promptly collapsed. The cast gathered around while a doctor pronounced Frederick dead of a massive stroke. After a few minutes the manager hesitantly went on stage to tell the audience that the cast would not be taking a bow and explained why. There was a stunned silence. The audience had just seen Frederici—or rather his ghost—take his bow. Apparently unable to accept his sudden death, Frederici has been seen many times since. The dress circle is a favorite venue for his hauntings, as is the backstage area.

Poltergeists: Things That Go Bump in the Night

Poltergeists are perhaps the most troublesome ghosts. These hauntings are characterized by bangs, raps, and unearthly noises, often accompanied by flying objects, outbreaks of fire, the sudden disappearance of objects, and their equally baffling reappearance.

Bare Bones

- The word poltergeist comes from the German for noisy ghost.

- Unlike most other spirits, these beings delight in tormenting humans by producing unnerving noises, flinging objects around violently, starting fires, and even attacking people.

- Poltergeist activity is often centered around an adolescent. Whether troubled youngsters attract some sort of spirit, cause the disturbances themselves through some sort of unconscious psychokinesis, or merely set out to deceive is the subject of hot debate.

A FAMILY AFFAIR

One of the earliest poltergeist hauntings to be recorded as fact rather than discounted as mere superstition was that which afflicted the household of farmer George Gilbertson in Yorkshire, England, in the 1780s. A local gentleman named William Henderson recorded the events. What attracted Henderson's

Maurice Grosse, the investigator sent by the Society for Psychical Research, shares some artifacts from the Enfield poltergeist case.

attention was the fact that the mischievous spirit attached itself to the Gilbertson family, not merely to the house in which they lived.

Henderson recorded that the Gilbertsons were subjected to a range of attacks of the kind that would become familiar to later investigators of poltergeists. The trouble began when the youngest boy was playing in the kitchen. He noticed that the wood had fallen out of a knot hole at the back of a cupboard. Picking up a stick, he pushed it through the hole to see how far it would go. The boy was shocked to feel the stick being pushed back out toward him with some force.

Thinking that some animal nested in the wall, the boy told his siblings. Over the next few days the children had much fun poking sticks and other objects into the hole, only for them to fly out again. Once, a stick struck a child hard on the forehead, so the parents stopped the game. The poltergeist, however, had other ideas. Always invisible, the intruder came out from behind the wood-work to tip over bowls of food, snatch bread from the table, and play other tricks. It took to pushing the children into closets or cupboards, then slamming and locking the doors to trap them. When one child took a tumble downstairs, Mrs. Gilbertson declared that she had had enough. The Gilbertsons sacrificed their lease on the farm and found another farm nearby. The family packed up, loaded its belongings on to some carts, and started for their new home. Mr. Gilbertson was supervising the packing of the last cart when a friend, John Marshal, came by.

"And so are you flitting at last, then, George?" Marshal asked.

"Aye, I'm forced to it," Gilbertson responded. "That damned boggart torments us so we cannot rest neither night nor day. It seems to have such a terrible malice against the poor bairns, it almost killed my old woman with fright. And so we're off leaving, you see."

There was a sudden knocking sound from inside an empty milk churn, and a sneering voice called out, "Aye, lad, we're all off leaving, you see."

"That damned boggart," muttered Gilbertson. Then he called to his wife. "Turn back," he shouted. "We might as well be

The Enfield Poltergeist

One of the most investigated cases of a modern poltergeist was the one that afflicted the Harper family of Enfield, England, for 13 months from August 1977. The visitation began with faint shuffling sounds upstairs, but Mrs. Harper soon saw the chest of drawers in her daughters' bedroom move, by itself, across the floor. Mrs. Harper quickly dragged her children next door and sent her neighbor to investigate.

The neighbor heard loud knocking noises and found that more furniture had been moved, so he called the police. They arrived in time to witness a chair dancing around the living room. The police ruled out trickery or an attack by intruders, and eventually Mrs. Harper was put in touch with the Society for Psychical Research (SPR). The SPR at once recognized the work of a poltergeist and sent a team of investigators.

Over the months that followed, several investigators witnessed objects being moved around and thrown about, and even the children being pushed around the rooms. Some of the investigators came to the conclusion that the children were faking at least some of what was occurring. Others remained convinced that the poltergeist visitation was truly a supernatural event. At any rate, the activity wound down after March 1978 and had ceased altogther by September.

What's in a Name?

The word poltergeist is German and means noisy ghost. Although the word has caught on, it is not a fair description of the typical poltergeist. The word noisy fails to do justice to the full range of terrifying phenomena of which a poltergeist is capable. It also isn't entirely clear if the link with ghosts is justified.

Most ghosts are visible, and if they cannot be identified as the wraith of a particular person, they are at least clearly apparitions of people from a past era. In fact, the phenomenon today labeled as poltergeist has gone by various names. In colonial America such outbreaks were frequently blamed on witchcraft. The famous Bell Witch would today be labeled a poltergeist.

tormented in our good old house as in another that's not to our liking."

Henderson records that the poltergeist continued to play its tricks on the Gilbertsons for a few weeks more, then it left them.

MISCHIEVOUS SPIRITS

Over the years, the poltergeist phenomenon has become recognized as something distinct from a normal haunting. In 1960 a girl in Alloa, Scotland, was plagued by repeated knocking and hammering sounds coming from inside the furniture in her bedroom. These lasted for some months, then ceased. A few years earlier a 14-year-old girl, Shirley Hitching, in Battersea, England, was likewise the focus of disembodied rapping. In this case the poltergeist went on to scrawl graffiti all over the walls of the house and to deface posters. Other common poltergeist activities include the throwing of stones, the moving of household items such as clocks, keys, or furniture, and the swift removal of sheets and blankets in the middle of the night. In some more potentially dangerous cases poltergeists have even been blamed for starting unexplained fires.

In 1984 Tina Resch, then age 15, became the focus of what the media dubbed the Columbus Poltergeist. The case included the normal run of phenomena, but with unusually numerous instances of fires erupting. The case hit the headlines when the local newspaper, the *Columbus Dispatch*, printed a photo of Resch with a telephone floating in midair in front of her. Several journalists investigated the case and collected some sensational evidence, but many of the journalists who visited came to believe that Resch was faking at least some of the evidence to gain notoriety and financial reward.

TEENAGE ANGST?

What emerges from all these cases is a general pattern of behavior for poltergeists, although there are always some variations. The visitations tend to start gradually with minor events. They then build over a period of months to a climax before trailing off again.

The manifestations can be unnerving and at times downright terrifying, but rarely is anybody actually hurt, and serious injury almost never results.

Moreover, the disturbances are almost always focused around a teenage girl, sometimes a boy. This person is generally undergoing a stressful change in his or her life, such as attending a new school or indulging in a first romance. Exactly what happens during a poltergeist attack is a matter of dispute. Some researchers believe that the phenomena are mere trickery. They usually put the blame on the teenager, claiming that he or she is causing the disturbances to gain attention.

Those seeking a paranormal explanation tend to take the events at face value. Some believe that the teenager is temporarily endowed with unconscious psychokinetic powers. Thus, the teenager will move objects around without realizing that they are doing so as a release for pent-up teenage emotions. Still others think that the disturbances are caused by a spirit that is attracted to the overwrought teenager.

A scene from the 1982 movie *Poltergeist,* which opens with a group of disembodied spirits trying to communicate with a young girl through television static. The plot of the movie featured many aspects of a real poltergeist, but its explanation of events had more to do with traditional horror movies than with paranormal investigations.

Possession: Losing Your Mind

Possession is one of the more alarming and controversial of the visitations by paranormal entities. Put simply, a possession occurs when a disembodied entity takes over a human mind and/or body. That entity can then use the human to perform all types of heinous acts, usually against the will of the human involved. In most instances the people involved perceive possession as evil or mischievous. These spirits are definitely indifferent toward the feelings or well-being of the person they possess.

Bare Bones

- Possession occurs when a supernatural entity of some kind takes over the mind of a living human being.

- According to medieval theology, a person can be possessed against their will or can enter into a pact and forfeit their soul in return for earthly gain.

- The reality of possession was taken for a fact in biblical times and through the Middle Ages, but since the eighteenth century, symptoms of possession have been increasingly blamed on mental illness.

Many investigators do not believe that there is any such thing as possession. They view all alleged cases of possession as being due to mental illness of one kind or another. Some forms of mental illness do, in fact, manifest themselves in ways similar to possession. The subject has also become overlaid with all sorts of religious belief and doctrine, which vary in different parts of the world and in most areas influences how cases of possession are viewed both by those who are afflicted and by those who investigate the cases.

In the Western world most views on possession are drawn, directly or indirectly, from the Christian faith. In large part these derive from the Bible, but medieval theology and folk belief also play a role. The ancient peoples of the Middle East also believed that evil spirits walked in the world of humans, and medical treatises that survive from both Egypt and Mesopotamia blame these spirits for disease and sickness. Although generally the spirit was blamed for only causing the illness, in some cases it was said to actually take possession of the doomed person.

THE CHRISTIAN VIEW

The Old Testament of the Bible contains numerous references to angels and demons, but possession is not specifically mentioned until the New Testament. Christ worked largely among the poorer and least-educated members of society, and it was there that he met and overcame demonic possession.

The Gospel of Matthew makes clear distinctions between people who had mental illness, were struck with palsy, or suffered assorted illnesses, and those, "who were possessed with devils." On five different occasions, Matthew records that Jesus cast out devils or demons that had possessed a person. Each time Matthew says that Jesus cast them out with his words, while those suffering more mundane diseases are cured by touch or the laying on of hands. At one point the Gospel reads, "They brought unto him many that were possessed with devils; and he cast out the spirits with his word."

After Jesus' ascension into heaven, the Apostles are also recorded to have cast out demons in the name of Jesus. On one occasion in Macedonia this got Saint Paul into trouble. The demon he cast out of a young woman slave had the gift of prophecy. When the woman's owner realized that his slave had lost the ability to foretell the future—from which he had made much money—he had Paul flogged in the marketplace and then thrown into prison.

By the later medieval period, Christian theology had ruled both that demons were real spiritual entities and that they could possess humans. Indeed it was generally accepted that all cases of possession involved demons. The Church devised a list of signs by which clergy could identify a case of possession. A possessed person was thought to be compulsively driven to blaspheme—often in a foreign language, to find hidden objects, and to predict the future. A possessed person might also be able to lift incredibly heavy objects and would vomit or excrete objects that they had not eaten. Folk belief also held that a possessed person would show fear of the Bible, crucifix, and other holy objects, and lacked the ability to speak the word "Christ."

It was often thought that the more extreme forms of blaspheming were caused by the conflict between the demon and the person it was possessing. The struggle for possession of the body created an inner turmoil that resulted in the outer manifestations, including blasphemy. More subtly, a person completely under the control of a demon might exhibit few, if any, of these signs. This victim

Possession in the Spotlight

Possession is a favorite theme among writers, dramatists, and moviemakers. The themes that the concept assembles are not only terrifying but also make for dramatic imagery and sudden shocks.

The classic of the genre is the 1973 film *The Exorcist,* which is a dramatization of a 1971 novel of the same title. This was based on the documented exorcism of a 14-year-old boy in 1949. It has been much copied and much parodied, providing a blueprint in the popular imagination for the behavior of victims of possession: the ability to vomit odd objects, turn their heads completely around in a circle, and launch frenzied attacks.

A more recent offering, which also claims to be based in fact, is the 2005 movie *The Exorcism of Emily Rose.* This is the story of German student Anneliese Michel who died after an attempted exorcism. So-called "true story" films have followed both of these successful movies. *Possessed* tells the story behind *The Exorcist,* while *Requiem* is a German-language film that claims to tell the true story of the Anneliese Michel possession.

Selling Out

Selling one's soul to the devil for some gain, usually wealth or power, is often a pact fraught with danger. As Faust found out in the oft-dramatized German legend, one never knows when the devil will come to claim his prize.

Sir Roland Alston, who lived at Odell in Bedfordshire, England, in the seventeenth century was a notorious womanizer, gambler, and rake whom locals claimed sold his soul to the devil.

In 1644 a tall dark man came to see him, prompting Sir Roland to leap on his horse and ride at top speed to the church. He was found dead by the door with scorched claw marks beside him.

Luckier was Jack O'Kent who lived in Herefordshire, England, 600 years ago. He sold his soul to the devil and promised he would surrender his soul on his death, "whether I am buried in the church or outside it." He escaped the consequences of the pact by having his tomb built into the wall of the church so that he was neither inside nor outside.

would instead be a tool of the demon and thus undertake activities of outright evil and malice.

In medieval times it was believed that there were two types of possession. With the first the possession was entirely the work of the demon. It moved into the person's body against the human's will on business of its own. In the second type the human instigated the possession by seeking to gain occult powers by partnering with a demon. This type of possession was later divided into two classes. The first involved those who sold their soul to the devil in return for earthly wealth or power. The second involved witchcraft, when witches invoked demons to perform magic. By the eighteenth century neither form of voluntary possession was considered a possession in the true sense since the demon was under the control of the human, not the other way around.

POSSESSION IN SALEM

A classic case of possession that crossed the boundaries of the two definitions was that which came to the Massachusetts village of Salem. Most people have heard of the witchcraft trials of Salem, but few realize that, at the time, demonic possession was thought to be at the heart of the matter. The trouble began when seven teenage girls attempted to see into the future, primarily to find out whom they would marry. On Christmas 1691 they poured an egg into a crystal wineglass and followed some rituals to try to predict this information.

It did not work, but the girls seem to have been psychologically traumatized by the event. Five of the girls subsequently collapsed in fits during which their bodies were twisted into abnormal and painful postures. They awoke claiming to have seen devils and demons that attacked and beat them. As the outbursts continued, Rev. Samuel Parris, the minister at Salem's church, consulted a doctor, and together they announced that the girls were suffering at the hands of the devil. Mary Sibley, an aunt of one of the girls, thought that a witch must have summoned the devil. She went through a ritual designed to break the power of a witch, and consequently her niece named three local women as the witches to blame. These

The trial of Martha Corey during the Salem witch trials of 1692. The trials at Salem were not outstanding at the time because of the charges of witchcraft, nor was it unusual due to the conviction of local women, instead, it was notable because of the fervor with which the death penalty was sought and executed.

were Sarah Good, Sarah Osburn, and the slave Tituba, all three of whom had local reputations as healers or witches.

The three women were arrested and brought before Magistrate John Hathorne. His opening questions showed not only that he had little doubt of their guilt but also what he thought they had done. "What evil spirits have you familiarity with?" he demanded. "Have you made contract with the devil?" Hysteria proceeded to grip the community of Salem. The girls suffered protracted fits and apparent possession. Only one, Mary Warren, ceased to suffer. Her sudden cure came when her employer—a farmer named John Proctor—dragged her back to work and separated her from the others. Meanwhile, the remaining girls accused person after person of consorting with the devil. No less than 19 people were hanged and one pressed to death before the state court halted the judicial hearings.

The events at Salem were driven by a sincere belief in the ability of demons and the devil to possess innocents.

THE DEMON PRIEST

The Catholic Church was just as convinced of this reality. In 1632 Father Urbain Grandier turned down an offer to become the priest confessor of the Ursuline Convent in Loudun, France. Despite his clerical status, Grandier was a notorious womanizer. The abbess at Loudun, Sister Jeanne, was no less active and had invited him to attend the church in the hopes of seducing him. When he refused, she accused Grandier of trying to seduce her and added an accusation of black magic. These allegations were ignored. Some months later other nuns also said that they had been seduced by a demon named Asmodai, who had been sent on his infernal mission by Grandier. They said that they had not only had sex with this demon, but also had been possessed by him and driven to commit diabolical acts.

Grandier was arrested and charged with summoning the demon to possess the nuns. His rooms were searched and several documents found. These were written in Latin, some backward and were signed by Grandier, Asmodai, and other hands that bore demonic-sounding names. One document read:

> We, the influential Lucifer, the young Satan, Beelzebub, Leviathan, Elimi, and Astaroth, together with others, have today accepted the covenant pact of Urbain Grandier, who is ours. And him do we promise the love of women, the flower of virgins, the respect of monarchs, honors, lusts, and powers. He will go whoring three days long; the carousal will be holy to him. He offers us once in the year a seal of blood, under the feet he will trample the holy things of the church and he will ask us many questions; with this pact he will live 20 years happy on the earth of men, and will later join us to sin against God.
>
> Bound in hell, in the council of demons. Lucifer Beelzebub Satan Astaroth Leviathan Elimi. The seals placed the Devil, the master, and the demons, princes of the lord.

Grandier denied all charges but was found guilty and burned at the stake. As soon as he was dead, the nuns were released from their fits and hallucinations.

Since the eighteenth century in the Western world, people have held demonic possession to be a fact in only a few cases. On occasion people have claimed demons to be responsible for a variety of illnesses and outbreaks of evil, but in most cases the intervention

A scene from the 1973 horror movie *The Exorcist*, in which Linda Blair starred as a 12-year-old girl suffering from possession. The film took some established features of possession but, as is often the way with Hollywood, exaggerated them for dramatic purposes to produce a true horror movie.

of doctors has led to a diagnosis of mental illness being given, and accepted, instead.

The Catholic Church, however, still believes in the reality of the devil and in his ability to possess humans. Most Protestant Churches similarly retain these beliefs in their doctrine. Most Christian denominations, however, now hold that most cases that match the definition of possession are, in fact, medical conditions.

Followers of Wicca, who claim to be the inheritors of what Christians called witchcraft, are clear that the allegations that their forebears used demons are untrue. They hold that their religion is quite separate from Christianity and has no space for such creatures, which they do not recognize.

Other religions often have a belief in spiritual entities that have been termed demons in written documents by Christians. Both Hinduism and Buddhism, for instance, hold that there are entities that tempt humans to sin, and certain Islamic cultures hold a widespread belief in spirit possession. In voodoo, possession by spirits is a tenet of faith and an integral part of ritual.

Exorcism: Banishing Spirits

Exorcism is the ritual that seeks to banish ghosts, demons, and other spirits from a person or a place. Most religions and spiritual traditions have exorcism rituals of some kind or another, but there are some notable exceptions.

Bare Bones

- Exorcism is the ritual that seeks to banish ghosts, demons, and other spirits from a person or a place that they are infesting.

- Most spiritual traditions have exorcism rituals of one sort or another, notable exceptions being the Sikh and Jain religions.

- Although exorcisms were on the decline for some years, there now appears to be a resurgence in demand for this service, and in recent years some tragic cases have been reported where fatal results have ensued.

Exorcism presupposes that the phenomena being experienced are not only real but are also caused by an outside entity, be it the spirit of a deceased human or a demon. Skeptics do not believe the phenomena to be real, and even among those that do accept the reality of the situation, there is no consensus that a distinct spiritual entity is to blame.

MODERN EXORCISM

By the middle of the last century, Christian exorcisms were conducted only on a rare basis. The major churches believe that most people who show signs of possession are suffering from mental illness, while most hauntings are more likely due to natural factors or human pranksters. In the Catholic Church an exorcism may be performed only with the written permission of the local bishop and after careful examination to rule out more mundane causes. In 1999 the church produced a revised Rite of Exorcism, though many still prefer the older Latin rite. The rite involves prayers, blessings, and invocations and is believed to be a dangerous act for the priest who conducts it.

The Anglican Church likewise holds that exorcism is a dangerous business that should be done only with permission from a bishop. Ordinary vicars are not allowed to perform the rite, only specific clergy who have had some experience. In neither the Protestant nor the Catholic faiths is the exorcism ritual confined to the traditional apparatus of "bell, book, and candle."

In his book, *Diabolical Possession and Exorcism*, Father John Nicola describes one case, which occurred in Earling, Iowa, during the last century. The unidentified victim of the possession, referred to as Mary, was a 40-year-old woman who had been suffering with symptoms inexplicable by doctors and psychologists since the age of 14. These included hearing voices and foaming at the mouth when being blessed by a priest. In 1928 the woman was taken to a Poor Clares community where a Capuchin friar, Father Theophilus, and his friend Father Joseph Steiger began a series of exorcisms, which took place over the course of three weeks.

During the course of the exorcisms, a number of alarming phenomena occurred, including the vomiting and excretion of large quantities of noxious substances by the victim. The demons possessing Mary spoke through her, threatening the life of Father Steiger, then subsequently claiming responsibility for a car crash he suffered. On December 23, in a final ritual, Father Theophilus declared, "Depart ye fiends of hell. Begone Satan, the Lion of Judah reigns." At this Mary first screamed, "Hell, hell, hell," then sat up and pronounced, "Praise be to Jesus Christ." Her tormentors, it appeared, had departed, and she lived the rest of her life untroubled by unwelcome visitors.

GHOSTS OF THE PAST

In the past belief in spirits and demons was much more widespread than today, and the clergy performed more exorcisms. Any ordained priest could exorcize a person or place, though it was often thought that certain clergy were more skilled at the task than others.

In the eighteenth century the people of Little Lawford in Warwickshire, England, resorted to exorcism to dispose of a troublesome ghost. The ghost in question was that of One Handed Boughton, a squire of Tudor times who had lost his hand fighting the Spanish. Twelve clergymen were hired for the event and brought to Little Lawford Hall. The phantom of One Handed Boughton laughed at the clergymen and put out their candles one by one until only one remained alight: that held by Parson Hall of Great Harborough. Try as he might, the ghost could not distract the parson, but equally the parson could not overcome the ghost. As dawn approached, the ghost suggested that the two make a

Fatal Exorcisms

The rituals involved in exorcism are usually fairly benign but on occasion can lead to inadvertent physical or psychological injury and even death. In 1976 a 24-year-old German college student named Anneliese Michel died after months of prolonged exorcism rituals left her physically and mentally drained. At a subsequent trial her parents and two Catholic priests were convicted of causing her death through negligence.

Kyung-A Ha died in 1995 in California after an exorcism ritual conducted by members of the Jesus-Amen Ministries, which involved beatings.In 1998 a Voodoo exorcism ritual being performed in New York went badly wrong and resulted in Charity Miranda being suffocated with a plastic bag. In Milwaukee in 2003 members of the Faith Temple Church of the Apostolic Faith conducted an exorcism on eight-year-old Terrance Cottrell. This involved the pastor lying on top of the boy, an act that resulted in chest injuries, which in turn led to fatal medical complications.

Hostile to Exorcism

The Sikh religion is perhaps the only developed faith that not only has no tradition of exorcism but is positively hostile to the concept. Sikhs do not believe in the existence of demons, angels, or other quasi-divine beings. It follows, therefore, that such entities cannot infest a place or person.

The Jain faith also denies the reality of such entities and has no exorcism ritual, but Sikhism goes further. Sikh theology concludes that, because it has no exorcism rites, any person who conducts what purports to be an exorcism is tricking the recipient in a way that denies the Sikh faith. If money changes hands or favors are performed in payment for the ritual, this is considered a real sin. Any ordained Ghiyanhi, or Sikh priest, has the power to exclude from the faith anybody who they believe has conducted a purported exorcism.

deal. The ghost agreed to confine himself to a marl pit on the estate, as long as he was free to ride over his former lands for two hours every night between midnight and 2:00 A.M. Thereafter, the ghost of One Handed Boughton was seen only by those brave enough to venture out late at night on to his old estates.

The ghost of Margaret Leigh, who died in Burslem, Staffordshire, England, in 1748, was more easily pleased. Margaret's ghost was seen several times sitting on her tombstone and asking to be buried sideways. The local vicar eventually called in workmen who dug the grave so that it lay north–south instead of the conventional east–west. The ghost was never seen again, and the sideways tomb remains.

DIFFERENT TRADITIONS

Judaism does not have such a strong belief in spirits as does Christianity. Nevertheless, it does hold that disembodied entities may become linked to a person or place. This link may be broken by a ceremony that could be classed as exorcism. A rabbi forms a circle with 10 other people, each of whom recites Psalm 91. The rabbi then blows the shofar, or sacred horn, in a specific pattern that is believed to loosen the ties that bind the spirit and enable it to speak. The rabbi then converses with the spirit to seek its purpose. Prayers designed to heal whatever hurt the spirit may be feeling subsequently follow, enabling the spirit to move on.

Islamic belief is slightly different. Muslims believe in spiritual entities called jinn. These creatures were born of fire. They are thought to be neither inherently evil nor good, but capable of both. A jinn may take possession of a person or place, but can be removed by an exorcism. These rituals usually involve the invocation of the powers of Allah by means of prayers repeated at specific times of the day over a period of several days or even weeks.

Hindus draw their exorcism rituals from their ancient holy books, the four *Vedas*. Of these the most important is the *Atharva Veda*, which contains verses and incantations related to magic and medicine. Sections of the *Vedas* may be read out loud by relay

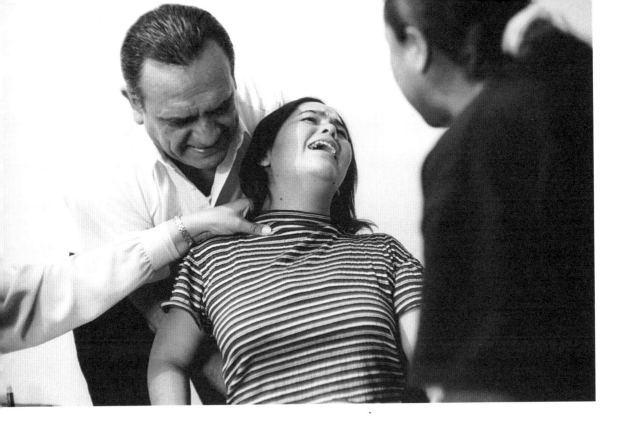

readers for days on end to ensure that a site is cleansed. Incense may be burned while this happens, and water from holy rivers may be scattered about.

A contemporary exorcism takes place in Mexico. The recent upsurge in requests for exorcism rituals has been blamed on the media, though some suspect that an increase in demonic activity may be to blame.

ON THE RISE

The practice of exorcism seems to be undergoing a resurgence in the West. In February 2005 about 100 Catholic priests signed up for a Vatican course on exorcism. According to the *Los Angeles Times*, "In Italy, the number of official exorcists has soared during the last 20 years to between 300 and 400, church officials say. But they aren't enough to handle the avalanche of requests for help from hundreds of tormented people who believe they are possessed. In the United States, the shortage is even more acute." In his book *American Exorcism: Expelling Demons in the Land of Plenty*, Michael Cuneo blames media portrayals of the phenomenon for this upward trend, "...[I]t isn't much of an exaggeration to say that exorcism today is actually the invention of the popular entertainment industry: the product, above all else, of Hollywood hype and Madison Avenue hucksterism."

Necromancy: Raising the Dead

Necromancy, the art of raising the dead or spirits by magic to gain control over them, is an ancient art. It has long been regarded as the highest accomplishment to which a magician or witch can aspire and is considered extraordinarily dangerous. The rewards are, however, great. With a ghost or demon at one's command, many things are possible.

Bare Bones

- Necromancy is the art of raising spirits by magic in order to profit from their powers.

- It is considered to be difficult and dangerous, because the spirits thus raised are powerful and prone to deceiving those who summon them.

- Only a few magicians have claimed success in raising spirits in this way—among them are John Dee and Aleister Crowley.

It is the element of control that distinguishes between what magicians do in necromancy and what mediums seek to do when speaking to the spirits of the dead. The first is undertaken with the express intention of producing a profound effect on the human world, the latter simply for the purposes of communication.

Occultists disagree among themselves regarding exactly what sort of spirits can be raised by necromancy, and to what ends they may be used. Much of what has been written is affected by the writer's cultural and religious background. In Christian lands, for instance, it is often assumed that the spirits being raised are those of demons or even the devil, and therefore the results can only be evil. Many magicians, however, claim that they are raising the spirits of dead humans or elemental beings that are indifferent to humanity. Theologians counter that evil demons are quite capable of pretending to be the phantoms of harmless old ladies in order to win the magician's confidence and gain access to the world of humans. The one thing on which everyone seems to agree is that necromancy is a dangerous business.

Numerous books, ancient and modern, give instruction in powerful magic including necromancy. These involve incantations to be said and detailed instructions for rituals to be followed. There are, however, few examples of magicians who can seriously claim to have succeeded in summoning a spirit through magic.

JOHN DEE

One of the earliest cases that has survived in any detail is that of John Dee. Dee was born of humble parents in Surrey, England, in

1527, but went on to become a lecturer in Greek and a Fellow of Trinity College, Cambridge.

In 1582 Dee joined his former student Edward Kelley to engage in serious occult research and practice. Within a year the pair were practicing necromancy on a frequent basis. Sadly, Dee did not write down in his journal the rituals that they followed, only the results. Dee believed that the spirits with which he and Kelley were communicating were angels, though he had only the word of the spirits for that.

Kelley and Dee also raised the dead, most famously conjuring up a dead woman complete with burial shroud in the churchyard of Walton-le-Dale in Lancashire, England. These types of spirits were not as communicative as the angels, and Kelly and Dee seem to have abandoned the practice. But in 1587 a new angel, named Madimi, appeared. This angel instructed Dee and Kelley to have sex with each other's wives. Dee refused and began to suspect that Madimi was a demon, not an angel, but Kelley was more enthusiastic. Eventually the deed was done, but Dee grew increasingly worried about the magic he was doing. He soon gave up necromancy and returned to his classical studies.

ALEISTER CROWLEY

The twentieth-century self-proclaimed master magician, Aleister Crowley, was less concerned with the effects of his magic. He proclaimed himself to be the Wickedest Man Alive and encouraged tales about orgies and sacrifices to circulate. Crowley made many claims, but one event, at least, was witnessed by an observer.

In 1909 Crowley traveled into the Sahara with the declared intention of summoning the demon Choronzon, the Dweller in the Abyss, to do his will. Poet and writer Victor Neuberg, who had an interest in the occult, went with him. Once in a remote spot that Crowley thought suitable, the ritual began. Crowley began by drawing a magical circle and other symbols in the sand. Neuberg was told to stand in the circle and not to leave, no matter what happened. Crowley then donned a black robe, sacrificed three pigeons, and squatted on the sand.

Summoning the Devil

While most necromancers believe that they can perfect their art only after many years of careful study, preparation, and ritual, others believe that the trick can be performed with minimal preparation and no skill at all. What is needed is simply to be in the right place at the right time and to carry out a simple ritual.

Take, for instance, the ancient earthworks of Winklebury Camp in Wiltshire, England. The devil is thought to sit on this hill, gazing out over Wiltshire and planning his evil works whenever he comes to the county. Those who are brave enough can summon the devil here at any time. All that is needed is for a brave soul to climb this steep hill after dark, find the ancient earthwork fortifications and run around them seven times. It is believed that the devil himself will then appear mounted on a terrifying horse with jet-black coat.

Having been thus summoned, the devil is bound to grant one wish to the person who has called him. Being the devil, of course, he has a habit of sticking to the letter of the wish, and also of tricking the misguided folk who summon him into giving away their souls or those of people close to them.

Aleister Crowley photographed in a typically theatrical pose and wearing robes of his own design. Crowley declared himself to be the Wickedest Man Alive and flamboyantly set out to raise demons to do his bidding. Whether or not he succeeded is a matter of controversy.

After repeated incantations and more sand drawing, Crowley went into a trance. He announced that Choronzon was arriving. Seconds later a beautiful woman came strolling up. Neuberg thought he recognized her and was about to step forward to warn her to leave when he recalled Crowley's instructions and stayed put. The woman promptly changed into demonic form; it was Choronzon seeking to lure Neuberg out of the circle. The demon then vanished. Crowley crawled toward Neuberg begging for water, but Neuberg suspected another trick and remained still. It was Choronzon again. Thwarted, the demon stood up and stated, "I feed upon the names of the most high. I churn them in my jaws. I void them in my fundament." After some more ominous but essentially meaningless talk and another attempt to attack Neuberg, Choronzon left. Crowley then came to, unable to recall what had happened.

That, at least, is what Neuberg said had happened. To what extent he was telling the truth, or to what extent he had been tricked by Crowley in his pursuit of a magical reputation, there is no way of knowing.

DEMONS OR DECEPTION?

The question of what happens during necromancy is as difficult as anything in the study of the unseen world. On the one hand, it may all be trickery and lies on the part of the magician, designed to convince his followers that he does, indeed, have great powers. Given that some male magicians like to use their powers to exploit their female followers sexually or to drain cash from others, there is a clear motive for the necromancer to exaggerate his success. That said, Dee was quite clearly convinced of his own success, and other magicians appear equally confident.

Even if one accepts that necromancers do conjure up spirits, it is not always clear what spirits have been brought forth. Dealing with spirits is a notoriously difficult and treacherous business. As Neuberg learned, demons intent on evil will assume all sorts of forms and trickery to get their way. Whatever spirits a necromancer may believe he has summoned, there is no guarantee that the supernatural being before him is the one intended. Necromancy is an uncertain and unreliable practice. Although it promises much in the way of worldly power to its practitioners, it puts them at considerable peril—be it of ridicule or of demonic possession.

The Second Pentacle from *The Key of Solomon*. *The Key of Solomon* is a medieval book that contains many arcane symbols and instructions on performing magical rituals, including necromancy and curses.

Apports and Asports: Out of Nowhere

Apports and asports are two sides of the same phenomenon. An apport is an object, usually some small everyday item, that appears from nowhere by supernatural agency. An asport is a similar object that vanishes instead of appearing. Apports and asports can come and go in a variety of settings and appear to have a variety of causes.

Bare Bones

- Apports are objects that are produced, seemingly out of thin air, by paranormal means.

- Asports are objects that disappear, again by apparently paranormal means.

- Apports and asports were common in the late-nineteenth-century heyday of physical mediumship and are also sometimes associated with poltergeist hauntings.

- It has been alleged that apports and asports are more likely to be produced by conjuring tricks than supernatural intervention, but some accounts do suggest evidence to the contrary.

MYSTERIOUS ORIGINS

A continuing dispute among those who investigate these matters concerns the origin of apports and destination of asports. Some believe that apports are objects transported from some remote location to the spot where they supernaturally appear. Others think that the objects are quite literally created out of nothing. Similarly, asports may be moved by unseen hands to some distant location, or they may cease to exist completely. As yet, there is no way of knowing for certain what is happening, but one incident in 1904 hints at an answer.

Ernesto Bozzano was an Italian investigator of the paranormal, who in March of that year was investigating a medium who claimed to be able to produce apports. On several occasions he sat in on séances held in darkened rooms, during which small ornaments, flowers, and other items were produced, seemingly out of thin air. The apports were usually preceded by twitching from the medium, which made Bozzano suspect that the apports were, in fact, objects secreted in the medium's clothes, which were shaken loose at the appropriate moment.

Bozzano decided that at the next séance he would ask the medium to produce something precise and definite, but to exclude any possibility of trickery, he would not decide what until the séance had begun. When the evening came, Bozzano decided to ask for a lump of pyrite that was sitting on his desk at home over a mile away. The medium, speaking in the voice of his spirit guide, said that his powers were weak at that time but that he would try. The usual twitching began, but no thump of a falling object was heard. Bozzano was convinced that he had exposed the fraud. But when the lights were put on, scatterings of pyrite dust around the séance table and in patches on the floor were revealed. When he got home Bozzano found that part of the pyrite block on his desk was missing.

As the Bozzano story indicates, apports and asports are usually associated with séances and with mediums, especially mediums who claim to produce physical phenomena. These phenomena were more common in the early years of public mediumship than they are today. The years 1850 to 1930, when the popularity of the Spiritualist movement was at its height, were filled with reports of apports, and less often asports. Today few mediums claim to have this power.

A lump of pyrite. A block of this mineral was featured in a famous test of the ability of a medium to produce an apport on demand.

STAGE TRICKS

Those who have reviewed early accounts of physical mediums are often skeptical of the powers claimed. There was a lot of money to be made by mediums. Most charged an entrance fee to attend a séance. Some mediums passed on messages that encouraged the living to hand over objects and cash to the medium. Even those that did not resort to such chicanery may have been earning a good living from being a medium when their only powers were those of an effective conjuror. An ability to produce apports, whether supernaturally or not, was a marketable skill.

In the wake of World War I, a barrage of bereaved parents, widows, and orphans sought messages from men killed in battle. Unscrupulous fraudsters moved into the market to produce false messages and faked photographs. To prey on the emotions of the bereaved was viewed as a low crime and a phrase was coined to describe such false mediums: spook crooks. Some paranormal investigators went to considerable lengths to unmask the guilty, not only to convict them of fraud, but also to try to clear the name of the genuine mediums.

One of the foremost investigators of the time, Harry Price, had his secretary Ethel Beenham learn to reproduce many aspects of physical mediumship—including apports—through stage conjuring tricks. The results were most impressive.

It is noticeable that, like the medium studied by Bozzano, many of those claiming to produce apports did so in a way that conjurors could easily mimic. Some produced apports from their mouths, even when their mouths were previously examined and found to be empty. The ability to regurgitate small objects is a well-known trick. Others produced items supposedly from their navels, but actually they came from hidden pockets that stage magicians had sewn into their vests. Some mediums were unmasked as frauds at the time; others were not but were viewed with suspicion.

> "I think...that the accusations of fraud against mediums have been much exaggerated."
>
> —SIR ARTHUR CONAN DOYLE, AUTHOR

GHOSTLY OFFERINGS

Not all apports are produced by mediums. Poltergeists are also widely reported to produce apports and asports. The Bell Witch was in the habit of dropping fresh fruit on to the dining table, while the Demon Drummer of Tidworth, active in England in the seventeenth century, preferred to drop stones. The rather controversial ghost at Borley Rectory in Essex, England, was a famous producer of apports. It apparently dropped stones, sugar lumps, and other small objects on to the floor on frequent occasions.

A particularly bizarre apport purportedly came from the Stratford Poltergeist, which plagued the Phelps family of Stratford, Connecticut, in the spring of 1850, with all the phenomena associated with a classic poltergeist haunting. The spirit apparently materialized a potato in thin air and then promptly dropped it in the middle of the breakfast table.

In the 1960s a poltergeist at Kilakee House, a stately home in Ireland, produced both apports and asports. The asports were milk bottle tops that vanished with regularity. These began to vanish early in the haunting and continued to go missing for months, no trace of them ever being found. The apports took the form of cloth caps and hats that were found in various rooms. Dozens of caps turned up, though only for a short period of time.

Another poltergeist, this time in Bavaria in 1969, took to moving toy dolls around the house. They were seen by members of the family in the process of moving several times and were quite clearly being carried rather than thrown. They did not fly in a straight line or land with a bump. Instead, they floated smoothly around corners and down corridors, then were put down gently. Even when they were placed in a locked cupboard, the dolls would still turn up elsewhere, though the cupboard door remained locked. They had presumably passed straight through the solid door.

> "Paranormal phenomena are in the eye of the beholder. They happen between human ears, not outside of them."
>
> —GERARD 'T HOOFT, PHYSICIST AND NOBEL PRIZEWINNER

Materializations: Seeing Things

Materializations come in many shapes, forms, and types. The way in which they are perceived by the people seeing them can tell us as much about the culture that a person is from as about the materialization itself. Some commonly reported materializations—ghosts, angels, and UFOs—are explored elsewhere in this book, but that leaves a large number of entities that fit into no clear category.

Bare Bones

- A materialization can be defined as any unexplained apparition. Apart from ghosts and angels, other materializations include doppelgangers, companions, and crisis apparitions.

- Doppelgangers are apparitions of living people who appear in one place while their counterpart is somewhere else. They are rarely seen by their living double.

- Companions appear to bring comfort and relieve loneliness in times of hardship, while crisis apparitions are phantoms that appear in one place at the precise moment their living body is dying elsewhere.

These manifestations, though not necessarily linked, likely have a distinct cause, or they may all be different manifestations of the same underlying reality. Or, as the skeptics maintain, they may simply be products of over-active imaginations.

DOPPELGANGERS

The first type of manifestation usually goes by the German term of doppelganger, though it is sometimes termed an astral double. This is a materialization that is identical in all respects to a real living person, who is usually fairly close to where the materialization is seen.

The case of a Mrs. Milman who worked in the British Houses of Parliament for some years between the wars is typical. When she was at work at her desk, an exact double of herself would be seen walking the corridors as if checking up on the various tasks and duties her staff were supposed to have done. Mrs. Milman never saw the double herself but one day came close to doing so. A colleague was chatting to Mrs. Milman at her desk, then left to carry some files to another room. As she exited the room, the colleague saw the doppelganger coming down the corridor toward her. In some alarm the woman shrank back against the wall and watched the double walk past her, getting as close as three feet (just under 1 m) away, and then walk past the open door of the office where the real Mrs. Milman was working. Unfortunately, Mrs. Milman did not look up to see her double walk past, being engrossed in her own paperwork.

In 1951 a Mrs. Smith saw her own doppelganger when she was sick in bed with a virus infection. This doppelganger came into the room and sat on a chair beside the bed. It was dressed in a dress that Mrs. Smith had thrown out a year or so earlier. The double looked sternly at Mrs. Smith and said, "If you wish to recover, you must stop taking those tablets the doctor has given you at once or they might finish you off." The doppelganger then faded from view. Mrs. Smith was so shaken that she did as instructed and quickly got better. She told the doctor, who only then discovered a rare side effect of the drug that could have proved dangerous.

THE COMPANION

Another reasonably common materialization is the companion. This is again a human figure, but one that is neither a double nor recognizable as anyone in particular by the witness. One particularly famous witness was the polar explorer Sir Ernest Shackleton. On his 1914 expedition his ship was wrecked on a remote shore, and he was faced with a 100-mile (160-km) trip over a mountain range to reach help. He made the trip with just one colleague but soon realized that there was a spectral companion with them. Shackleton said nothing at the time, fearing he was suffering hallucinations. But he found out sometime later that his living colleague had also seen the phantom companion and had likewise stayed silent, thinking that he had gone mad.

A similar companion appeared to climber Frank Smythe on his abortive 1933 attempt on Mount Everest. He became so convinced of his companion's reality that he shared a block of Kendal mint cake with it. That these companions are not restricted to emergencies is shown by the case of pilot Edith Foltz-Stearns. If she has to fly alone a companion will materialize next to her soon after takeoff and remain there for the duration of the flight. At first she found the apparitions alarming, but soon grew used to them.

CRISIS APPARITIONS

Crisis apparitions are most decidedly of a real, identifiable person. Usually the materialization involves a person known to the one who

Hypnogogic Entities

Some people experience what are known technically as hypnogogic visions, or more colloquially as waking dreams. These visions are experienced in the borders between sleeping and waking. They are generally thought to occur when the part of the brain that creates dreams has not caught up with the fact that the rest of the brain is waking up.

The same experience that occurs as a person is falling asleep, hypnopompic visions, are similar but more rare. The witness usually sees people or things that are quite unfamiliar to them but appear for a few seconds to be completely real. These might take the form of a person in the room or, more elaborately, an entire landscape, as if the witness has been transported many miles away.

Quite how this mechanism works is unclear, though there is nothing supernatural about it. It does indicate that the human brain can access visions that, for a while at least, appear to be solid and real.

Ernest Shackleton was an Irish polar explorer who prided himself on the fact that as a leader, he had never lost a single man. In 1914 he escaped from a shipwreck with the aid of a phantom apparition.

sees it. As the name suggests, they usually occur when the person whose apparition is seen is undergoing a crisis of some kind.

On December 7, 1918, Lt. David McConnel of the British Royal Flying Corps (RFC) was asked to fly an aircraft the 50 miles (80 km) from Scampton to Tadcaster, then return by train. He left his room at 11:30 A.M. telling his roommate, a Lt. Larkin, to expect him back around tea time—tea was customarily served at about 4:00 P.M. At 3:20 P.M. Larkin was in their room reading when he heard the door open and McConnel's familiar voice call out, "Hello, boy." Larkin turned around to see McConnel in full flying garb, standing in the open door with his hand on the doorknob.

"Back already?" asked Larkin.

"Yes, got there all right. Had a good trip." Then as he stepped back and closed the door, McConnel added, "Well, cheerio."

A few minutes later Lt. Smith came in and asked Larkin when McConnel would be back because they had planned to go out together that evening. Larkin told him that McConnel was already back and guessed he was washing up and changing out of his flying suit. Smith went off but was unable to find McConnel anywhere.

Much later that evening, word came through that McConnel had been forced down by fog at Doncaster, taken off again as the fog cleared, only for the mist to close in once more. At 3:20 P.M. McConnel had tried to land at Tadcaster but had misjudged his height in the fog and crashed. He was killed instantly, at the moment that his apparition was seen and heard by Larkin.

Such apparitions are reported reasonably often. What distinguishes that of the unfortunate McConnel is that Larkin and Smith were seen and heard by many of their colleagues going around the base trying to find the missing pilot some time before news arrived of the crash. Such independent corroboration is rare.

Similar was the case of Robert Bowes, an elderly farmhand in Ireland. In 1926 his employer, Miss Godley, went to see him as she had heard he was dangerously sick in bed. She left in her horse and trap, accompanied by her friend Miss Goldsmith and driven by her steward. As they came down to a lake near the sick man's home, all three saw Bowes steering a boat across the waters. Miss Godley called out, but the man ignored her and vanished as his boat entered reeds on the far side. Assuming that Bowes must have recovered, Miss Godley returned home. Later that evening, the doctor came by to tell Miss Godley of her employee's death. Miss Godley was surprised because she thought Bowes fully recovered, but it turned out that death had occurred at about the time she and her companions had seen his ghost on the waters.

"A mind that is stretched by a new experience can never go back to its old dimensions."

—OLIVER WENDELL HOLMES, ASSOCIATE JUSTICE, U.S. SUPREME COURT

Resources

ORGANIZATIONS IN THE UNITED STATES

American Association for Parapsychology
Box 225
Canoga Park, CA 91305
(818) 883-0887

American Society for Psychical Research, Inc.
5 West 73rd Street
New York, NY 10023
(212) 799-5050
www.aspr.com

Association for Research and Enlightenment
215 67th Street
Virginia Beach, VA 23451
(257) 428-3588
www.are-cayce.com

Institute of Noetic Sciences
101 San Antonio Road
Petaluma, CA 94952
(707) 775-3500
www.noetic.org

International Association for the Study
of Dreams
1672 University Avenue
Berkeley, CA 94703
(209) 724-0889
www.ASDreams.org

National Spiritual Alliance
P.O. Box 88
Lake Pleasant, MA 01347
www.thenationalspiritualallianceinc.org

National Spiritualist Association of Churches in
the USA
General Offices
13 Cottage Row
P.O. Box 217
Lily Dale, NY 14752
(716) 595-2000
www.nsac.org

Parapsychological Association, Inc.
2474-342 Walnut Street
Cary, NC 27511
www.parapsych.org

Rhine Research Center
Institute for Parapsychology
2741 Campus Walk Avenue, Building 500
Durham, NC 27705
(919) 309-4600
www.rhine.org

IN CANADA

Paranormal Studies & Investigations Canada
117 Runnymede Road
Toronto, Ontario M6S 2Y4
executive@psican.org

IN AUSTRALIA

Australian Institute of Parapsychological Research
P.O. Box 445
Lane Cove, NSW 2066
Australia
www.aiprinc.org

WEB SITES

www.deanradin.com: Dean Radin's Conscious Research Laboratory Web site.

www.themystica.com: A developing online encyclopedia providing useful basic information about some aspects of the paranormal.

www.randi.org: Web site of the James Randi Educational Foundation.

www.skepdic.com: Online version of the Skeptic's Dictionary.

www.skeptic.com: Web site of The Skeptics Society.

www.blavatskyarchives.com: Online information on the teachings of Madame Blavatsky.

www.survivalafterdeath.org: News and articles on mediumship, psi, and survival after death. Posts are updated every week.

www.coldspot.org: Canadian Web site for Coldspot, a paranormal research and investigation unit.

ADDITIONAL READING

Blum, Deborah. *Ghost Hunters*, Penguin, 2006.

Carroll, Robert Todd. *The Skeptic's Dictionary*, Wiley, 2003.

Luckhurst, Roger. *The Invention of Telepathy*, Oxford University Press, 2002.

Radin, Dean. *Entangled Minds: Extrasensory Experiences in a Quantum Reality*, Pocket Books, 2006.

Randi, James. *An Encyclopedia of Claims, Frauds, and Hoaxes of the Occult and Supernatural*, St. Martin's Press, 1997.

Sagan, Carl. *The Demon-Haunted World*, Random House, 1995.

Targ, Russell, and Hal Puthoff. *Mind-Reach. Scientists Look at Psychic Ability*, Dell Publishing/Delta Books, 1977.

Index

Page references in boldface indicate boxes. Italic page references represent illustrations.

Photo Credits

Every effort has been made to contact copyright holders where necessary. If any omissions have been inadvertently made, please contact the publishers.